Police Discretion in India

This book is the first empirical study of police discretion in India. Going beyond anecdotal accounts, it addresses the issues and concerns of arrest discretion behaviour of police with analysis of available literature internationally, testing the validity in the context of police in India and explaining the gap that exists between the legislative intent and field law enforcement. It establishes how extralegal determinants like subculture, environment and situations influence arrest discretion as much as legal determinants such as statutes, rules, manuals and court rulings. It also provides vital explanations on the working of the police system in India.

The volume will be of great interest to policymakers, police leaders, officers of judiciary, scholars and researchers of criminology and criminal justice, sociology and social anthropology and South Asian studies.

Satyajit Mohanty belongs to 1988 batch of Indian Police Service. In a career spanning over more than three decades, Mohanty has been posted at senior leadership positions in a number of Police Districts and Ranges, Police Commissionerate, Police Headquarters, Prisons and Correctional Services and Fire and Civil Defence Organisation in Odisha, India. He has also served as the Chairman of the Odisha Public Service Commission.

He holds M.Sc. and LL.B. degrees from Utkal University, Master's degree in Human Rights from Pondicherry University, and PGPPM from IIM Bangalore and Maxwell School of Public Policy, Syracuse University, USA. He has been awarded Ph.D. degree in Law by the National Law University Odisha, India.

He is a recipient of Police (Antrik Suraksha Seva) Medal, Police Medal for Meritorious Service and President's Police Medal for Distinguished Service.

"Police discretion is a vast domain of power which can be used for doing reasonably good for those who are subject to it. Police play a significant role in weighing the balance in the life of the people it governs. One of the attributes of such exercise of discretion is the power to arrest, which exercised judiciously benefits and when abused, harms. This academic work by Dr. Satyajit Mohanty, IPS (retd) is significant in understanding and broadening one's view on such discretion used by the police and how it can evolve for the greater good".

Justice K.G. Balakrishnan, *Former Chief Justice of India*

"An outstanding book meticulously researched and the fact that it is written by an insider (former police officer) makes it insightful. The author's extensive research and work on a subject which concerns every individual yet has rarely been written about, provides a critical analysis of Indian policing and what ails it and where we need to look to reform Indian policing. It was an eye opener for me!!"

Sidharth Luthra, *Senior Advocate, Supreme Court of India*

"Discourse on police discretion in the context of Indian police is mostly anecdotal as rarely any empirical study has been attempted. The book seeks to address the issues and concerns while the police exercise discretion in their powers of arrest, and explaining at the same time the gaps that exist between the legislative intent and actual law enforcement with compelling findings".

Prakash Singh, *(formerly) Director General of Police Assam, Uttar Pradesh and DG BSF*

"Police discretion in arrests can make a critical difference not only to the maintenance of law and order but also to public trust in the institutions of a democracy like India. Combining considerable primary research and rigorous academic method, and drawing on the author's decades of experience as a police officer, this book is incredibly important for scholars, lawmakers, and security officials interested in police and law reform".

Amitav Acharya, *Distinguished Professor of International Relations, American University, Washington, DC*

"The wide and discretionary arrest powers of police have been the subject of critical debates over the past seventy-five years of Indian independence. An outstanding book written by a distinguished police officer, it explores the processes and methods to prevent its abuse in the best interests of society and police. It is a must read for teachers, scholars, judges, police officers, policy makers and all those who are concerned with the study of abuse of power by the police and its accountability".

Professor Srikrishna Deva Rao, *Vice Chancellor, National Law University Delhi*

Police Discretion in India

Legal and Extralegal Factors

Satyajit Mohanty

Routledge
Taylor & Francis Group
LONDON AND NEW YORK

First published 2024
by Routledge
4 Park Square, Milton Park, Abingdon, Oxon OX14 4RN

and by Routledge
605 Third Avenue, New York, NY 10158

Routledge is an imprint of the Taylor & Francis Group, an informa business

British Library Cataloguing-in-Publication Data
A catalogue record for this book is available from the British Library

ISBN: 978-1-032-49638-2 (hbk)
ISBN: 978-1-032-52434-4 (pbk)
ISBN: 978-1-003-40667-9 (ebk)

DOI: 10.4324/9781003406679

Typeset in Sabon
by Apex CoVantage, LLC

Dedicated to my mother

Contents

Figures

Tables

Foreword

One can count a handful of police officials who have successfully aspired to pursue academic and doctoral research on policing in India. The reasons for this are varied and complex but it remains true, even after several decades of curricular and pedagogic reforms in the Indian legal education, that the police studies are not promoted by law schools and law research institutions. Even if that past lack is inexcusable, the law schools now should facilitate research studies that may before long convert the police organisation into a decent law-abiding and human rights protective force.

It therefore comes as good news that the National Law University of Odisha has recognised the importance of such studies and Professor Srikrishna Deva Rao (himself a noted scholar-teacher of criminal law, and now heading the National Law University at Delhi) has found time to painstakingly guide the scrupulous effort of Dr. Satyajit Mohanty.

But what is even rare is an engagement with the realms of police discretion and accountability, and even rarer still is a direct focus on the role of "extra-legal" dimensions in the use/abuse of police discretion. Despite law reforms and judicial progressivism, a notable feature of police culture and conduct that remains notoriously pervasive is the elementary social fact that arrest is the rule rather than exception. This book in your hands shuns easy moral judgements about police organisation as a whole but rather seeks to explain various reasons why and offers a systematic research account of what may be done to change this state of affairs.

Dr. Satyajit Mohanty combines a dexterous knowledge of comparative criminal law and policing landscapes and offers a wealth of empirical skills – a total of 360 police officers of different criminal law, including 138 officers from the Indian Police Service from different states of India and 195 offender respondents as participants have been consulted and the leading "situational" determinants stand fully identified by the adroit use of socio-economic survey, simple frequency tables, cross-tabulations and multiple regression which guide data analysis and interpretation.

While this study is empirically engaged with the Odisha police force, the results also "inductively" extend to "pan Indian characteristics of arrest discretion behaviour of the police". Even if some research *cognoscenti* may contest this extrapolation, Dr. Mohanty justifies it because the sample includes a survey of on-training police officers at Sardar Vallabhbhai Patel National Police Training Academy at Hyderabad and various IPS officers across India.

The work is important for many reasons. It admirably stresses, first, that while discretion in human affairs cannot (and perhaps should never) be eliminated, it can and should be controlled and held accountable in a rule of law society. The author notes that discretion "will continue to remain an inescapable part of policing" and "enforcement without discretion would be harsh and painful to the people", and serves as a "lubricant" to the administration of criminal justice in India,[1] and reminds us of the colourful expression of Ronald Dworkin that it is like "the hole in doughnut". Dr. Mohanty admirably maintains at the same time that "it should be fair, reasonable, and in conformity with public policy" and valuably urges police and law academics in India to continually study the potential, promise and peril of police discretion to arrest.

Second, mere law reform will not result in curbing it or succeed in making discretion accountable. The work reveals that the amended Section 41 of the CrPC (which introduced a new provision of "service of notice" instead of a formal arrest of an accused person, if the commission of the offence is punishable with imprisonment up to seven years) had virtually little or no effect on the arrest discretion behaviour or structure; and the fact that majority of offences carry this sentence resulted in "very insignificant reduction in the arrest figure".

Third, although the role of "extralegal factors" in the abuse of arrest discretion raises high hopes of a frontal discussion on political and governmental interference, the author's careful attention is focused primarily on significant "organisational, subcultural and environmental determinants" of arrest discretion behaviour (see Chapters 5 and 6). The extralegal factors that the learned author has in view are "the demeanour" and "social stratification including race, gender and education of the offender". Also, an important aspect is the size of the Indian police force and its vast jurisdiction. Each "covering more than few thousand square kilometers and with manpower no fewer than tens of thousands", the police "decision-making is more likely to be influenced by the policing environment and subcultures than the organizational policies".[2]

But these determinants, fourthly, are invariably influenced by the socio-economic status of the offender. Dr. Mohanty rightly observes, "People with more education and greater culture in their lives are more likely to have law mobilized to protect their interests". In other words, and as I have said often, citizens who *go* to the courts of their own accord remain minuscule compared to the multitude who are *taken* to courts!

Taking recourse to important studies in the "behaviour of law" which may yield a theory that generates a number of hypotheses regarding how extralegal characteristics influence the "likelihood of law being implemented", Dr.

Mohanty hypothesises that in the "Indian context", the "poor and marginal are less likely to have law mobilized to protect their interest". He ruefully observes that while "the spirit of the amended arrest law in India is more of a rights-based approach", the police behaviour and organisation "still provides wide discretionary latitude to bypass the core ethos of the law".[3]

At the same time, the learned author notes that "there is some basis for each of these subcultural truths and each alienates police from the citizens". The "truths" are [1] It is "impossible to win the war on crimes without bending the rules"; [2] "Public are potentially hostile and untrustworthy"; [3] "Citizens are unsupportive and make unreasonable demands"; [4] The "police are the only real crime fighters"; [5] "Loyalty to colleague counts more than anything else" and [6] "No one understands the nature of police work but fellow officers". The police beliefs about overall alienation remain distinctive to policing cultures and organisation and contribute considerably to a culture of policing that virtually claims impunity from the demands of trust and accountability. Dr. Mohanty's suggestion to follow the ideals and practices of neighbourhood policing suggest important ways ahead to mitigate the distance (even stereotypes) among the police, citizen and constitutional cultures.[4]

Throughout this work, the author is explicitly concerned with debunking various "myths". The first is that the "amended arrest law will reduce the number of avoidable arrests and decongest the prisons" and the second is that the "provisions of amended arrest law (Section 41 CrPC) will restrict the wide discretionary power the police enjoyed in the pre-amendment period". The idea that arrests "are made on the basis of evidences in accordance with the provision of the statutes" constitutes the third myth; and so, does the fourth myth resting on the view that legal "considerations dominated the arrest discretion behaviour more than extralegal factors". The destruction of these four myths is successfully accomplished and archived in this work.

Dr. Mohanty concludes his fine book in these words: "People in the democracies across the world want more say in the way they would like to be policed and, in a way, reject the existing accountability mechanisms of the organization." In this considered view, the "[t]wenty-first century is likely to usher in a new era of police accountability – accountable to the people – two centuries after the advent of the modern police". In many senses, the global turn towards reconsidering administration of criminal justice is suggested by recent instance of "police excess in George Floyd's arrest in Minneapolis, whose tragic death prompted worldwide protests against racially biased policing".

Yet, one may justly ask: how long would one want, and continue, to say *Amen*? If the not-so Utopian moment seems at hand, why does the vastness of dystopian global reality of arrest behaviour by the police continue to consume the lifeworld of citizens and societies?

Dr. Mohanty, given decades of discipline of police and public service, does not directly raise this question, but as a citizen of the world he acknowledges that "the malaise is much deeper". And so it is, both nationally and globally.

For far too long, slow-acting legislatures and leaders have acted merely as forces of law and order and managers of collective human security. They have under that banner and name alienated policing in which hostile stereotypes both about the police and citizens take roots and prevail. Now, the global social policy change movements have somehow facilitated the growing need and serve the growing human demand, to convert a repressive police organisation into a democratic service agency. The Indian state and civil society have a pioneering global partnership role to play in this direction, enriched as they are by promising reform agendum and progressive judicial demosprudential leadership in the co-governance of the nation.

Upendra Baxi
Emeritus Professor of Law, University of Warwick and Delhi
May 28, 2022

Notes

1 Elsewhere, I have elaborated why our administration of criminal justice still awaits transformations to a criminal justice system: see Baxi, U. (2020). Human rights in the administration of criminal justice. *Journal of the National Commission on Human Rights*, 19, 1–22.

2 Dr. Mohanty invites our attention to the fact that as of 2020, there were "16,955 police stations, 800 police districts, 189 police ranges, 95 police zones and sixty-three Commissioners of Police in India" and as many as "3,38,000 officers empowered to 'arrest without a warrant' ".

3 But note that there exist "the five rider clauses to the amended provisions of arrest" which are "but wide discretionary latitudes given to the police officer which cannot be vouched for not being subject to potential misuse". Dr. Mohanty wryly notes that these clauses exist despite that section being dubbed "as archaic being unable to pass the constitutional test of reasonableness" and which "allows too much of discretion and subjectivity at the hands of police". See *Prakash Singh v. Union of India* 2006 (8) SCC 1. However, the legislative ambivalence results here in escalating a culture of police unreasonableness, and even lawlessness.

4 The suggestion for a "democratic police" force which is fully responsive and responsible to the people has been a constant refrain, since the Independence of India; numerous state and national police reform committees and commissions have commended transition towards democratic or people's policing. See Baxi, U. (1982). *The crisis of Indian legal system* (pp. 115–120). New Delhi: Vikas. More recently, as Dr. Mohanty explains in this work, the Supreme Court has suggested structural reforms as well as small steps to transform the situation. Needless to say, neither has been fully adopted by the legislatures!

Acknowledgements

This book is the outcome of my research on police discretion as a Ph.D. scholar at the National Law University Odisha and as a practitioner. As a maiden empirical study in the field of police discretion in India, against the backdrop of my lack of practical knowledge of complex statistical methods needed for data analysis, it is Prof. Rabindra Kumar Mohanty, Dr. Bigyanananda Mohanty and Mr. Shyamal Kumar Das, who gave me the initial confidence to go ahead with the idea. Not only did they process the complex data at hand, they were always readily available to explain the nuances and implications of the analysis in real-world situations.

I am also grateful to Prof. Srikrishna Deva Rao for his constant support and guidance as I researched on the subject and wrote this book. Despite many competing interests for his time, he always made time for me with an affable smile and genuine warmth.

I want to acknowledge the efforts of Mr. Anish Alok Mohanty and Ms. Anumita Chakrabarti for their painstaking efforts in editing the first manuscript of the book.

I am indebted to my wife, Dr. Lisa Patnaik, for patiently bearing with my unavoidable encumbrances during this period.

I am grateful to the National Law University Odisha, SVP National Police Academy, Hyderabad and the Odisha Police for giving me the platform to commence and complete the work.

Last but by no means least, my thanks to the Commissioning Editor Routledge and his team for their professionalism in publishing the book.

Abbreviations

Addl SP	Additional Superintendent of Police
AIR	All India Reporter
CrPC	Criminal Procedure Code
CAPF	Central Armed Police Force
DGP	Director General of Police
DySP	Deputy Superintendent of Police
IPC	Indian Penal Code
IPS	Indian Police Service
NPC	National Police Commission
NHRC	National Human Rights Commission
OBC	Other Backward Class
PMR	Police Manual Rules
PPMCC	Pearson Product Moment Correlation Coefficient
SC	Scheduled Caste
SCC	Supreme Court Cases
ST	Scheduled Tribe
SI	Sub-Inspector
SLL	Special and Local Laws
SP	Superintendent of Police
SPSS	Statistical Package for the Social Sciences

Preface

> "Policing is for the most part extralegal, for while police officers (often) work within the constraints of law, they seldom invoke the law in performing police work"
>
> – *Robert E Worden* (1989)

Prof. Worden's observation was exemplified by the recent instance of police excess in George Floyd's arrest in Minneapolis, whose tragic death prompted world-wide protests against racially biased policing. The charge against him was the use of a then allegedly counterfeit twenty-dollar currency note at a grocery shop[1]. Thousands of miles away from Minneapolis, at around the same time, a similar case was unfolding in Tuticorin, India where a shopkeeper Jayaraj and his son were arrested by the police on the charge of keeping their shop open beyond prescribed hours during the Covid-19 curfew. They were allegedly tortured by the police while in custody and died while receiving treatment in the hospital for injuries suffered in detention. This incident was called the "George Floyds of India" across mainstream media and social media.[2]

What is common to both these incidents is that in both cases, the charges – a counterfeit twenty- dollar bill and keeping the shop open beyond prescribed hours – were trivial. The police, in the first instance, could have examined the veracity of the allegation and in the second instance, could have initiated appropriate penal proceedings under the law. In both situations, the police in discharging their legally mandated brief as gatekeepers of the law at the ground level, needed to balance it with how vigorously they react, how much benefit of the doubt they give, whether they decide to arrest and how forcefully they exercise their power of arrest. These instances show the wide discretionary ambit of the police and the ramifications of the choices they make within this ambit. What prompted the police to abuse their discretion and use brute force during the arrests, directly leading to the loss of precious lives of the individuals in custody, is both intriguing and a matter of urgent public importance. How much do extralegal factors influence police decision making? And if they do, what accountability mechanisms are in place or can be introduced to guard against the colourable exercise of arrest powers or the abuse of discretion?

This power of arrest has been a matter of intense debate and controversy since the inception of the modern police force. Arrest decisions are strongly influenced by an intelligible assessment of live circumstances by the police officer and involve a considerable amount of discretion. Although discretion is an unavoidable and ubiquitous feature of police work, it is certainly susceptible to abuse. Lawmakers and courts across the globe have attempted to regulate this power and impose restraints on arrest discretion by introducing greater accountability through laws and rulings for over a century. A concerted effort has been made to constrain the unfettered exercise of arrest discretion through well-intentioned statutes, policies, rules and internal guidelines – incidents such as George Floyd's and Jayaraj's indicate that much needs to be done to improve accountability and curtail discretionary abuse.

This book has been written with the aim of exploring the dynamics of arrest discretion behaviour of the police and making recommendations to prevent its abuse with a view to improving police legitimacy and upholding the rule of law.

The century old arrest law of India as defined under Section 41 Criminal Procedure Code of India[3] was amended in the year 2009 on the basis of recommendations of the Law Commission of India in its 177th Report[4]. The objective was to reduce the number of avoidable arrests based on the legal principles of "reasonableness"[5], "necessity"[6] and "restraints"[7]. The amended law introduced a new provision of "service of notice" instead of formal arrest of a person accused of an offence punishable with imprisonment for less than or up to seven years. Analysis of substantive laws in India shows that the offences that prescribe punishment for less than or up to seven years constitute two-thirds of the total penal offences. Following the new amendment, the arrest figures in India should have been theoretically reduced by two-thirds as a similar proportion of offences are punishable with imprisonment up to or less than seven years in the substantive laws of India. If not to that extent, avoidable arrest figures would have been reduced considerably as the amended law authorises the police to let off the accused with a "service of notice" in a significant proportion of previously "arrest-only"[8] offences as this was one of the key legislative intents behind the 2009 amendment of arrest provisions. But a study of arrest figures for the pre- and post-amendment periods shows that there has been a very insignificant reduction in the arrest figures – 1.18 arrest per offence in the post-amendment period as against 1.19 in the pre-amendment period (from 2006 to 2015 with 2009 as mid-base year)[9]. This leads to the inquiry if the statute, departmental guidelines, court rulings, police manual rules etc. have any influence on the arrest decision of the police or are there other factors that have escaped our scrutiny?

Research establishes that the perception that police made arrest decisions simply on the basis of whether or not law has been violated was an inaccurate portrayal of how police worked. Studies establish that police use enormous amount of discretion, which is at the core of police functioning (Kelling, 1999). Police make far more discretionary determinations than any other class of administrators and a good deal of discretion is illegal or has questionable legality (Davis, 1969). While the empirical research leaves little doubt that legal factors significantly influence arrest outcomes, Worden (1989) argues that arrest decision is not solely influenced by law, and policing is for the most part extralegal. Literature review establishes that factors like organisational, situational, subcultural, environmental and individual determinants are at the forefront of influencing the arrest decision on behalf of the law enforcement (Gaines & Kappeler, 2003, Groeneveld, 2005, Hidayet, 2011). Out of the five determinants, the organisational determinant comprises legal variables like statute, court directives, departmental guidelines etc., while components of the situational determinants are partly guided by legal factors like seriousness of the offence, offender's criminal record etc. and partly by some extralegal factors like demeanour of the offender and individual officer's characteristics. The other determinants are extralegal, complex and intangible in nature while considerably influencing the arrest decision.

Though controversial and much debated, use of discretion by the police has remained a lesser researched topic in India than it is in the West. This study is the maiden empirical inquiry to test if the determinants of arrest discretion (empirically validated in the Western world) are valid in the Indian context, how they interplay and which among the determinants has dominant influence over arrest decision. Besides, in this study, validity of a few theoretical concepts and hypotheses on arrest discretion behaviour have been tested in the context of police in India. This study contributes to fill the research gap that exists in the field of police discretion and aims to be interpretive, providing explanations for the results obtained in this study through the analysis of background study of Indian police, laws and policies in India, and by considering the association of variables in this study.

The major approach in this study is quantitative data analysis. The variables under each determinant have been operationalised with appropriate response statements and respondents have been asked to express their degree of agreement or disagreement with each item on a classical Likert scales with five choices. A total of 222 police respondents from Odisha police and 138 officers from the Indian Police Service from different States of India have participated in the study. For study of situational determinant, a separate socio-economic survey has been conducted with 195 offender respondents as participants. Combination of simple frequency table and cross tabulation have been employed for data analysis.

The study establishes that organisational, subcultural and environmental determinants are significant for police in India and positively correlated to arrest discretion behaviour. It empirically establishes that subcultural and environmental determinants influence arrest discretion behaviour as much as the organisational determinant, contrary to the popular perception that it is the organisation, through statutes, rules and compliance to court directives, that constrains the arrest discretion. The decision making process within the discretionary boundary is a complex exercise of legal-extralegal considerations. The colourable exercise of arrest power or abuse of arrest discretion is often clothed as a legitimate exercise because the boundary between legal and extralegal considerations is thin and not well defined universally. This study brings a certain degree of clarity into the arrest decision making process so that the police leaders can identify the factors contributing to the discretionary abuse and put proper accountability mechanism in place to prevent abuse.

A majority of the police respondents endorse that scope for personal judgment exists in arrest decision beyond the boundary of statutes and rules. Still a larger percentage of the study population believe that arrests in some instances precede formalities like collection of evidences. This casts doubt on the efficacy of accountable mechanisms of the police organisation against intentional violation of arrest guidelines. The study thus empirically establishes the inadequacy of the existing accountability mechanism to prevent discretional abuse.

The book is divided into seven chapters. In chapter 1, I have discussed the legislative intents behind the amendment of the arrest law in 2009. The objectives were to make the law more in conformity with the Constitutional principles, to reduce the number of avoidable arrests and to decongest the prisons. But some secondary data crunching of arrest figures in India taking 2009 as the mid-base year does not reflect the legislative intents. The findings led me to probe further into the causes of non-realisation of the legislative intent by the field law enforcement in the post amendment period. A set of questions have been raised fundamental to the study of arrest discretion in the context of India.

In chapter 2, I have reviewed the existing literature on discretion, traced how the concept developed as a discipline in the criminal justice system during the 50s and 60s of the last century and evolved over years. Besides, the rulings on police discretion by the national Courts of England, USA and Canada over the years have been discussed to give an overview of judicial interpretation of the police discretion. On the basis of literature review, a set of hypotheses have been developed, out of which few important ones have been chosen for this study for empirical validation in the context of the police in India.

Chapter 3 presents an overview of the history of policing in India, laws and policies that have shaped the police discretion in post-independence period. Important decisions of the High Courts and Supreme Court of India on arrest, police discretion and directives that largely influenced the legislative amendment of the arrest law have been discussed.

One of the major challenges in the study was the operationalisation of the determinants of arrest and their empirical tests in the Indian context. This has been discussed in chapter 4. Factors or variables defining the conceptual space of each determinant have been carefully chosen from the literature and have been operationalised. Twenty such variables have been selected for the organisational, subcultural and environmental determinants whereas three variables each for the individual and situational determinants. Each variable under a major a determinant or concept has been qualified with a statement which is meaningful to the "world of experience" and collectively they represent the concept. The process of scoring is achieved by assigning numeric value to the response format. The classical Likert scales with five choices have been chosen for this study. A socio-economic survey of offenders has been taken up for empirical testing the situational determinants. In this study, the state of Odisha is taken as a universe. Besides, random selection of senior officers from India Police Service from across different states and union territory polices of the country on training course at National Police Academy, Hyderabad have been taken as respondents. Therefore, inductively, the research findings are expected to mirror pan Indian characteristics of arrest discretion behaviour of the police.

Cross-comparison of frequency table data are the main tools of data analysis in this study. Chapter 5 and 6 deal with data analysis. I have dealt with the interplay of organisational, subcultural and environmental determinants in chapter 5 and individual and situational in chapter 6, primarily for two reasons. Firstly, the variables under the first three determinants have been measured, compared and analysed through a uniform methodology as opposed to those under individual and situational determinants. Secondly, the data analysis of the first three determinants has challenged the popular narratives on arrest discretion and deserves to be treated exclusively.

In addition, this study aims to be interpretive, where I intend to provide appropriate explanations for the results that have been obtained in this study by analysing the background study on police discretion internationally, laws and policies in India, and by considering the association of the variables in this study. The final chapter, while summing up the findings, debunks a few popular narratives on police discretion, accountability mechanisms and subcultural ethos. Here are some myths;

Myth 1

The amended arrest law will reduce the number of avoidable arrests and decongest the prisons.

The amended Section 41 of the CrPC introduced a new provision of "service of notice" instead of a formal arrest of an accused person, if the commission of the offence is punishable with imprisonment up to seven years. Analysis of substantive laws in India shows that the offences which prescribe punishment up to or less than seven years is two-third of the total penal offences. Had the legislative intent been followed in true letter and spirit of the amended law, the arrest figures in India would have been reduced by two-thirds. But analysis of arrest figures for the pre- and post-amendment periods shows that there has been very insignificant reduction in the arrest figures (1.18 arrest per offence in the post-amendment period as against 1.19 in the pre-amendment period). The annual figures for comparative study have been taken from 2006 to 2015 with 2009 as mid-base year[10].

Analysis of prison statistics for the years, 2016, 2017 and 2018 shows that the total prison population during the period was 4,33,033, 4,50,696 and 4,66,084 respectively. They were overcrowded with 113.7, 115.1 and 117.6 percent occupancy rates[11]. A more granular view of the proportion of under trial prisoners as against the total prison population, which is an even better metric to gauge the overcrowding of prisons, revel a steady rise from 67.7 to 69.4 percent during this period[12].

Myth 2

The provisions of amended arrest law (Section 41 CrPC) will restrict the wide discretionary power the police enjoyed in the pre-amendment period.

The provisions under 41(1)(b)(ii) of CrPC is the rider clause to the amendment, which states that the police can arrest any person without warrant if such person has committed a cognizable offence punishable with imprisonment up to seven years provided that the police officer is satisfied that such arrest is necessary—

(a) to prevent such person from committing further crime, or
(b) for proper investigation, or
(c) to prevent such person from tampering with evidence, or
(d) to prevent such person from making any inducement, threat to any witness, or
(e) to ensure the presence of such person in the Court whenever required.

Otherwise, the person can be served with notice under Sec 41A.

Data analysis shows that an overwhelming 88 percent respondents endorse that the five conditions under Sec 41(1)(b)(ii) provide plenty of choices for exercise of discretion whether to arrest an accused person involved in "noticeable" offence. True, the discretion is an inescapable part of the criminal justice system and discretionary choices are available to the investigating officer to arrest repeat offenders (under proviso (a)), habitual criminals (again under proviso (a)) and criminals who could influence or intimidate witnesses (under provisions (c) and (d)) even if the offence committed is punishable with an imprisonment up to or less than seven years. For instance, police invariably arrest and deny bail to recidivist vehicle lifters who are booked under theft, an offence punishable by imprisonment of up to three years. If one goes by the strict letters of the amended arrest law, the offender could have been entitled to service of notice, and not necessarily arrest. But the arrest of such repeat offender, by invoking proviso (a) of the rider clause above, reposes public faith in criminal justice administration. Interestingly, while one hand the law makers amended the century old arrest law dubbing it as archaic being unable to pass the constitutional test of "reasonableness" and that allows too much of discretion and subjectivity at the hands of police, the five rider clauses to the amended provisions of arrest are but wide discretionary latitudes given to the police officer which cannot be vouched for not being subject to potential misuse. Besides, the investigation officer may take shelter of the rider clauses as lawful safe haven against the colourable exercise of arrest power.

Myth 3

Arrests are made on the basis of evidences in accordance with the provision of the statutes.

One of the response statements significant for this study is designed to elicit information on how much operational independence the officer enjoys beyond the four walls of departmental guidelines and rules. More than 73 percent of the respondents either agree or strongly agree to the response statement that investigating officers sometimes make arrest decisions based on their personal judgment as opposed to guidelines. This is revealing of the fact that a larger proportion of population believes that the scope for personal judgement exists within the boundary of the statute. Another statement under this dimension is designed to elicit a response on the oft criticised police practice to arrest an accused person before the collection of evidence in spite of a litany of court directives and requirements of the statue to do the contrary. 75.8 percent of the respondents believe that arrests in some instances precede formalities like collection of evidences. This casts doubt on the efficacy of accountable mechanism of the department against intentional violation of arrest guidelines.

Myth 4

Legal considerations dominate the arrest discretion behaviour more than extralegal factors

One of the key assumptions of this study was that factors, such as organisation through its policy, process and value dimensions, informal organisational or subcultural ethos, operating environment within which the police function, situational and individual determinants, either individually or in combination, influence the arrest discretion behaviour of the police. Out of the five determinants, the first three determinants – organisational, subcultural and environmental determinants – have been operationalised for statistical analysis with several anchor variables. One of the tasks is to find out the relative importance of the three key determinants – organisational, subcultural, environmental – in influencing the arrest discretion behaviour and to find out the extent to which the three determinants are perceived to influence arrest discretion behaviour.

Based on an empirical study it was found that environmental and subcultural factors are perceived to impact arrest discretion behavior almost similarly or even more than the organisational determinants which are well defined with rules, regulations, statutes, departmental sanctions etc. What could be the reason behind these findings which appear to be counter-intuitive?

One explanation for the variations may be the degree of subjective interpretation that the concerned determinants undergo. More the subjective interpretation, more would be the impact on arrest discretion behaviour. Organisational determinants are more objective with rule, regulation, court directives, and organisational sanctions against violation being in place. The discretionary latitude here is well defined and sanction awaits anyone against breach of discretionary boundary. The conceptual space within the subcultural ethos or environmental determinants is complex and intangible therefore likely to be more susceptible to subjective interpretation. Where there is more scope for subjective interpretation of a situation, the decision making is more likely to be non- uniform. This has been showed empirically in forthcoming chapters, where we find the least amount of variation as the response statements to questions on organisational determinants which are based on statute, departmental circulars, police manual orders, and departmental sanction against procedural transgression etc.

It is recommended that discretion, as a discipline, should be a part of the training curriculum of the police training academies. It is suggested that police leadership consider the practice of community policing to improve the department's operational image and to overcome the negative aspects of police culture. Some of the directives of the Supreme Court in the Prakash Singh case[13], such as establishment of Police Complaint Authority, selection procedure of the state police chief and fixed tenure for field level police officers will go a long way towards establishing proper accountability mechanisms and giving much needed operational independence to the police.

As there was no empirical inquiry related to arrest discretion behaviour of the police in India, the framework of this study is based on theoretical inquiries from Western literature. Literature suggests that situational, subcultural, environmental, individual and situational determinants are at the forefront of arrest discretion behaviour. Study on all five determinants is a challenge but it is the sheer academic inquisitiveness and desire to empirically test the relevance of all the determinants in the Indian context that motivated me to proceed ahead with the task. Therefore, I hope that this study serves as an exploratory investigation that provides useful insights for further studies on arrest discretion behaviour of the police in India.

Discretion will continue to remain an inescapable part of policing, as enforcement without discretion would be harsh and painful to the people.

Discretion acts as a lubricant to law enforcement mechanisms with the caveat that it should be fair, reasonable, and in conformity with public policy. The question of accountability assumes importance to ensure that discretionary determinants remain free from abuse. Discretion and accountability are linked intrinsically (Pepinsky, 1984). The global outcry demanding fairness in policing procedures following the tragic death of George Floyd in police custody or for that matter, people clamouring for justice in Jayaram's death in India, points towards the lack of robust accountability mechanisms in the police organisations against the abuse of discretionary powers. The institution of the police is imperative to maintain social harmony, but what is really needed is policing that is more accountable to the people. The twenty-first century is going see a fundamental shift in the philosophy of policing as the people in democratic societies demand an increasing say in the way they wish to be policed.

Notes

1 Evan Hill, et.al., "How George Floyd was Killed in Police Custody," *The New York Times*, 8 July 2020, https://www.nytimes.com/2020/05/31/us/george-floyd-investigation.html
2 R.K.Vij, "India must adopt zero tolerance policy for torture and death in police custody", *The Outlook*, 13 July, 2020 https://www.outlookindia.com/magazine/story/india-news-opinion-india-must-adopt-zero-tolerance-policy-for-torture-and-death-in-police-custody/
3 The contents of the provisions of arrest under Section 41 of the Code of Criminal Procedure retained its original text in the statute from 1898 till 2009 when major amendments were introduced to the Code of Criminal Procedure.
4 The Law Commission, in its 177th Report, took up the matter of arrest suo motu in order to clearly define the law relating to arrest without warrant. The Commission recommended sweeping changes in the arrest laws in its Report in the year 2001 which were later inserted in the Criminal Procedure Code by amendments in the year 2009.
5 Law has to be reasonable, just and fair.
6 Police can exercise powers only when it is genuinely necessary.
7 Liberty of an individual can be interfered only where circumstances necessitate them.
8 Prior to the amendment, arrest was the only recourse in cognizable offences. The police did not have the option of "service of notice" on the accused.
9 Sourced from Crime in India published annually by National Crime Records Bureau, MHA, Government of India.
10 Sourced from Crime in India published annually by National Crime Records Bureau, MHA, Government of India.
11 Sourced from Prison Statistics India published annually by National Crime Records Bureau, MHA, Government of India.
12 ibid.
13 2006 8 SCC 1.

1 Introduction

1.1 The Background

> Arrest and detention in police lock-up of a person can cause incalculable harm to the reputation and self-esteem of a person. No arrest can be made in a routine manner on a mere allegation of commission of an offence made against a person. It would be prudent for a police officer in the interest of protection of the constitutional rights of a citizen and perhaps in his own interest that no arrest should be made without a reasonable satisfaction reached after some investigation as to the genuineness and bona fides of a complaint and a reasonable belief both as to the person's complicity and even so as to the need to effect arrest. Denying a person of his liberty is a serious matter.
>
> – Supreme Court of India[1]

A sovereign government derives its legitimacy by virtue of the social contract with its citizens. The police, as the agents or representatives of the government, are expected to uphold the obligations of the social contract (Young 2011) because the "authority of police is derived from the people through social contract and this power is held in public trust" (Moll 2006). Based on this philosophy, the police perform multifarious functions including safeguarding the basic tenets of dignified life, liberty and the pursuit of happiness of the members of society by keeping criminal and deviant characters at bay with exercise of the coercive powers of arrest, detention and search. Therefore, the power to arrest the suspect or the accused of an offence is one such legitimate authority of the police. However, the subject of arrest has been a matter of intense debate and controversy since the inception of modern police in the mid-nineteenth century. Lawmakers across the globe spent the last century working on new laws and rulings on how to regulate this power and impose restraints on the arrest decision of police so as to ensure more accountability.

Until the 1950s, the usual narrative for police administrators was that the police investigated every crime and ensured compliance with and enforcement of every law, with equal priority and diligence. Police chiefs made

DOI: 10.4324/9781003406679-1

public announcements that all offences, regardless of the seriousness of the offence, were investigated with equal effort and that all laws were enforced with the same priority. But the ground reality has always been far from this premise. Prioritisation of a multitude of tasks has often been dictated by resource constraints and a variety of other factors. When to arrest, whom to arrest first among group of offenders and the mode of arrest are decisions that the police officers take on a daily basis. These decisions are subject to an intelligible assessment of circumstances by the police and naturally involve the exercise of a fair amount of discretion.

Interestingly, only in the mid-twentieth century, legal scholars and academics "discovered"[2] that this wide discretional latitude is at the heart of police functioning. Decisions such as whether to arrest a person, to let them off with a mere warning, whether to detain a person on suspicion and whether to stop a vehicle for over-speeding are governed by a police officer's discretion at that very moment. But discretion should never be unfettered as flexibility and discretion have the potential risk of delivering injustice and abuse of power (Fisk 1974). It has been found that the "police use a much higher amount of discretion than most other criminal justice officials, and there is no close second" (Davis 1975). This is likely because the "police are the first point of call acting as gate-keepers of any criminal justice system" (Halliday 2009), and while statutes, codes, departmental guidelines etc. provide directions for addressing the issues, most circumstances would necessitate discretionary decision-making by the police based on professional judgements and standards. Therefore, the exercise of discretion should be fair, just, reasonable and meant for public good (Fisk 1974).

Arrest laws in India have seen few discernible changes over the years. The police under the Criminal Procedure Code (CrPC), the main statute on criminal procedure in India, are given vast powers of arrest to enforce the laws of the land and to maintain an orderly society. These wide powers of arrest remained unchanged for over a century, through Indian independence and the advent of the Indian Constitution. It was only after a long hundred and ten years[3] that the law of arrest was amended in 2009. However, the subject of arrest still carries a fair amount of discretion. In subsequent chapters of this book, the factors influencing the arrest discretion behaviour of the police are discussed in detail.

Following the recommendations of the 177th Report of Law Commission of India (2001),[4] the provisions of arrest were amended in the CrPC in the year 2009. The 2009 amendment was premised on both Article 21 of the Constitution of India which guarantees that "no person shall be deprived of his life and personal liberty except according to the procedure established by law" and the Supreme Court's ruling in seminal Maneka Gandhi case,[5] where it was held that the procedure established by law must be "right, just and fair and not be arbitrary, fanciful and oppressive". This postulated that any law not conforming to the "reasonableness" test of the Maneka Gandhi case could be struck down as unconstitutional. The Law Commission argued that the language of the provisions of arrest without warrant enjoined in Section 41 of the CrPC (pre-amendment) falls short of "reasonableness" test as constructed in Maneka Gandhi and the decision to arrest is left entirely to the sole and absolute discretion of the police officer making the arrest. Besides, taking into account the observations of the National Police Commission Report (1979–1981)[6] on arrest and avoidable arrest, and having due regard to the rulings of the Supreme Court in Joginder Kumar[7] and D.K. Basu,[8] the Law Commission of India suggested sweeping changes in the form of amendments to the provisions of arrest without warrant. The law was amended in the year 2009 with the provision that the police may arrest a suspect involved in offences with maximum punishment of up to seven years only after certain conditions are justified in writing by the investigating officer, otherwise a "notice" can be served on the suspect with undertaking to produce himself for investigation as and when required. The lawmakers thus introduced a new category of offence by this amendment, that is, "noticeable offence". The legislative intent was to reduce avoidable arrest figures and overcrowding of the prisons, and regulate police arbitrariness and discretion in arrest law.

1.2 Ground Reality of Arrests in India

A study of offences defined in the substantive laws of India shows that 33.5 percent, that is, approximately one-third of such laws prescribe punishment for more than seven years while two-thirds of such offences entail punishment for less than seven years. The offences prescribed in the Indian Penal Code (IPC), India's major penal code and in other substantive statutes of India were studied. Out of the 296 penal sections in the IPC, 198 sections cover offences for which the punishment prescribed is less than or up to seven years and the other 98 offences prescribe punishment of more than seven years. The analysis of forty-nine minor substantive statutes shows that out of 131 offences prescribed in those statutes, eighty-six prescribe imprisonment for up to or less than seven years and the other forty-five prescribe imprisonment of more than seven years. The classification of offences based on punishment up to and more than seven years is placed in *Appendix A*. This effectively means that two-thirds of the cognisable offences in substantive laws in India are to be treated as "noticeable" by the police following the 2009 amendment. The figures of arrest should have been proportionately reduced but the figures show a disquieting trend, contrary to the intent of the lawmakers.

An analysis of arrest figures, when it comes to arrests without warrants in the pre- and post-amendment periods, shows that there has hardly been any reduction in the number of arrests. The average arrests per offence between 2006 and 2009 stand at 1.19 whereas in the post-amendment period from 2010 to 2015, the ratio shows only a negligible decline and is pegged at 1.18. The official statistics for arrest and registration of offences are published by the Ministry of Home Affairs through its National Crime Records Bureau, in its annual compendium, "Crime in India". The decennial statistics for the period from 2006 to 2015 were culled out from the annual issues to compare and contrast the trends in arrest figures by police in the pre- and post-amendment periods. Table 1.1 presents the abstract of decennial statistics.

The figures under Columns 4 and 7 reflect the total number of cognisable offences registered by police, under the Indian Penal Code, as well as Special and Local Laws, and the number of persons arrested from 2006 to 2015. The graph on Table 1.2 captures the decennial figures on offences registered

Table 1.1 Abstract of decennial statistics

Year 1	*Number of IPC cases registered* 2	*Number of SLL cases registered* 3	*Total number of cases registered (IPC+SLL)* 4	*Number of persons arrested in IPC cases* 5	*Number of persons arrested in SLL cases* 6	*Total number of persons arrested (IPC+SLL)* 7
2006	1878293	3224167	**5102460**	2653683	3554222	**6207905**
2007	1989673	3743734	**5733407**	2780559	4087246	**6867805**
2008	2093379	3844725	**5938104**	2882286	4255988	**7138274**
2009	2121345	4553872	**6675217**	2849025	4902606	**7751631**
2010	2224831	4525917	**6750748**	2947122	4842815	**7789937**
2011	2325575	3927154	**6252729**	3145845	4312413	**7458258**
2012	2387188	3654371	**6041559**	3270016	4150075	**7420091**
2013	2647722	3992656	**6640378**	3523577	4467963	**7991540**
2014	2851563	4377630	**7229193**	3790812	4804382	**8595194**
2015	2949400	4376699	**7326099**	3636596	4857230	**8493826**

NB: Source: Crime in India, NCRB, MHA, Government of India; IPC – Indian Penal Code, SLL – Special and Local Laws

Table 1.2 Decennial figures on offences versus arrest

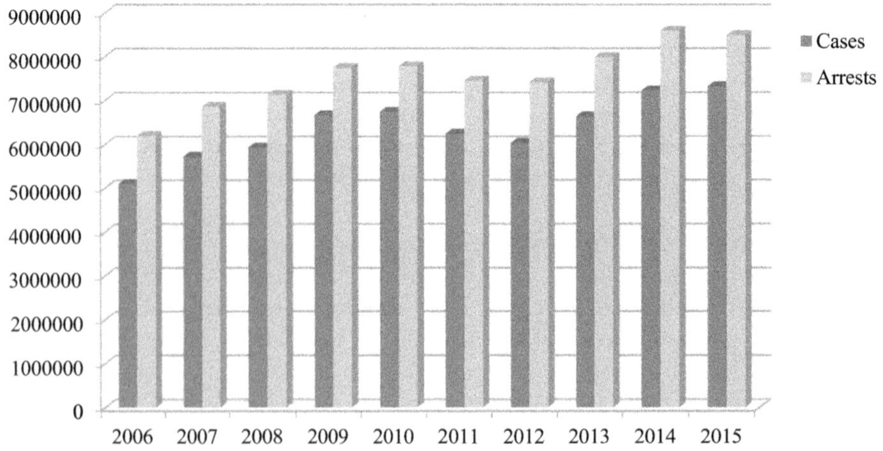

Table 1.3 Decennial arrest per offence figures

Year	*Ratio of arrest per offence*	*Average arrest per offence*
2006	1.21	
2007	1.19	**1.19**
2008	1.20	
2009	1.16	
2010	1.15	
2011	1.19	**1.18**
2012	1.22	
2013	1.20	
2014	1.18	
2015	1.15	

and persons arrested. It is interesting to note that the numbers of arrests show a steady upward trend vis-à-vis the number of registration of offences. But, having regard to the offences to be treated as "noticeable" following the amendment of arrest law in 2009, a downward trend in arrest per offence is what is expected as the outcome of the legislative intent behind the amendment. A glance at Table 1.3 reveals a contrarian picture.

These figures may not show a definite trend but one thing that clearly emerges is that the average arrests per offence in the post-2009 period – year 2009 being taken as the datum since the law was amended then – do not show any appreciable decline as was expected following the amendment. The decline should have ideally followed the percentage of offences which are deemed "noticeable" by the amended provision of Section 41 CrPC in 2009, that is, by a margin of two-thirds but interestingly what it reflects is a very negligible decline in a statistical comparison. The average of arrests per offence during the four-year period from 2006 to 2009 was 1.19 and that during the six-year period from 2010 to 2015 is 1.18 – a marginal drop of 0.01 per offence. Whereas, had the legislative intent been translated ideally, the decline would have been in the range of 0.5–0.7 (two-thirds of the offences being noticeable). On the ground, it would have been translated as one arrest per two offences in the post-amendment period as against more than one arrest per offence in the pre-amendment period. But the rates of arrest in the post-amendment period almost mimic the trend of pre-amendment period.

The book delves into the reasons behind this gap as to why the legislative intent has failed to be translated into reality. What is it that shapes the ultimate implementation of law on the ground level apart from the statutory guidelines, manual rules, and departmental and court directives? This book intends to explore if the determinants of arrest discretion collected on the basis of literature review from the West are valid in the Indian context. An empirical study has been designed to test a few hypotheses and to identify the dominant effect of the determinants on arrest discretion behaviour of the police in India. This may provide an insight into the factors, both legal and extralegal, that shape the arrest decision behaviour of police. Finally, a set of recommendations has been made on how to regulate police discretion so that the police leaders and policymakers can ensure that the use of discretion is fair, just, in the public interest and free from abuse.

1.3 The Determinants of Arrest Discretion

Research by police scholars, social scientists and literature studies establish that factors such as organisational, informal organisational or subcultural, environmental, individual and situational determinants are a few key factors that influence discretionary decision-making by law enforcement agencies (Gaines and Kappeler 2003; Groeneveld 2005; Hidayet 2011).

The organisation through its policy, process, value and training creates a structure that considerably constrains discretionary behaviour (Groeneveld 2005). For a long time now, policy has been regarded as one of the most constructive methods of directing police decision-making. The law, court directives, police manual rules, departmental circulars, disciplinary action for wilful violations of procedure etc. define the policies of the police organisation. The more extensive and detailed policies within the organisation are, the more control the organisation has over discretionary decision-making.

The informal organisational culture refers to the "unwritten culture comprised of individual values and traditions that are communicated informally across from officer to officer" (Walker and Katz 2005). This is referred to as police subculture. Subculture is defined as "a culture within a broader culture that may deviate in some aspects from the broader culture and influences daily decisions" (Herbert 1998). These discrete sets of values are woven together to form a perceptual net that guides individual decisions (Brown 1988).

Environmental determinants, such as political culture, media and public opinion, considerably influence the decision-making by the police. Each of these components either independently or in combination creates a complex maze within which the decision-making by the police is processed.

Individual determinants examine the relationship between the officer's gender, work experience, education, position in the organisation, social class, etc. on one hand and the police behaviour on the other. Literature review and research on individual determinants produce mixed results with strong and weak relationships, which means other variables remaining constant, the officer's relative experience and seniority may have certain degrees of influence on the decision-making.

Situational determinants are by far the most influential of the determinants on discretionary behaviour, as shown in various studies. The situational variables are factors concerning the "degree of interaction between law enforcement and citizens within the community and offender attributes" (Halliday 2009). "Thus, police discretion is influenced by the surrounding situation in which an officer finds himself and how an offender presents himself before the police" (Halliday 2009). According to Black's (1971, 1976) general theory of legal control and the nature of law, "arrest decisions are influenced by social stratification" including race, gender and education. "People of disadvantage are less likely to be successful in having law mobilised to protect their interest and more likely to have the law successfully applied to their behaviours" (Eitle 2005). In the Indian context, it may be hypothesised that the poor and marginalised are less likely to have the law mobilised to protect their interests.

Out of the five major determinants of arrest discretion behaviour, organisational determinant has the maximum level of objectivity, with written rules, statutes, departmental guidelines, court directives etc., while the other four determinants are based on extralegal, complex and often intangible behavioural factors. The arrest decision is processed through a complex maze of structural and extralegal filters and is therefore often difficult to predict. If in spite of the amended provision of the procedural law on arrest and with a catena of court directives and departmental guidelines, the arrest figures in India do not show any appreciable decline, contrary to the intention of the lawmakers, the inescapable conclusion that follows is the dominating role played by the complex set of extralegal factors in arrest decision. In the absence of literature on police discretion and study on the subject in India, this research intends to explore these factors and their influence on arrest discretion with empirical testing of some of the hypotheses in Indian context based on the literature available internationally.

1.4 Explanation of Terms

This study mentions several concepts and terms, including discretion, arrest, cognisable offence, accountability, police subculture and extralegal factors and needs brief explanation.

Discretion: "Discretion concerns an officer's perspective as to how much resource can be allocated to enforce law in terms of time and effort" (Hidayet 2011). The definition of discretion offered by Kennet Culp Davis (Davis 1969) is amongst the most quoted ones. It states that a "public officer has discretion whenever the effective limit on his power leave him free to make a choice among possible courses of action or inaction". This, of course, is a very wide definition which creates no differentiation between the acceptable and unacceptable bases for discretion. Further, Davis went on to point out that policies and guidelines aimed at controlling the acceptable use of discretion help structure, restrict and limit the discretion allowed to officials. The discretion allowed, therefore, is "fettered" by such policies and guidelines. This understanding of Davis is reflected and aptly put forth in the Concise Oxford English Dictionary's definition of discretion as the "liberty of deciding as one thinks fit, absolutely or within limits". These limits are essential to ensure that "decisions are principled rather than arbitrary and they respect human and civil rights" (Bronitt and Stenning 2011).

Arrest: According to Halsbury's Law of England, "arrest consists of the actual seizure or touching of a person's body with a view to ensuring his detention. The mere pronouncing of the words of the arrest is not an arrest unless the person sought to be arrested submits to the process and goes with the arresting officer. Words may, however, amount to an arrest if, in the circumstances of the case, they are calculated to bring to a person's notice that he is under compulsion and therefore submits to the compulsion".[9] Black's Law Dictionary explains arrest as to "deprive a person of his liberty by legal authority or taking, under real or assumed authority, custody of another for the purpose of holding or detaining him to answer a criminal charge or civil demand".[10]

The procedural or substantive laws of India do not provide a definition for the word "arrest", but Section 46 of the Criminal Procedure Code, 1973 (CrPC) contains the provision regarding the procedure of arrest. In Roshan Beevi,[11] the Madras High Court's full bench, while explaining the meaning of the term "arrest", observed that "the word 'arrest' when used in its ordinary and natural sense, means the apprehension or restraint or deprivation of one's personal liberty. The question of whether a person is under arrest or not depends not on the legality of arrest, but whether he has been deprived of his personal liberty to go where he pleases. When used in legal sense in the procedure connected with criminal offences, an arrest consists in taking into custody of another person under authority empowered by law for the purpose of holding or detaining him to answer a criminal charge or of preventing the commission of a criminal offence". Tyagi (2014) argues that "the essential elements to constitute an arrest are that there must be an intent to arrest under the authority accompanied by a seizure or detention of the person in the manner known to law, which is understood by the person arrested".

Cognisable offence: Section 41 CrPC deals with the circumstances when the police can make an arrest without having a warrant or an order of the Magistrate. Under the provisions of the section, police may arrest any person "who (a) commits a cognizable offence in the police officer's presence, (b) against whom a reasonable complaint has been made, or credible information has been received, or (c) a reasonable suspicion exists that he has committed a cognizable offence".[12]

It is pertinent to explain here what is meant by cognisable and non-cognisable offences. Section 2(c) of CrPC defines a cognisable offence: "cognizable offence means an offence in which police officer may, in accordance with First Schedule of the or under any other law for the time being in force, arrest without warrant". The First Schedule of the CrPC gives details of classification of offences defined in the Indian Penal Code (IPC) under six columns, such as, 1. Section of law, 2. Offence description, 3. Punishment, 4. Cognisable or non-cognisable, 5. Bailable or non-bailable, and 6. Triable by what court. To illustrate an example, offences related to marriage under Chapter XX of IPC like remarriage within the life period of a spouse, adultery etc. are non-cognisable offences though imprisonment for seven and five years have been prescribed, respectively, upon conviction in those offences. Offences like murder, rape, grievous hurt, robbery, theft etc. are classified as cognisable offences even if only imprisonment for three years is prescribed for conviction in a theft case. Therefore, it is not the quantum of punishment that differentiates whether an offence is cognisable or non-cognisable but probably the classification is based on the offences which require immediate police intervention without order from the court. However, this remains debatable and the scope of this research is not to go into details of the debate. Suffice is to say that the number of cognisable offences in the IPC far outnumbers that of non-cognisable offences.

Besides the cognisable offences under the IPC, one of the Criminal Major Acts, a large number of offences under Criminal Minor Acts, sometimes referred as Special and Local Laws (SLL), have been classified as cognisable offences, for example, offences under Arms Act, Explosive Act, Narcotics Drug and Psychotropic Substance Act and State Excise Acts. Police have the power under Section 41 CrPC to arrest persons involved in cognisable offences under minor criminal Acts too.

The scope of this study is limited to the arrests made by police without warrant under Section 41 CrPC for involvement in cognisable offences under both IPC and SLL, not the preventive arrests as authorised under CrPC (Sec151) or under any other law for the time being in force.

Accountability: Discretion and accountability are linked intrinsically. Pepinsky (1984) argues that "accountability means having to answer for one's actions or inaction. Accountability is synonymous with responsibility. Having to answer for one's action makes sense only if one could have chosen to do otherwise". According to Davis (1969), discretion means choice of action. Pepinsky (1984) concludes that accountability implies discretion. Besides, as the "authority of police is derived from the people through the social contract and the power is held in public trust" (Moll 2006), the police must remain accountable to the public for its action. National Police Commission (1981b) in its Report VIII on accountability and police performance recommends that police should remain accountable to the people, to law and to the organisation – in that order. It also emphasises that accountability can be ensured by active supervision and depends upon the awareness of people of their rights and their willingness to exercise the same.

Police subculture: The police subculture is the "informal organisational culture or unwritten culture comprised individual values and tradition that are communicated informally across the organisation from officer to officer" (Walker and Katz 2005). "The broadest definition presents police culture as a means to cope with the strains of the occupation based on experience, structural cultural, and perceptions of the meaning of being a police officer" (Ingram, Paoline and Terrill 2013). Subculture is a "culture within a broader culture that may deviate in some aspects from the broader culture and influences daily decisions" (Herbert 1998). Anthony (2018) argues that the "culture of the police department equates to organizational culture". The culture of police officers in the street is a subculture. "A police department has many of the components of organizational culture found in other organizations and industries, but what differentiates police culture from other organizational cultures is the constant potential for life-and-death encounters combined with the unique stresses and strains that originate in the policing environment" (White and Robinson 2014). An "individual's organizational identity is related to organizational culture" (Alvesson and Sveningsson 2015), indicating that an officer's identity and behaviour are shaped by police culture.

Extralegal: Extralegal is not synonymous with illegal. Extralegal factors are those factors in decision-making which are not regulated or sanctioned by law, yet have influence on shaping the final outcome of the decision. Mastrofski (1981) argues that "extralegal influences on arrest include characteristics of victims (including race, wealth, and social status) and suspects (including race, wealth, age, gender and reputation); the degree of resistance shown by the suspect to officer authority". Legal factors include those "set forth explicitly in written law for making arrest, as well as strategic considerations such as victim preference for making an arrest, seriousness of the offence, and strength of evidence". The factors like negative influences of subculture and the role of environment within which police operate, such as the media, political culture and the public opinion, play significant roles in decision-making and may be categorised as extralegal factors.

Determinants: The lexical meaning of determinant is a factor which decisively affects the nature or outcome of something. In this study, the determinants that affect the arrest discretion behaviour are taken as organisation, subculture, environment, individual characteristics and the situation. Often, in this study, the term determinant has been synonymously used as "variable" or "independent variable" or "predictor variable". Variable is any characteristic, number or quantity that can be measured or counted. Independent variables are those variables believed to affect the dependent variable. Dependent variable in this study is the arrest discretion.

Predictor variable has similar meaning as an independent variable but is used in regression, which is one of the data analysis methods for this study.

1.5 Context of the Study

The book has been written in the context of the Indian police. Article 246 of the Constitution of India read with List II of Seventh Schedule essentially identifies the police as a subject within the State list, which implies that the state governments of the Union of India have the responsibility of maintenance of law and order, and they formulate the regulations governing the police force in their state, in the form of police manuals for each state. As on date, there are 28 state police and 8 union territory police organisations in India.[13]

The Director General of Police (DGP) leads the police force in each state. The DGP is answerable to the state government regarding the administration of the police force and provides advisory assistance to the government as regards police matters. The DGP is at the top of police hierarchy in a state. The structure of hierarchy of police in India represents a vertical alignment, which consists of senior officers drawn from the Indian Police Service (IPS) and the police services at the provincial level in a supervisory role and the upper subordinates (inspectors, sub-inspectors and asst. sub-inspectors) usually at the level of police stations. Then comes the police constabulary, which constitutes almost eighty percent of total police strength. The constabulary is given the task of patrolling, inspection, guarding and law and order work.

States have been split into smaller administrative areas known as districts. The Superintendent of Police is the officer who leads the police force of the district. The Inspector General or Deputy Inspector General of Police is responsible for larger units known as "ranges", which are groups of districts clubbed together for administrative purposes. Further, in some states, ranges have been clubbed together into "zones", which are placed under an officer of the rank of an Inspector General or Additional Director General of Police. In order to address the law and order problems of highly populated urban areas, Commissioner of Police posts have been created by statute which additionally confers power of executive magistrates to the officers to address the urban disorders.

Districts are further divided into smaller units called subdivisions. The officers having the ranks of Assistant Superintendent of Police or Deputy Superintendent of Police are responsible for each subdivision. There may be multiple police stations in each subdivision, depending on its area, population and volume of crime. In some states, the police stations in a subdivision are clubbed together to form circles, headed by an Inspector of Police.

Police stations are the fundamental units of the police mechanism in districts. Under the procedural law, all crimes have to be recorded at the police station and all preventive, investigative and law and order work are executed from the police station. Even within the police station, there are smaller units called beats. The constables perform the duty of patrolling, surveillance and collection of intelligence in the beats. An officer in the rank of Inspector of Police is put in charge of each police station, especially in cities and metropolitan areas. However, in smaller police stations or rural areas, the officer in charge is usually of the rank of a Sub-Inspector of Police.

Entry to the Indian police occurs at three or four levels. The highest level entry is at the level of Assistant Superintendent of Police who has to qualify for an all-India test to be a member of the Indian Police Service. Article 312 of the Constitution of India provides for this All India Service and regulates the service conditions of the officers. They rise in the rank to become senior supervisory officers and hold leadership positions in the police organisation.

They are trained in leadership, police science, criminal law, field crafts and tactics etc. for two years before taking up the field assignment. Next in hierarchy of direct entry is the Deputy Superintendent of Police who is recruited by the state governments and undergoes training at state police academies for two years before getting a substantive post. The third direct entry is at the rank of Sub-Inspector of Police which is the cutting-edge level of the organisation. The officers manage the police stations, register offences, investigate, arrest suspects, search and seize material evidences, regulate traffic and remain responsible for the overall law and order situation in their jurisdiction. The minimum educational qualification for all these three direct entries is graduation. The last and lowest level of direct entry is that of a constable. Their minimum educational qualification is high school certificate or in some States, junior college (plus two) and training varies from nine months to one year. A constable rises in the rank as head constable, Assistant Sub-Inspector and even Sub-Inspector on promotion, if he maintains a good service record.

Data on the police organisation, published by the Bureau of Police Research and Development of the Ministry of Home Affairs, Government of India, annually, shows that in the year 2020 the sanctioned strength of civil police is more than 1.67 million out of which one-fifth, that is, approximately 3,38,000 are officers. Effectively, that is a massive number of officers empowered to arrest without warrant. There are 16,955 police stations, 800 police districts, 189 police ranges, 95 police zones and sixty-three Commissioners of Police in India.[14]

Despite twenty-eight State police and eight Union Territory police organisations and diversity in police forces, there is quite some commonality among the organisations. This is due to the following main reasons:

1. The structure and working of the State Police Forces are governed by the Police Act of 1861, which is applicable in most parts of the country, or by the State Police Acts modelled mostly on the 1861 legislation.
2. Major criminal laws, such as the Indian Penal Code, the Code of Criminal Procedure and the Indian Evidence Act are uniformly applicable to almost all state and union territories of the country.
3. The Indian Police Service (IPS) as an All India Service provides bulk of the senior officers to the state police forces, guided by uniform service rules with training curriculum.
4. The quasi-federal character of the Indian polity, with specific provisions in the Constitution, allows a coordinating and counselling role for the Centre in police matters and even authorises it to set up certain central police organisations. (CHRI, 2002)
5. The rulings of the Supreme Court of India on police matters are applicable and binding on all state and union territory police organisations.

The empirical study on factors influencing arrest discretion behaviour of the police in India has been undertaken by taking samples from the Odisha

State Police and simple random samples of IPS officers from different State and Union Territory polices of India. Inductively, the research findings are expected to shed light on arrest discretion behaviour of the police in India.

1.6 Purpose of the Study

From the foregoing discussions, it is apparent that since eighties of the last century, starting with recommendations of the National Police Commission on avoidable arrest, the debate on how to tame the enormous power of arrest vested in the police in India and how to regulate the discretion associated with exercise of such power continued till the nineties, which marked the delivery of two landmark judgements by the Supreme Court of India (Joginder Kumar and D.K. Basu) and finally culminated in the 177th Report of the Law Commission of India (2001). The recommendations of the Law Commission of India paved the way for sweeping changes in the arrest law with the amendment of the procedural law of India, the CrPC, in the year 2009. The legislative intent reflected in the parliamentary debates before the amendment, which has been discussed at length in the succeeding chapter, was strong and unanimous in curtailing the arbitrariness in exercising the power of arrest vested in the police in India for a century. The lawmakers were supportive of other recommendations of the Commission including service of notice in certain category of offences instead of formal arrest. The amended arrest law introduced a new category of offence, that is "noticeable", though it is not a legal term and neither has it been defined anywhere in the CrPC following the amendment. But the term has been used extensively in this book for convenience with a view to categorising those offences which are punishable with imprisonment up to or below seven years and the police have the options under law to issue notice to such offenders instead of formal arrest. The analysis of arrest figures in India for five years preceding and following the amendment does not show any significant reduction in the number of arrests contrary to the legislative intent. Thus, the question that naturally comes to mind is whether there are some factors beyond the statutes that influence the arrest decisions that act counter to the letter and spirit of the law.

A large body of literature on arrest decision behaviour or arrest discretion in the West establishes that departmental guidelines, regulations, court directives, organisational policy, and processes influence the arrest discretion but there are several other factors, like situational, subcultural, environmental and individual determinants of arrest discretion (Davis 1975; Mastrofski, Worden and Snipes 1995; Gaines and Kappeler 2003; Groeneveld 2005; Walker and Katz 2005; Hidayet 2011). Study on police discretion shows that officer's behaviour is not solely guided by law, as policing is for most part extralegal and that police work within the constraint of law but seldom invoke law in performing police work (Worden 1989). There is an imperative need to study whether these determinants influence the arrest discretion behaviour of the police in India by testing their validity in the Indian context.

Study on police discretion is an untouched area in India. There is barely any literature on police discretion, let alone any empirical inquiry. This warrants serious academic inquiry as to why the legislative intent does not get reflected in the field law enforcement and why the amended law on arrest fails to impact the law enforcement as one of its main objectives was to restrict the power of arrest on the basis of "principle of necessity" and "principles of restraint". The "principle of necessity" advocates that the police can exercise powers of arrest only when it is genuinely necessary to do so for detection and prevention of crime. The "principle of restraint" states that the liberty of an individual and his freedom should be interfered only when circumstances necessitate the same (177th Law Commission 2001).

With these background issues, the purpose of this book has been set; to analyse the reasons as to why the legislative intent of the amended arrest law is not being reflected in the field law enforcement and if the determinants of arrest discretion collected on the basis of literature review from the West have validity in the Indian context. An empirical study has been designed to test few hypotheses and to identify the interplay and effect of determinants on arrest discretion behaviour of the police in India. This may provide an insight into the factors, both legal and extralegal, that shape the arrest decision behaviour of police. The study would recommend ways and means to regulate police discretion on the basis of research findings so that the police leaders and policymakers can ensure that the use of discretion is fair, just, in the public interest and free from abuse.

1.7 Queries That Need to Be Answered

The following queries need to be answered while exploring the factors influencing arrest discretion behaviour of the police in India.

1. Are the discretional latitudes wide enough in the amended arrest law of Section 41 CrPC to deny realisation of legislative intent?
2. Are the determinants of arrest discretion behaviour in Western literature significant for police in India?
3. Do the extralegal determinants like subculture, environment and individual characteristics impact the arrest discretion behaviour of the police in India?
4. Which among the three determinants, such as organisational, subcultural and environmental determinants, is the dominant one in influencing arrest discretion behaviour?
5. Do the police in India have an arrest bias against "socially and economically marginal" people as an equivalent of "racial profiling" in Western literature?

On the basis of literature review of arrest discretion behaviour of police from the West, a number of key factors or determinants of arrest discretion have been identified. The determinants have been operationalised in the Indian context and suitable response statements have been devised for each determinant and its associated dimensions. The reactions of the respondents to the response statements have been scaled with numerical weightage. Correlations between the determinants and arrest discretion behaviour have been analysed to answer the queries by adopting suitable quantitative methods of data analysis.

1.8 Academic Significance of the Study

The study has the potential to contribute to the knowledge of arrest discretion behaviour of the police in India. Although the topic of police discretion has been extensively researched with a rich body of literature in the West, the study of police discretion is an untouched area in India. The study is the maiden attempt to empirically test if the determinants of arrest discretion (empirically validated in the Western world) are valid in the Indian context. Besides, in the course of the study, a few theoretical concepts and hypotheses on arrest discretion behaviour have been tested, results of which are likely to provide insight into the functioning of the police in India. Police organisations in India are large, hierarchical and legalistic. In such organisations, the discretionary latitude is expected to be low (Hidayet 2011) and that appears to be the perception of the top leadership in the organisation. In investigating the three proposed models of organisation – rational, constrained rational and loosely coupled – Mastrofski, Worden and Snipes (1995) argue that the size of an organisation is an essential element in validating the models. They conclude that the decision-making of an officer is widely influenced by the policing environment and peer culture in larger bureaucratic departments, while organisational policies become essential instruments in regulating behaviour in smaller departments. This may be a good hypothesis to test in the present study, considering that in the Indian context, state police organisations are large bureaucratic set-ups.

According to Black's (1971) general theory of legal control and the nature of law, "arrest decisions are influenced by social stratification including race, gender, education, etc.". "People of disadvantage are less likely to be successful in having law mobilised to protect their interest and more likely to have the law successfully applied to their behaviours" (Eitle 2005). People with more education and greater culture in their lives can be reasonably expected to have the law mobilised to safeguard their interests. A number of hypotheses may be drawn from Black's theory, relating to how extralegal characteristics influence the implementation of the law. In the Indian context, it may be hypothesised that the poor and marginal are less likely to have the law mobilised to protect their interest. This is equivalent to the concept of racial profiling in the Western world. The study is meant to test if the police in India have an arrest bias against "poor and marginalised" people.

Police subculture as a determinant of arrest discretion has been operationalised in the Indian context and studied to assess its impact on arrest decision. Any positive correlation is likely to contribute to the literature as no such study has been done in the context of police in India.

1.8.1 Practical Significance of the Study

The interest for this study emerges from the analysis of arrest figures in India in the pre- and post-amendment periods with 2009 as the mid-base year. The figures do not show any significant decline in the arrest figures as was expected in the post-amendment period. State police organisations in India are very large hierarchical organisations with centralised command and high degree of elements of structural control like statutes, rules, codes and written guidelines governing the organisation. It is generally expected that such organisations would provide little leeway for discretionary behaviour. But it is paradoxical to note that the statute (Section 41 CrPC), court directives (Joginder Kumar, Arnesh Kumar etc.), police manual rules, departmental circulars etc. fail to translate the legislative intent of reducing the number of avoidable arrests following the amendment of century-old arrest law. Therefore, it has become imperative to inquire further into the problem and to identify if there are factors beyond the strict elements of structural control that influence the arrest decision of the police. The study explores if the extra-legal determinants of discretion like situation, subculture or environment in addition to legalistic organisational determinants influence the arrest decisions. And if it is validated empirically, police leaders and policymakers need to take note of these factors and devise methods to regulate the determinants in order to ensure that their effects do not derail the organisational objectives and are in consonance with public policy.

Discretion being an inescapable part of policing, the study recommends robust accountability mechanism in the police organisation to limit discretionary abuse. Discretion and accountability are linked intrinsically. Pepinsky (1984) argues that "accountability means having to answer for one's actions or inaction. Accountability is synonymous with responsibility. Having to answer for one's action makes sense only if one could have chosen to do otherwise". The study examines the existing accountability mechanism of the police in India and their efficacy. It also recommends if more needs to be done to develop a robust accountability mechanism as the power exercised by police is held in public trust.

Literature on police subculture from the West suggests that police subculture affects the decision-making of officers at various encounters (Cockcroft 2012). Herbert (1998) argues that subculture may separate itself in letter and spirit from the broader culture, and influence daily decisions. Some of the adverse ethos of police subculture like, "Dirty Harry dilemma", "us and them", "thin blue/khaki line" and "code of silence" have been operationalised in this study in the Indian context to inquire into their impact on arrest decisions. These attitudes may lead to the abuse of authority, selective enforcement and illegitimacy of use of authority (Wood 1997). By identifying the extent to which the subculture affects arrest discretion, the police leadership may take measures to ensure that police misconduct arising out of subcultural ethos is curbed. Besides, the findings of this study will be important for the police leadership to design training curriculum to institute reforms.

The police organisation cannot function in isolation. The external environmental determinants of discretion like political culture, media and societal pressure will continue to shape the decision-making process within a democratic government, where the police are owned by the state. The study will examine if such influences are in the public interest and recommend if the police need more functional autonomy.

On the whole, the study is expected to contribute to the police discretion literature in India as an academic work, and the study outcomes may have practical significance in the form of policy recommendations for the police leaders and policymakers.

Notes

1 Joginder Kumar v. State of UP, 1994 AIR 1349.
2 In 1953, Justice Robert H. Jackson of the American Supreme Court called for a nationwide study by the American Bar Association (ABA), of criminal justice agencies, believing that the criminal justice system was in shambles. The findings of the decade-long research, adopting methodology of field observation and "law in action", were starling that brought about a paradigm shift in the understanding of discretion in criminal justice system.
3 The CrPC was legislated in the year 1882 and underwent major amendments in 1898 and 1973. But the provisions of arrest by police in cognisable cases remained as such from 1898 to 2009, when major amendment took place.
4 The Law Commission, in its 177th Report, took up the matter of arrest suo motu in order to clearly define the law relating to arrest without warrant. The Commission recommended sweeping changes in the arrest laws in its Report in the year 2001 which were later inserted in the Criminal Procedure Code by amendments in the year 2009.
5 Maneka Gandhi v. Union of India, A.I.R. 1978 SC 597.
6 The National Police Commission (NPC) was set up by the Government of India in the year 1977, with its scope covering various facets of the police as an organisation, such as its character, duties, relations with public, influence of politics in its working, potential misuse of its power, performance evaluation, etc. This Commission, which was the first Commission set up at the national level post-independence, suggested multiple reforms in the police set-up, producing eight reports between 1979 and 1981.
7 Joginder Kumar v. State of UP, 1994, 2 Crimes 106 SC.
8 DK Basu v State of West Bengal, A.I.R. 1997 SC 610.
9 Halsbury's Law of England, 3rd Edition, Vol 10, Page 342.
10 Black's Law Dictionary, 5th Edition, 1979.
11 Roshan Beevi v. Joint Secretary to Govt. of Tamilnadu (A.I.R. 1984 N.O.C. 103, Mad).
12 S. 41(1), (2), Code of Criminal Procedure, 1973.
13 Crime in India, 2020, National Crime Records Bureau, Ministry of Home Affairs, New Delhi.
14 Data on Police Organisation, 2020, BPR&D, MHA, Government of India.

2 Police Discretion

Factors Influencing Arrest Discretion

2.1 Police Discretion

Although the use of police discretion has become the subject of global controversy and debate in the recent past, it has long been a pertinent internal challenge faced by police forces across the world. Discretion, defined as "the freedom to decide what should be done in a particular situation" by the Oxford English Dictionary and "the ability and right to decide exactly what should be done in a particular situation" by the Longman Dictionary of Contemporary English, has wide-ranging ramifications on public life, when it comes to its interpretation as well as its practical exercise in the context of the police.

Like in most other professions, discretion is quite an inevitable and intrinsic characteristic of police work as well. The concept of discretion was a key part of the mutual pledge system in the ninth century as it is of the consensual system of policing of the modern day, that is, in both cases a certain level of discretion has been allowed to individuals who wield the legal authority to enforce laws made by the government. For instance, the constables of the middle ages in England, as well as thief-takers, used their discretion to not arrest certain persons due to their social standing or because of their friendship (Palmiotto and Unnithan 2011). Nevertheless, up until the 1950s, the usual narrative by police administrators was that the police investigated every crime, and ensured compliance with and enforcement of every law with equal priority. Police chiefs made public announcements to this effect, claiming that all offenses committed, regardless of the seriousness of the offense, were accorded the same importance and investigated with equal effort. But ground reality has always been at stark departure from what was claimed by the police. In reality, there is an inevitable prioritisation of tasks due to (often crippling) resource constraints. Decisions such as when to arrest, whom to arrest first (among a group of offenders), the mode of arrest, and whether to handcuff the offender are taken by police officers as per their own discretion on a daily basis. These decisions are generally subject to an intelligible assessment of the circumstances by the police officer, and therefore involve fair amount of exercise of discretion.

Despite being both an ambiguous and contentious subject in equal measure, discretion was regarded as a subject worthy of academic attention only after a

DOI: 10.4324/9781003406679-2

considerable amount of time since the establishment of formal police organisations. It was not up until 1956, when a survey conducted by the American Bar Foundation (ABF) showed that discretion is intrinsic to the criminal justice system and operated through every level of the same, and that the subject gained its long overdue attention. Following that, the issue of discretion became a topic of key interest for police researchers around the world by scholars like Kenneth Culp Davis,[1] Wayne LaFave,[2] Joseph Goldstein,[3] Samuel Walker,[4] Harold E. Pepinsky[5] and Ronald M. Dworkin[6] among others. Besides academia, courts in the UK, Canada and the USA also began interpreting and reinterpreting police discretion in common law through their rulings and pronounced guidelines on proper exercise of discretion by the police.

2.1.1 Defining and Interpreting Discretion

The definitions and interpretations of discretion need detailed discussions in order to properly and contextually understand the concept.

Black's Law Dictionary explains that "when applied to public functionaries, discretion means a power or right conferred upon them by law of acting officially in certain circumstances, according to the dictates of their own judgment and conscience, uncontrolled by the judgement or conscience of others".

One of the earliest definitions of discretion was given by Pound (1940). He defines discretion as "an authority conferred by law to act in certain conditions or situations in accordance with an official's or an official agency's own considered judgment and conscience. It is an idea of morals, belongs to the twilight zone between laws and morals".

The definition of discretion offered by Kennet Culp Davis (Davis 1969) is amongst the most quoted ones. He states that a "public officer has discretion whenever the effective limit on his power leaves him free to make a choice among possible courses of action or inaction". This, of course, is a very wide definition which creates no differentiation between the acceptable and unacceptable bases for discretion. Further, Davis went on to point out that policies and guidelines aimed at controlling the acceptable use of discretion help structure, restrict and limit the discretion allowed to officials. The discretion allowed, therefore, is "fettered" by such policies and guidelines. This understanding of Davis is reflected and aptly put forth in the Concise Oxford English Dictionary's definition of discretion as the "liberty of deciding as one think fit, absolutely or within limits". These limits are essential to ensure that "decisions are principled rather than arbitrary and they respect human and civil rights" (Bronitt and Stenning 2011).

Certain aspects of the definition provided by Davis need special discussion. According to Davis,

> discretion is not limited what is authorised or what is legal but includes all that is within the effective limits of officer's power. This phraseology

> is necessary because a good deal of discretion is illegal or has questionable legality. Another facet of the definition is that a choice to do nothing; perhaps inaction decisions are ten or twenty times as frequent as action decisions.
>
> (Palmiotto and Unnithan 2011)

"Discretion is not limited to substantive choices but extend to procedures, methods, forms, timing, and many other subsidiary factors".

Galligan (1992) notes how discretion is generally defined as the freedom that a decision-maker enjoys while choosing between alternatives. Terming such an understanding as simplistic, he argues that the standards used by the decision-maker and the reasoning behind the choice are crucial. According to Galligan, discretion denotes "good judgement" and implies choice exercised by a decision-maker based on proper reasoning and supported by intelligible standards (Satish 2016).

Halliday (2009) describes discretion in law enforcement as "an official action that is taken by a criminal justice official i.e., police officer, lawyer or judge etc. in which they use their own individual judgement to decide the best course of action. In theory, the criminal justice official considers the totality of circumstances before determining whether or not legal action should be taken by an individual. Discretion is further a permission, privilege or prerogative to use judgement about how to make a practical determination. There are embedded constraints in exercise of discretion, which are bound by laws, rules, norms, and guidelines" (Kleinig 1996).

Yale Law Professor, Ronald Dworkin (1967) likens discretion to "hole in the doughnut". He notes that

> police officers exercise discretion within this space. The surrounding boundaries represent laws, regulations, standards, rules and policy which supposedly constrict and restrict discretion. Ambiguity and vagueness create cracks in the boundary of the structure that results in policy failure. Thus, the cracks allow the discretion to seep outside the boundary and causes police officers to err.
>
> (Dworkin 1967)

"A police officer operating in this manner on the edge of law inevitably leads to a chain of related events with significant impact. A minor incident of abuse of discretion leads to a chain reaction down the 'slippery slope' which can establish arbitrary behaviour" (Young 2011).

2.2 The "Discovery of Discretion" and Subsequent Developments

As briefly mentioned before, knowledge on discretion before the 1950s was at a very rudimentary level. This was largely due to the supposition that discretion did not exist in the criminal justice system and that "discretion in policing and furthermore in the criminal justice system was seen as illegal and improper" (Kelling and Coles 1996). The police were assumed and expected to be working "by the book" in fulfilling their law-enforcement duty. "With the era of policing mired with corruption, recognising that discretion was evident and played a large and important role in day to day police work was just unacceptable" (Sherman 1984).

This premise was prominently questioned for the first time in 1953, when Justice Robert H. Jackson of the American Supreme Court called for a nationwide study of criminal justice agencies by the American Bar Association (ABA), based on the belief that the criminal justice system was in shambles. The research wing of the ABA, the American Bar Foundation (ABF), took up the research under the stewardship of Frank J. Remington, Professor of Law at University of Wisconsin and Lloyd Ohlin, Professor of Criminal Justice at Harvard Law School. The findings of this decade-long research, which adopted the methodology of field observation and "law in action", were startling and brought about a paradigm shift in the understanding of discretion in the criminal justice system (Kelling 1999).

ABA through its survey empirically established that the exercise of discretion was apparent in every level of criminal justice organisation. "The idea that police, for example, made arrest decisions simply on the basis of whether or not a law has been violated- as a generation of police leaders led the public to believe- was simply an inaccurate portrayal of how police worked" (ibid.). The results further showed that "police work is complex, that police use enormous amount of discretion, that discretion is at the core of police functioning and that police use criminal law to sort out myriad problems" (Kelling 1999). Throughout the 1960s and 1970s, scholars were intrigued and awed by the discovery of discretion, and studied police functioning with empirical data. As expected, several studies taken up after the ABA survey only confirmed these findings: that the work carried out by the police is quite complicated, criminal matters take up a small portion of time spent by the police on police work, and discretion is intrinsic to police work. Furthermore, it was also brought to light that the police actually use discretion much more than other officials in the criminal justice system. "This is because police are the first point of call acting as 'gate-keepers' of any criminal justice system" (Halliday 2009).

Kenneth Culp Davis (1969), Professor of Law at the University of Chicago as well as Harvard University and a former practitioner of law, reflected on these findings and supposed that approximately half of all the exercises of discretion by criminal justice agencies were actually carried out by the police. He added, "the police are among the most important policy makers of our entire society. And they make far more discretionary determinations in individual cases than any other class of administrators; I know of no close second" (Davis 1969).

As a result, scholars and policymakers started looking for ways of controlling and regulating discretion. At this point, however, their thoughts started diverging out into two different directions. While one school of scholars like

Davis (1975) believed in the efficacy of rule-making, regulations and accountability to tame unfettered discretion, others like Goldstein (1960) advocated for the elimination of discretion altogether. Belonging to the former school of thought, Pepinsky (1984) famously argued that "discretion is a desirable part of policing" and although it may be misused, "there can be no justice without discretion". I look at both of these perspectives at some length in the following sections:

I. Discretion as an unavoidable pragmatic necessity
   There are four primary reasons, as described by scholars, as to why discretion is an essential element of police work, some being pragmatic while others being more normative (Bronitt and Stenning 2011):

   1. No legislature has been able to formulate laws which encapsulate all behaviour and actions intended to be criminal and in exclusion of all other conduct (Walker and Katz 2005).
   2. Inability to dispose of and repeal the laws, which are ineffectively drafted and out of date, necessitates discretion in order to ensure fairness.
   3. It is important to note that due to a scarcity of resources, it is impossible to enforce all laws against everyone who breaks them (Gaines and Kappeler 2003).
   4. Unwavering application of laws without discretion to exclude application would lead to "harsh and intolerable results" (La Fave 1969).

II. The perils of discretion

On the flip side, the arguments against discretion include the perils of allowing the police to "selectively enforce" laws, which would allow officers "to redefine justice in terms of their own priorities, which might not correspond to the priorities of the wider community" (Wortley 2003). Secondly, by allowing the police to exercise complete discretionary power without requisite training and education needed to fairly exercise it, potential misuse and its direct consequence on individual's liberty will be more prominent (Halliday 2009). Thirdly, discretion offers an opportunity to treat offenders differently based on their gender, race, religion, age etc. inappropriately. A good example of this would be racial profiling which includes instances of police discretion being exercised on the basis of racial disparities. According to the American Civil Liberties Union, racial profiling "refers to the discriminatory practice by law enforcement officials of targeting individuals for suspicion of crime based on the individual's race, ethnicity, religion or national origin". The term "driving while black or brown" was formulated after multiple studies in the United States and documented that "the people of black or Hispanic origin are more likely to face traffic stops than their white counterparts" (Halliday 2009). Another major argument against police discretion is that it allows for corruption within the department by abuse of discretion and misuse of authority. An instance of abuse of discretion could be clothed as proper exercise of power since the line between the two is often very thin and blurred.

It is apparent from the discussions in the foregoing paragraphs that the "discovery" of discretion in the day-to-day functioning of the police by the research of ABF in the 1950s and 60s gave rise to a wave of legal and social science academia interest on the subject which helped look at the concept empirically. This eventually contributed towards the formulation of policy guidelines and regulatory mechanisms to check police organisations' unfettered discretion and ensure that they remain accountable for any abuse.

Since the police are the gatekeepers of the criminal justice system, by virtue of being the very first point of public contact in the dispensation of justice, many of its functions are subject to judicial scrutiny. Besides, citizens have the right under the common law remedies to knock on the door of the courts to protect their rights and against abuse of authority. The pronouncements of courts in the USA, UK, Canada, India etc. have shaped the police discretions over the years by bringing the abusers to justice, compensating the victim, defining the limits of discretion, engaging in the process of judicial rule-making or even amending the legislation. Some of the landmark judgements of different national courts are briefly discussed in the next section to appreciate the role of the courts in defining, tempering and regulating discretion. The interpretations of Indian superior courts have been separately dealt with in the next chapter.

2.3 Interpretation of Discretion by National Courts

2.3.1 English Courts

The Blackburn[7] case is the most seminal English judgement on the question of police discretion. In this case, the question of full enforcement of gambling laws and anti-pornographic laws by the Police Commissioner of London was the matter before the Court of Appeal, England's second highest court. It was held that Courts should interfere with arrest decisions in "extreme cases" and that the "Police Commissioner has complete discretion to decide deployment of officers, their activities and how they should perform their duties" (Williams 1989).

The issue of police discretion arose again in Holgate-Mohammed.[8] Here, the House of Lords considered the question of abuse of discretion by a police detective in making an arrest. The detective, during the investigation of a burglary, decided to arrest the suspect, Ms. Holgate-Mohammed, and hold her under custodial interrogation for her suspected involvement in the offence. The custodial interrogation proved to be fruitless as no confession could be produced and since there was no evidence linking her to the crime, she was released. Following her release, she filed for damages against the police for false imprisonment. The trial court accepted her claim, but the police appealed before the House of Lords. The House of Lords examined the case on Wednesbury principles, which decided the factors appropriate for examination to establish whether an office has exercised discretion in a proper manner. "Unreasonableness, attention given to extraneous circumstances, disregard for public policy etc." have been referred to as relevant matters for consideration. The House of Lords exonerated the appellant sergeant as he had arrested the respondent in good faith. Holgate-Mohammed establishes the general rule that if there is reasonable cause to bring about an arrest, the decision to make that arrest cannot be challenged. The rules laid down in Holgate-Mohammed and Wednesbury, while emphasising discretion being an essential aspect of police work, spell out the limitations of discretion too.

The courts in England effectively created a set of principles to adjudicate police discretion, through this and a few other notable cases (Coxhead,[9] Dytham[10]). First, there are particular standards and guidelines for reviewing arrest discretion. In determining police discretion, the courts usually look at relevant statutes to determine if discretion may be permissible. The determinants for improper exercise of discretion include "unreasonableness, disregard for public policy, and various other extraneous circumstances". Second, the department has the authority and responsibilities to enact or bring about general rules for officers to abide by while exercising discretion. Third, it is impermissible to have a wide-ranging policy for non-enforcement of law. Fourth, non-action by the police could also amount to abuse of discretion in a situation that casts an obligation on the officer to the contrary. These principles effectively crystallise the complexity of understanding, evaluating and exercising police discretion.

2.3.2 *The US Courts*

The multiplicity of the U.S. Supreme Court decisions seems to have been necessitated by the need to bring about a certain level of "control" over police discretion. Palmiotto and Unnithan (2011) argue that 1960s and 1970s were decades that emphasised the constitutional rights of citizens at the expense of police discretion. Before the U.S. Supreme Court began questioning police actions and deeming them unconstitutional, the police maintained order in the manner they pleased. Most states had vagrancy, loitering and disorderly conduct laws, which gave the police a great deal of authority and room to operationally impose order in the manner they deemed fit. The state statutes on these laws were so vague that the police could virtually arrest anyone. For an extended period of time, the police were able to get away with the exercise of such discretion while enforcing laws such as disorderly conduct. They tended to conduct rampant arrests, completely refrain from conducting arrests or arrest those citizens who lacked political clout.

During the 1960s and 1970s, the U.S. Supreme Court rendered many landmark judgements that required the police to follow guidelines established by the Court. The Bill of Rights was invoked as a means to bring about a certain level of control over police actions, which resulted in the aforementioned guidelines. The Supreme Court has the authority to interpret the U.S. Constitution and the Amendments to the Constitution. In 1803, the U.S. Supreme Court, under Chief Justice John Marshall in the Marbury case,[11] decided that the Supreme Court of the United States is vested with the power of judicial review, and therefore it can adjudicate on the legality of actions carried out by the legislature and executive. The Marbury v. Madison case determined that the judges were responsible for protecting the rights of individuals. The U.S. Supreme Court has the right to review actions performed by the executive branch of the government. The police fall under the executive branch of government and therefore the Court has been reviewing police actions for decades on such principles.

One of the major cases of the 1960s is the Miranda case,[12] which laid down the rule that the police have a duty to inform any suspect of their constitutional rights against self-incrimination, and rights to call for an attorney. These rights include that a suspect does not have to speak to the police if asked any questions about a crime and if he decides to speak, then he has the right to have an attorney present. Also, the suspect is warned that anything they say can and will be used against him in a court of law. Finally, Miranda requires that the police inform the suspect that if he can't afford to pay for legal representation, then an attorney would be appointed to handle the matter prior to questioning the suspect. The Miranda case falls under the Fifth Amendment, which requires the police to inform a suspect of his constitutional rights. The police represent the government; therefore, the Bill of Rights has been interpreted in conjunction with the Fourteenth Amendment to protect citizens from illegal and inappropriate police actions. The Fifth Amendment states,

> nor shall [he] be compelled in any criminal case to be a witness against himself, nor be deprived of life, liberty, or property, without due process of law.

The Fourth Amendment is an important Amendment that protects citizen rights and provides guidelines on police discretion. This Amendment deals with police activities such as arrest, due process, probable cause, search and seizure, warrants, line-ups and hot pursuit. The Fourth Amendment states,

> The right of the people to be secure in their persons, houses, papers, and effects, against unreasonable searches and seizures, shall not be violated, and no Warrants shall issue, but upon probable cause, supported by Oath or affirmation, and particularly describing the place to be searched, and the persons or things to be seized.

In Weeks v. United States,[13] the Supreme Court decided that illegally obtained evidence seized by federal law enforcement officers would not be admissible evidence in a federal court. This decision became known as the "exclusionary rule". However, it was not until 1961 that the "exclusionary rule" became applicable to all the states. In Mapp,[14] the Supreme Court extended the applicability of the Weeks rule to the law enforcement officials at the state level. Mapp decided that illegally obtained evidence could not be used in state courts.

In Terry,[15] the Supreme Court ruled that the police could detain an individual without any probable cause for questioning. Stopping a person is permitted and does not constitute an arrest when unusual behaviour has been observed leading to a reasonable suspicion that a criminal act may be likely. It should be noted that reasonable suspicion has not been defined as strictly being a probable cause. The police officer can select specific facts to justify his suspicion.

Therefore, a police officer may frisk a person, if he believes that the suspect may be dangerous, but he may search only for weapons and not for evidence.

In addition to the Fourth and Fifth Amendments, the Supreme Court has also used the Sixth Amendment to control police discretion. An important issue pertaining to the Sixth Amendment, with regard to criminal investigations, is that of the line-up. The line-up is one of the methods used by the police to identify the potential suspect of a crime. The police place several suspects in a line for the express purpose of having either the victim or a witness identify the suspect as being the criminal. Once the suspect has been formally charged with a crime, the Supreme Court considers a line-up to be a "critical stage of the proceedings" which requires counsel to be present. In Wade,[16] the courts ruled that the use of line-ups by the police for identification purposes must be fair and free from any bias. For example, the individuals in the line-up should be of the same sex, approximately the same age and height, with similar skin texture and hair colour, and should be wearing similar clothes.

2.3.3 Canadian Court

The case of Beaudry v. The Queen[17] in the Supreme Court of Canada adjudicated and laid down an important precedent on the issue of police discretion. The case of Beaudry involved an allegation of obstruction of justice levelled on a police officer for an exercise of his discretion in not investigating numerous grave offences related to driving by an off-duty police officer. This allegation against the officer gave rise to an implication of criminal liability and at the trial, the officer justified his non-investigation by stating that it was a proper exercise of police discretion. At the time of the trial, the police officer had not concealed his action of discretion, and he nonchalantly reported the stoppage of the off-duty officer in an intoxicated state to his superior officers. He justified his discretion to not administer the off-duty officer with the breathalyser test or investigate further on the basis of the contention that this duty was experiencing "emotional and relationship issues" and needed help, not admonition. Upon the rejection of this justification by the superior officers and an order to prepare an impaired driving report, the police officer denied it and consulted the police union for compliance or non-compliance of the order. He was convicted of obstruction of justice, and in his appeal the Supreme Court on an inspection of the nexus between the exercise of police discretion and obstruction of justice upheld his conviction on a majority of 5:4. In this decision, a considerable convergence was perceived between the minority and majority decisions summarised in the following points:

"i. Police officers exercise an essential discretion in relation to the discharge of their duties to enforce the law and investigate crime.
ii. Police discretion is not absolute or unfettered. An exercise of police discretion must be justified rationally. The justification has both subjective and objective elements. The subjective aspect relates to whether discretion has been exercised 'honestly, transparently and on the basis of valid and reasonable grounds'. The objective factors supporting the justification focus on 'the material circumstances' in which the officer's discretion was exercised. Justifications offered must be proportionate to the seriousness of the conduct and it must be clear that the discretion was exercised in the public interest.
iii. Police discretion is inherent in the office of the constable, and in common with prosecutors, must be exercised independently of the executive. Police discretion is neither constrained by administrative directives nor by the roles and functions of the prosecutor.
iv. The liability for the abuse of discretion (obstruction of justice in this case) has to be approached in two stages. First, to determine if the exercise of discretion was valid. If not, the next stage required proof of the elements of the offence beyond any reasonable doubt. According to majority, the improper exercises of discretion are not ipso facto criminal" (Bronitt and Stenning 2011).

2.4 Factors Influencing Arrest Discretion

Most of the studies relating to arrest decisions were conducted through observational and other methods of empirical fact-finding such as questionnaires and interviews. The first ever comprehensive study of discretion in criminal justice system including the police was undertaken by the American Bar Foundation (1956–1965) with "serendipitous" mix of the University of Wisconsin Law School's "law in action" tradition as embodied by Remington and the Chicago School of Sociology's tradition of field observation as represented by Ohlin (Kelling 1999). The seminal work of Davis, "Police Discretion" (1975), is based on interviews with the Chicago police at all levels. Wortley (2003) based his methods on questionnaires and written interview schedules which were administered on police personnel of New South Wales for his work, "Measuring Police Attitude Towards Discretion". Alpert et al. (2006) preferred an observational method combined with quantitative processes for their research on "Police Officers' Decision-Making and Discretion: Forming

Suspicion and Making a Stop". Groeneveld (2005) employed "Arrest Discretion Scale" by employing several variables, preparing suitable questionnaires to measure a specified dimension of each independent variable and correlating them with scores on the arrest discretion scale. Hidayet (2011) for his research on organisational factors influencing police discretion of Turkish Police used sophisticated statistical and modelling method. A large number of police scholars have relied on secondary data such as official crime statistics, arrest details, officers' background details and victims' socio-economic status to find out if there are any correlations among the variables. Literature review shows that factors such as organisational, informal organisational/subcultural, environmental, individual and situational determinants are major factors that influence discretional decisions of law enforcement agencies (Gaines and Kappeler 2003; Groeneveld 2005; Hidayet 2011).

2.4.1 Organisational Determinants

Research on organisational elements of the police indicates that police officers' actions are shaped by departmental norms, rules, procedures and values (Groeneveld 2005; Smith 1984; Mastrofski 1981). According to Brown (1988), organisational constraints refer to the system of administrative rules, policies and managerial controls designed in conformity with administrative directives. These include organisational structure (degree of centralisation), types of organisational control (rules, incentives, recruitment and training procedures), and the behaviour of administrators and supervisors. Wilson (1968) in his pioneering work on police behaviour in different organisations suggested that the role of the police is influenced by organisational characteristics and goals. He opined that there are three types of police organisations: "legalistic", "watchman" and "service-oriented". Legalistic organisations emphasise that "the law is the law, no exceptions" and strictly follow the norms and rules. Service-oriented organisations stress upon community participation in policing functions and are less likely to emphasise on arrest. In watchman-style organisations, order maintenance is the prime goal. Selective enforcement of laws, therefore suits its organisational objectives.

Mastrofski, Worden and Snipes (1995) worked on the various possibilities of organisational impact on behaviour. The study finds that in the "rational model" the bureaucratic structure of the organisation brings about a deep impact on the behaviour of employees as this model emphasises on rule-making, adherence to the procedure and a strong review mechanism. The "constrained rational model" is similar to the rational model but with the difference that here political cultures shape the choice of the leadership which in turn influences police practices. In contrast, the "loosely coupled model" postulates that the impact of the organisation is relatively insignificant as the leadership is loosely linked with the frontline officers. It emphasises the importance of "environment, culture and peer influence" on decision-making. While discussing the three models, Mastrofski et al. (ibid.) argue that size of an organisation is a key determinant factor in validating these models. They conclude that "while the decision-making of an officer is widely influenced by the policing environment and peer culture in larger bureaucratic departments, organisational policies become essential instruments in regulating behaviour in smaller departments". This may be a good hypothesis to test in the present study, since in the Indian context the state police organisations tend to be large bureaucratic set-ups. An important finding of the organisational theories is that while organisational characteristics are positively correlated with how an officer behaves, as per the "constrained rational" and "loosely coupled models", external factors which are not dependent on the organisation, such as environment, subculture and situations can also exert a significant influence on the decision-making processes of rank and file (Eitle 2005).

Groeneveld (2005) in his seminal work on arrest discretion of field patrol officers has further classified the variables under organisational determinants of discretion in his research work. He argues that "the way an organisation creates structure for arrest discretion flows from four principal sources: official policy, process, training, and values. These dimensions capture the channels through which organisational management can attempt to influence or constrain the arrest behaviour of officers".

Historically, policy measures have been seen as the primary means to guide police judgement. Davis (1975) originally argued that administrative rule-making should govern every police action. Most of the police agencies rely heavily on rules and procedures to successfully accomplish their mission. Groeneveld develops the hypothesis from the literature that "the more the extensive and detailed policies are within the organisation, the more control over discretionary decision-making".

According to Groeneveld (2005), the process dimension involves the organisational imposition of procedures that must be followed by officers to effect an arrest. This includes departmental procedures to detect an instance of abuse of discretion, warning mechanisms as well as means to correct deficiencies.

The third dimension of organisational influence on officers' discretion addresses the issues of training. Groeneveld (2005) argues that "training represents the chief way in which policy and procedures are translated into behaviour expectations of the employees". The extensiveness and content of arrest procedure training and monitoring its effectiveness impact officer's discretionary behaviour. Young (2011) emphasises that "with the pervasive role discretion plays in policing, ensuring quality police work should be accomplished through a relevant training continuum throughout all levels of law enforcement".

And finally, with respect to value, Groeneveld (2005) argues that the "professional ethos of the organisation sets the tone for its members". Professionalism, independence, interpersonal relationship in the organisation, community policing approach and citizens' review of police work are strong indicators of value in a police organisation. According to Groeneveld (2005), "as police agencies work on developing relationships with the community, police executives need to find ways to guide discretion and police behaviour generally through increasing reliance on value instead of relying strictly on rules and protocols of accountability".

2.4.2 Subculture Determinants

The informal organisational culture refers to "the unwritten culture comprised of individual values and tradition that are communicated informally across from officer to officer" (Walker and Katz 2005). This may be referred to as police subculture. Police subculture has been the subject of immense research and discussion by scholars and practitioners alike. "It is understandable given that culture is noted as an obstacle to police accountability, as a reason why police reforms fail, as a cause of police abuse of authority, as a mechanism for officers to cope with the hostile and uncertain work environments, and an explanation for discretionary behaviour" (Ingram, Paoline and Terrill 2013).

Subculture is a "culture within a broader culture that may deviate in some aspects from the broader culture and influences daily decisions" (Herbert 1998). Anthony (2018) argues that "the culture of the police department equates to organizational culture. The culture of police officers in the street is a subculture". "A police department has many of the components of organizational culture found in other organizations and industries, but what differentiates police culture from other organizational cultures is the constant potential for life-and-death encounters combined with the unique stresses and strains that originate in the policing environment" (White and Robinson 2014). "An individual's organizational identity is related to organizational culture" (Alvesson and Sveningsson 2015) implying that the culture within the police mechanism impacts the officers' identity and behaviour.

Cox (1996) argued that police subculture is what teaches police officers "how to go about their tasks, how hard to work, what kinds of relationships to have with their fellow officers and other categories of people with whom they interact, and how they should feel about police administrators, judges, the law, and the requirements and restrictions they impose". For example, since police officers may be subject to physical risk during their daily functioning, they may conceptualise the world as a "potentially toxic and lethal work environment". This conceptualisation "often leads to arbitrary behaviour" (Young 2011). Some of the myths like, "the police represent the thin line between chaos and orders" ("thin blue line") and "public potential hostile and untrustworthy" ("us and them") are deeply internalised by the members across the police organisations. Several academic (McConville and Shepherd 1992; Reiner 1992) and Commission Reports (Wood 1997; Mollen 1994) confirm that "secrecy becomes a protective armour shielding the force as a whole from public knowledge of infraction". The "Code of silence" is a principle which applies all across the police organisation. These discrete sets of values are woven together to form a perceptual net that guides individual decisions (Brown 1988).

The police often have to work in a potentially hostile environment for long hours amidst resource constraints, with an objective to maintain order in society. Researches have established that members of the police organisation are guided by their own set of beliefs, attitudes and behaviour, which when put together can be termed as police subculture. According to the seminal work of William Westley (1970), "police subculture is a crucial concept in the explanation of police behaviour and attitudes". The subculture, in his view, "characterizes the public as hostile, not to be trusted, and potentially violent; this outlook requires secrecy, mutual support, and unity on the part of the police". Manning (1977) suggested that "the inherent uncertainty of the police work, combined with the need for information control, leads to police team work, which in turn generates collective ties and mutual dependency". "Police officers are influenced by the formal organisational structures and expressed organisational values and also by informal values, beliefs, norms, rituals, and expectations of the other police officers that are passed through the organisational culture and from one generation of police officers to another" (Scaramella, Cox and McCamey 2011). "Its influence begins early in the new officer's career when he is told by more experienced officers that training given in the police academies is irrelevant to 'real' police work" (Bayley and Bittner 1989). Sparrow, Moore and Kennedy (1990) argued that "police subculture creates a set of truths, according to which the officers are expected to live". These subcultural truths (listed below) do have some reasons backing them, and each of them alienates the police from the citizens.

- Bending the rules is sometimes necessary to win the war on crimes.
- Public are potentially hostile and untrustworthy.
- It is difficult for the police to deal with unsupportive citizens who make unreasonable demands.
- Police are the only law enforcement agency which has the daunting task of fighting crime.
- Loyalty to colleague counts more than anything else.
- Only the police officers understand the hardships involved in police work.

Researchers have gone into some detail when it comes to these subcultural truths and have come out with interesting findings. The first of these perceived truths is what sociologist Carl B Klockars (1985) terms as "Dirty Harry" dilemma which rationalises vigilante justice. Klockers adopted it from the 1971 Warner Brothers film where Sergeant Harry, in pursuit of a psychopathic killer who has kidnapped a minor girl for ransom, gets frustrated when he sees the culprit reneges his bargain, shoots his partner and escapes. Harry tracks him down and shoots him on his leg, torturing him into revealing where the victim has been hidden. Harry believes that a morally good end can employ whatever means necessary to accomplish the objective. The relevance and influence of this dilemma in everyday police operations including in arrests is significant. Police officers generally perceive the criminal justice system as too liberal or ineffectual to deal with the hardened criminals and justify street justice. In the Indian context, the theme may have a parallel in the movie, *Ardh Satya* (literally meaning half-truth) of 1983. The protagonist in the movie is a police officer like Harry and has become highly cynical with the environments he works and has finally taken law into his own hands.

"The dangers associated with policing often prompt officers to distance themselves from the chief source of danger – other citizens. Thus, the police officers, who are socially isolated from the public, and rely on each other for protection from a hostile and dangerous work setting, tend to develop an '*us versus them*' attitude towards public and a strong sense of loyalty towards fellow officers" (Terril, Paolin and Manning 2003).

Yet another distinct subculture that permeates the organisation is the feeling and understanding that the police have the real responsibility of fighting crime. The thin line between order and chaos is protected by them and once the police withdraw from the scene, disorder will descend, and chaos will prevail. In the 1950s, Bill Parker, the Chief of LAPD, coined the phrase, the "thin blue line" to reinforce the role of LAPD in fighting crime and maintaining order in Los Angeles. As Parker explained, "the thin blue line, representing the LAPD, is the barrier between law and order and social and civil anarchy" (Lasley 2012). These sentiments were echoed by police organisations in India during the stakeholders' meeting with the Law Commission of India for its 177th Report on "Law relating to arrest". In response to the consultation paper, the State of Odisha justified the pre-amendment powers of arrest by the police in cognisable offences by arguing that "the aggrieved public have come to see arrests of the culprits by the police as the first step in their yearning for justice. Any curtailment of this power will result in loss of public faith in the criminal justice system". It was further argued that "Indian society is generally perceived to be meek and relies considerably upon the armed police to keep order and hence police should not be weakened". The State of Haryana was of the view that the "Indian public do not expect the police to release the offender immediately after arrest. They would accuse the police of collusion in most such cases". The state police expressed grave concern on the proposed amendment stating that "the proposal to limit the power to arrest an accused in bailable offences, if implemented, would cause tremendous damage to maintenance of public order in the society". These strong sentiments of police organisations in India against the proposed liberal arrest laws betray the deep-seated ethos of this subculture across the police organisations. However, the term in the Indian context may be rephrased as "thin khaki line", having regard to the shade of the uniform donned by the Indian police (Mohanty 2019).

"Code of silence" is "a strong subcultural ethos in policing to denote the informal rule of secrecy that exists among the police officers not to report on colleague's errors, misconduct or brutality. Secrecy is a set of working tenets that loosely couple the police to accountability, that allow them to do their work and protect each other in the face of oversight interference" (Crank 2004). This ethos compliments the "us versus them" mindset and "Dirty Harry" dilemma. If the police perceive the public as non-cooperative, unappreciative and are critical of their work, and that the "rules are to be bent" for espousing a greater social cause, the loyalty to a fellow colleague acts as a premium one may have to pay to insure oneself against the professional hazards that one may encounter in the course of their career. This perceived feeling of being protected by colleagues against the abuse of power, particularly against illegal arrests or excesses during arrest, gives a sense of immunity to the officer and influences his discretionary powers.

2.4.3 Environmental Determinants

On environmental determinants of discretion, research suggests that "even when situational characteristics are similar, policing practices differ depending on community characteristics. Police officers develop behaviour models that are acceptable to community that is policed" (Hidayet 2011). Klinger (1997) argues that the police action in a specific neighbourhood is determined by the "officer perceptions of what appropriate behaviour is in the community". If the police believe that a particular community does not *deserve* their services, the community ends up getting a lower level of service. Fyfe (1981) contends that "crime rate in a community determines policing strategy as empirical studies show that the police are more inclined to behave harshly in communities with higher crime rates. Many researchers argue that variations in police behaviour can be explained by the degree of informal social control in the community" (Hidayet 2011). "Lower level informal social control requires greater formal social control. An inverse relationship exists between informal social control in a community and use of formal social control by the police in that community" (Alpert, Dunham and Piquero 1997). This means that the police may tend to become harsher while dealing with the people living in a slum area than with members of an affluent neighbourhood. In the Indian context, political, societal and media pressures are three strong determinants that could be included under this category. National Police Commission (1981a) in its Third Report, while highlighting the causes of police corruption, reports that "police are frequently pressed by the expectations of the public opinion in certain situation to make arrests, merely to create an impression of effectiveness. Press reports about sensational cases invariably end up with a comment on arrest by the police. The fact that no arrest has been made in the case is held against the police". "The NPC in its Third Report has recorded some typical situations or matters in which pressure is brought to bear on police by political, executive and other extraneous sources, like arrest or non-arrest of a person who is under investigation, release or non-release on bail after arrest, foisting false criminal cases against political functionaries for achieving political ends, discretionary enforcement of law with emphasis on severity and ruthlessness while dealing with persons opposed to the ruling party" (Joshi 2013).

With respect to arrests, the NPC enlists "typical situations or matters in which pressure is brought to bear on the police by the political, executive or other extraneous sources as follows:

1. Arrest or non-arrest of a person against whom a case is taken up for investigation by the police
2. Release or non-release on bail after arrest
3. Taking persons into preventive custody to immobilise them from legitimate political activity in opposition to the party in power
4. Discretionary enforcement of law while dealing with public order situations, with emphasis on severity or ruthlessness in regard to persons opposed to the ruling party
5. Manoeuvring police intervention by exaggerating a non-cognisable offence to gain advantage over another party"

In today's world, the media act as a powerful tool to shape the public opinion by not only exposing the excesses committed by the police, but often defining the standards of civility the police are expected to exhibit in the course of enforcement of laws.

> Media has a dual character. It is a medium as well as a creator of news, attitudes and agenda. It conveys as well as directs. Media reports alert policymakers, interest groups and political parties to emerging issues, and to threats and opportunities. As a powerful medium, information is often conveyed and commented upon with a view to shape the public agenda, mould public opinion and push action along a particular course towards a particular goal.
>
> (Ayyar 2009)

The media and the police world over have an ambiguous relationship. In most cases, the media narrative of police work takes on a critical tone and one rarely sees a major piece of police work receive the accolade of general approval. "Literature on the subject of police and media relations reaches a consensus that there is an extreme amount of animosity between these two groups. The literature also bears out the fact that this animosity had perpetuated itself over a long period of time and may even be the result of built-in biases that solidify in the morals of the officers and reporters before they ever even begin their jobs" (Bellew 2001). A study conducted by Selke and Bartoszek (1984) reveals that apparently "the animosity between journalists and police officers may have its seeds in the backgrounds and personal orientations of those who choose these professions. They further point out that the majority of recruits also believed that the media is not generally objective and is more concerned with printing what sells papers rather than merely covering new events". Skolnick and Fyfe (1993) argue "if any single instance of police action has ever been wholly satisfactory to all concerned, since an otherwise perfect example of police work is likely to be viewed less enthusiastically by the offender. The environment in which police must do their work is therefore certain to be unfavourable. Good immediate results are difficult to secure and may bring new and unexpected favours into the operation. The chain of circumstances thus forged proves a burden to even the best police organisation". Ghosh and Rustamji (1994), two distinguished police scholars, argue that the public and their mouthpiece – the press – are interested in every aspect of police work and the tone of press reporting and comments profoundly influences the public opinion.

Public opinion adds a layer of accountability to police functions. It is argued in earlier section that accountability and exercise of discretion are interrelated. Strong criticism by the media of mishandling a grave crime or police excesses or inaction brings the organisation under the scanner. The political leadership seeks immediate remedial measures often in the form of departmental action against negligent officers to counter the public criticism. The field functionaries in the organisation are therefore weary of undue media interest in police works. Besides, in India, most police organisations, at the level of district Superintendent of Police, maintain a system of collection of daily clippings of the newspaper reports that relate to their jurisdictions. In so far as the reports are critical of police functions, the concerned field functionary is asked to explain, and in some instances, an inquiry is ordered. Prompt arrests in the face of media criticism often save the police from further embarrassment. But in the process the procedural and legal formalities become a casualty.

Thus, the media, public opinion, public reaction and political culture create a complex maze within which the police often take decisions. Each of these components either independently or in combination influences the decision-making processes of the police.

2.4.4 Individual Determinants

Individual determinants have been studied under two categories: "how individual characteristics of officers on one hand and the officers' values, beliefs and attitudes on the other, are seen as correlates of police decisions" (Hidayet 2011). Multiple studies have been conducted which are aimed at examining the relationship between individual characteristics such as "gender, age, educational level, social class and experiences" and police behaviour. The studies produced mixed results with both strong and weak relationships. As regards officers' values, beliefs and attitudes having correlation with decision-making, Goldstein (1977) argues that "officers' responses in certain situations are derived from their perceptions on what policing means to them". Mastrofski, Worden and Snipes (1995) have reported that officers reflect their belief and idea of what's best for the community in their policing activities. "They use their own attitudes and policing style to make decisions about who is suspicious, who is to be arrested, and whose action needs to be investigated. Although many scholars argued that attitude can help in understanding the discretionary behaviour, the literature suggests that relationship between attitude and behaviour is not strong enough to judge whether a set of values can guarantee a certain kind of behaviour" (Hidayet 2011).

One of the factors of the individual determinants is the ethics and integrity of the officer. "Police corruption usually stems from misuse of authority and individual officer's integrity. Thus, by exercising discretion the police officers are at liberty of denying certain people their due process rights" (Kleinig 1996; Walker and Katz 2005). National Police Commission (1981a) in its Third Report stated that "the powers of arrest involve the exercise of considerable discretion in the day-to-day working of the police" and "therefore give scope for corruption and malpractices accompanied by extortion and harassment to the public".

Punch (1985) defines police corruption as taking place:

> when an official receives or is promised significant advantage or reward (personal, group or organisational) for doing something that he is under a duty to do anyway, that he is under a duty not to do, for exercising a 'legitimate discretion for improper reasons', and for employing illegal means to achieve approved goals.
>
> (emphasis added)

The definition provided earlier incorporates the notion that certain forms or acts of corruption do not originate in "personal rewards", but in rewards for the greater organisation such as the police in itself or for a wider group such as a special squad. This definition differs from Goldstein's (1975) which postulates that corruption originates in "personal gain" or "personal reward" for the police officer. Further, Punch widens the definition to include "approved goals" in addition to illegitimate ones. These "approved goals" are referred to misleadingly in relation to "noble cause corruption". Klockars (1980) argues that noble cause corruption, what he refers to as "Dirty Harry" dilemma mentioned earlier is a staple part of police life.

2.4.5 *Situational Determinants*

The situational variables are factors concerning the "degree of interaction between law enforcement and citizens within the community and the offender attributes. Thus, police discretion is influenced by the surrounding situation in which an officer finds himself and how an offender presents himself to him" (Halliday 2009). Halliday has summed up the situational variables under the following headings:

- "The seriousness of the crime
- Prior criminal record

- Strength of evidence
- Preference of the victim
- Relationship between the victim and suspect
- Characteristics of the victim
- Race, ethnicity and gender of the suspect
- Behaviour
- Visibility of the event i.e. media or witness
- Neighbourhood characteristics
- Individual officer characteristics (Gaines and Kappeler 2003; Walker and Katz 2005)"

Officers take into account one or more of these variables before making a decision regarding the course of action to follow. Halliday argues that the single most important factor concerning situational variables is the seriousness of the offence. If the crime is more serious, it is less likely for the officer to exercise their discretion to not arrest. Instead, it's more likely that the officer would follow the rules and arrest the offender.

"Empirical research has provided overwhelming support to the notion that police have a great deal of discretion in how they address a citizen's conduct and that both legal and extra-legal criteria can influence the outcomes of police – citizen encounters" (Smith and Visher 1981). This means that when an officer encounters a citizen, their decisions should ideally be guided by legal factors such as "seriousness of a citizen's conduct" or "evidence against a suspect". Therefore, it is not too much of a surprise that the empiric reality shows that there indeed is some discrimination on grounds of gender or race, in arrest decisions, and these are extralegal considerations. While the empirical study clearly shows that legal factors are significant in their influence over arrest outcomes, Worden (1989) notes that "Policing is for the most part extra-legal, for while officers (often) work within the constraints of the law, they seldom invoke the law in performing police work". As discussed earlier in this chapter, there is a strong correlation "between the demeanour of the offender and police decisions" (Black 1971). For example, disrespectful behaviours of offenders increase the likelihood of an officer making an arrest and using force towards those suspects (Hidayet 2011).

Black's (1971, 1976) seminal work on the social organisation of law gives an insight into how the law is mobilised (for example, an arrest decision) to protect or ignore the interest of an actor. According to his general theory of legal control and the nature of law, "arrest decisions are influenced by social stratification including race, gender, education etc". "People of disadvantage are less likely to be successful in having law mobilised to protect their interest and more likely to have the law successfully applied to their behaviours" (Eitle 2005). People with more education and greater culture in their lives are more likely to have law mobilised to protect their interests. Black's theory generates a number of hypotheses regarding how extralegal characteristics influence the likelihood of a law being implemented. In the Indian context, it may be hypothesised that the poor and marginal are less likely to have law mobilised to protect their interest.

In this study, conducted in the Indian context, the socio-economic survey of selected offenders has been conducted to find out if there is a correlation between poor and marginal and their being more likely to be arrested as compared to their affluent counterparts. It is presumed that the awareness about the legal rights or lack of it depends upon the socio-economic condition of the individual and it being so, whether the members of poor and marginal sections of the society are more likely to meet with discretionary abuse because of lack of legal awareness and access to legal assistance.

2.5 Measuring the Factors Influencing Arrest Discretion

From the foregoing discussions, it is found that the determinants or factors influencing the arrest discretion behaviour of the police have broadly been categorised under four major headings, such as organisational, environmental, individual and situational. The organisational determinant has further been subdivided into formal departmental policy and informal organisational culture. The latter has been explained in terms of police subculture. For the purpose of this study, informal organisational/police subculture has been taken as a separate determinant as the variables under this head are critical and distinctive enough to deserve a separate identity.

Various studies also suggest that environment and peer culture are dominant factors in influencing discretionary behaviour in many large police organisations, more than even organisational constraints. The average state police organisations in India are considered large or very large with manpower of tens of thousands within a vast geographical spread. The study is intended to empirically test if the proposition is true in the Indian context. Literature review further suggests that studies on individual determinants produce mixed results with both strong and weak relationships and that correlation between attitude and behaviour is not strong enough to understand whether a particular set of values can guarantee a distinct kind of behaviour. However, this study aims at collecting officers' gender, age, experience and position in the organisation for any possible co-relation with arrest discretion behaviour.

Situational determinants by far have maximum impact on the arrest discretion behaviour of the police. In the present study, a socio-legal survey has been conducted in respect of selected offenders who are involved in offences for which maximum punishment prescribed in law is up to or less than seven years. In such instances, according to the amended arrest law, the respondents are likely to be served notice instead of formal arrest. But, while many of them have been arrested instead of being served a notice, many others, however, are able to "have the law mobilised to protect their interest", that is, they have been served notice instead of a formal arrest. The awareness about the legal rights or lack of them depends upon the socio-economic condition of the individual. Members of poor and marginal sections of the society are more likely to be at the receiving end of discretionary abuse than their affluent counterparts. Having regard to these critical variables that influence arrest discretion, the determinant has been introduced for the purpose of this study as "Situational/Offenders' Determinants" by selecting relevant variables.

2.6 Key Hypotheses

On the basis of foregoing discussion, six hypotheses have been listed out on the subject of police discretion. The validity of the hypotheses is required to be tested by devising suitable methodologies to find out if these hypotheses are universal in their applicability to the Indian police.

1. *Organisational determinants positively constrain the arrest discretion behaviour of the police through channels such as policy, process and values.*

   Study of organisational features indicates that decisions of police officers are shaped by departmental norms, rules, procedures and values (Groeneveld 2005; Smith 1984; Mastrofski 1981). According to Brown (1988), organisational constraints refer to the system of administrative rules, policies and managerial controls designed in conformity with administrative directives. Groeneveld (2005) in his seminal work on arrest discretion of field patrol officers has further classified the variables under organisational determinants of discretion for his research work. He argues that "the way an organisation creates structure for arrest discretion flows from four principal sources: official policy, process, training, and values. These dimensions capture the channels through which organisational management can attempt to influence or constraint the arrest behaviour of officers". Organisational determinants positively constrain the arrest decision of officers by ensuring compliances to the statute and court directives, and by introducing policy, manual rules, regulatory circulars, disciplinary mechanism, training etc.
2. *Police subculture positively correlates with arrest discretion behaviour.*

   The informal organisational culture refers to "the unwritten culture comprised the individual values and tradition that are communicated informally across from officer to officer" (Walker and Katz 2005). This may be referred to as police subculture. Subculture is "a culture within a broader culture that may deviate in some aspects from the broader culture and influences daily decisions" (Herbert 1998). These discrete sets of values are woven together to form a perceptual net that guides individual decisions (Brown 1988). According to William Westley (1970), the police subculture is "a crucial concept in the explanation of police behaviour and attitudes. The subculture, in his view, characterizes public as hostile, not to be trusted, and potentially violent; this outlook requires secrecy, mutual support, and unity on the part of the police". Four distinct subcultural myths, "dirty Harry dilemma", "us versus them", "thin blue/khaki line" and "code of silence" have been operationalised in the Indian context to empirically test the impact of subculture on the arrest decision behaviour.

3. *The environmental determinants positively affect the arrest discretion behaviour.*

   Study of the environmental determinants indicates that even when the "situation characteristics" are identical practices of the police vary as per the characteristics of the community in which they originate. Officers develop a behaviour model which is approved by the community in which they exercise policing (Hidayet 2011). In the context of this study, environmental factors, such as media, public opinion, public reaction and political culture that create a complex maze within which the police take decisions, have been operationalised as variables. Each of these components either independently or in combination influences decision-making processes of police.

4. *Subculture and environmental determinants affect the arrest discretion behaviour more than the organisational determinants.*

   An important finding of the organisational theories is that while organisational characteristics have positive correlates with how an officer behaves, the "constrained organisational" and "loosely coupled models" imply that non-organisational factors, such as environment, subculture and situations can exert a significant influence on the decision-making processes of rank and file (Eitle 2005). In investigating the three proposed models, Mastrofski, Worden and Snipes (1995) argue that "size of an organisation is an essential element in validating the models. They conclude that the decision making of an officer is widely influenced by the policing environment, peer culture in larger bureaucratic departments, while organisational policies become essential instruments in regulation behaviour in smaller departments". The police organisations in India are relatively larger with vast geographical jurisdiction, each covering more than few thousand square kilometres and with manpower no fewer than tens of thousands. Large or very large being the police organisations in India, the decision-making is more likely to be influenced by the policing environment and subculture than the organisational policies.

5. *Individual determinants such as the officer's gender, work experience and position in the organisation impact differentially to the arrest discretion behaviour.*

   Many studies have examined the relationship between officers' characteristics, such as gender, age, educational level, social class and experiences, and police behaviour. The studies have produced mixed results with both strong and weak relationships.

6. *People with socio-economic disadvantage are less likely to be successful in having law mobilised to protect their interest.*

   The situational variables are "factors concerning the degree of interaction between law enforcement and citizens within the community and offender attributes. Thus, police discretion is influenced by the surrounding situation in which an officer finds himself and how an offender presents himself before the police" (Halliday 2009). According to Black's (1971, 1976) general theory of legal control and the nature of law, "arrest decisions are influenced by social stratification including race, gender, education etc". "People of disadvantage are less likely to be successful in having law mobilised to protect their interest and more likely to have the law successfully applied to their behaviours" (Eitle 2005). People with more education and greater culture in their lives are more likely to have law mobilised to protect their interests. Black's theory generates a number of hypotheses regarding how extralegal characteristics influence the likelihood of law being implemented. In the Indian context, it may be hypothesised that the poor and marginal are less likely to have law mobilised to protect their interest.

2.7 A Diagrammatic Representation of Arrest Drivers

The conceptual diagram of the study is presented in Figure 2.1. Literature establishes that the organisational, subcultural, environmental, individual

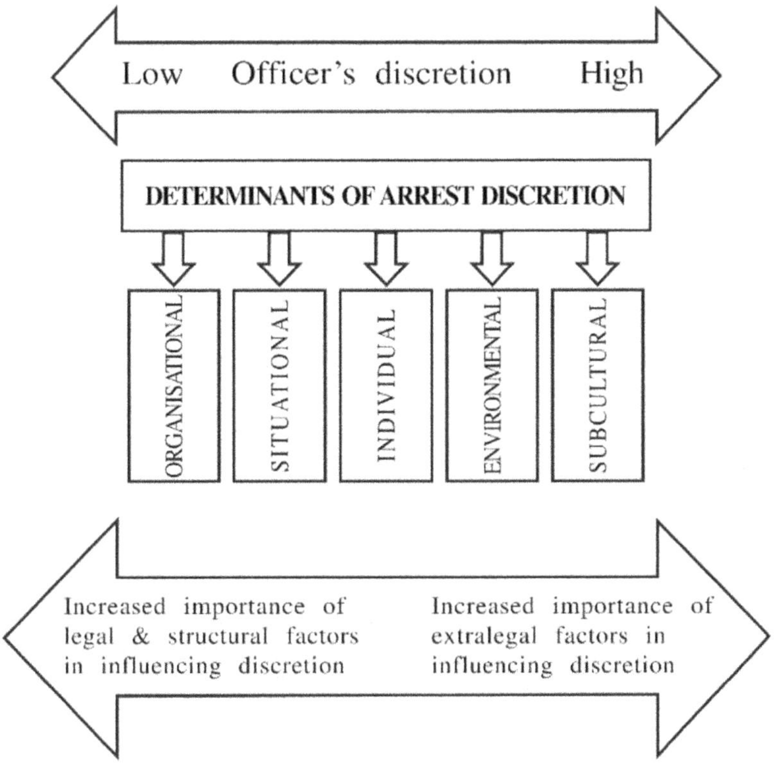

Figure 2.1 Conceptual diagram of the study

and situational determinants are at the forefront of the arrest discretion behaviour of police. Legal and structural factors in the organisation which include the existence of statutes, manual rules, guidelines and supervision mechanism tend to constrain an officer's discretionary behaviour and the exercise of discretion consequently becomes more regulated and remains within the acceptable limits. Some of the variables of situational determinants, such as seriousness of the crime, strength of evidence and prior criminal record, do invoke legal factors in arrest discretion. On the other hand, subcultural, environmental, individual and certain situational determinants (like offender's behaviour, race or ethnicity of the offender etc.) generate more subjective response, and are complex and intangible with large discretionary latitude. The diagram represents the concept graphically. The five determinants have been arranged as per the degree of legal (organisational and partly situational) and extralegal (individual, environmental, subcultural and partly situational) influences they exert on the arrest discretion behaviour. Arrest decisions are made within the complex maze of legal and extralegal factors. The extralegal determinants have the potential for discretionary abuse. On how the exercise of extralegal factors subverts the police legitimacy, Jauregui (2013) argues that "the police power of discretion in responding to situational exigencies is always already outside of law, bestowing on police – and burdening them with – authority to use force in ways that are not always clearly regulated by legal rules. This extralegal power to intervene with coercive force is a main reason why police are 'ambivalently feared and admired', a social status suggesting that their legitimacy is always already questionable at best". The challenge with the higher police management lies on how to regulate the influence of extralegal factors, as there is no one-size-fits-all solution to address the concerns.

In the next chapter, the subject of arrest discretion behaviour of the police in India has been traced out, although well-documented secondary sources in this regard are far and few between. This is essential for two reasons: firstly, it is necessary to round up all literature as well as judicial pronouncements on this subject to cohesively understand the way discretion has been perceived and treated in the context of the police in India, and secondly, to explore if these findings can serve as the reference points to operationalise the determinants in the context of Indian police.

Notes

1 Discretionary Justice: A Preliminary Enquiry, 1969, Police Discretion, 1975
2 The Need for Discretion, 1969
3 Police Discretion not to Invoke the Criminal Process, 1960
4 Taming the System: The Control of Discretion in Criminal Justice, 1993
5 Better Living Through Police Discretion, 1984
6 The Model of Rules, 1967
7 Ex Parte Blackburn, 1968, 1 All E.R. 763 C.A
8 Holgate-Mohammed v. Duke, 1984, 1, All E.R. 1054 H.L

9 Coxhead case, 1986 R.T.R. 416
10 Dytham case, 1979, 3 All E.R. 641
11 Marbury v. Madison case 5 U.S. 1 Cranch 137 1803
12 Miranda v. Arizona 384 U.S. 436, 1966
13 Weeks v. United States, 232 U.S. 383, 1914
14 Mapp v. Ohio 367 U.S. 643, 1961
15 Terry v. Ohio, 392 U.S. 1, 1968
16 United States v. Wade, 388 U.S. 218
17 Beaudry v. The Queen, 2007 1 SCR

3 Police Discretion

Laws and Policies in India

A brief discussion of the history of the police in India is essential to appreciate the complexities and nuances in the way it operates in its current form.

Due to the predominance of rural living in India, traditional policing emerged from the villages in India. The responsibility of policing was lying in the hands of the village headman and the structure of primary policing was dependent on the landholding pattern prevalent in the village. The presence of dominant landowners created a system in which such landowners inevitably ended up influencing the police, with the police even acting as mere agents for these landowners in numerous instances. In the absence of large landowners, the headman would be autonomous (Bayley 1969).

Up until the arrival of the British in the mid-eighteenth century, the systems of governance in India were autocratic and military. The ruler and his principal agents fulfilled the functions of military commander, revenue collector, head of police, judge and magistrate into their own persons (Curry 1932). Upon the arrival of the British, a centralised policing structure was developed. Curry (ibid.) in his book on the history of the Indian police, one of the earliest books to record the history of policing in India, explains that when the British took over the government of provinces one after another, they found that local self-government, which is a vital part of the Englishman's heritage, was missing and thus "policing in India, like her economic development, became of necessity the duty of central government". Bayley (1969) remarked that "the Indian police history can be written largely in terms of attempts to create an imperial system linking the indigenous fragmented system and making it responsive to orders of imperial capital". Thus, a state-owned and centralised police structure grew out of necessity for largely under-policed and disparate provinces, rather than being the outcome of an imperialist agenda to deliberately model the police organisation the way it developed then. The transition from localised and fragmented military autocracies to a fully developed civil police system was slow with a great deal of experiments being done that finally culminated into the existing system.

DOI: 10.4324/9781003406679-3

3.1 From Regulation of 1772 to Police Act 1861

By 1761, the East India Company had achieved a strong foothold in Bengal. The East India Company, as a matter of policy, did not interfere with the pre-existing administrative machinery in an area. However, the prevalence of crime and rampant violations of public order triggered a departure from this policy. Warren Hastings, the Governor of the Presidency of Bengal, brought about a change in this pre-existing machinery by the Regulation of 1772, which facilitated the establishment of criminal courts in each district of Bengal. However, at a later stage, remarking that the "court is giving encouragement to the evil doers, since the standard of evidence demanded makes punishment difficult", Hastings proposed a reversion to the Moghul system of "Foujdar"[1] policing; which required all landowners to assist them in these duties (Curry 1932). Where there was no "Foujdar", the old system of the village police being responsible to the "Zamindar"[2] was left in operation. An important feature of this system was the creation of a separate office for the receipt and management of information collected by the Foujdar. "This office was the germ from which sprang the fully developed police system in modern India" (Curry 1932). However, these arrangements were not found satisfactory and within a decade of their introduction, the "Foujdars" were withdrawn.

With the first British attempt to institute a system of policing in India having failed, violent crimes continued to grow. When Cornwallis became the next Governor-General of Bengal, he found that the criminal administration system in states was in utter chaos. Through the regulation of 1793, he introduced the following important measures:

i. The police in the country should be considered under the exclusive charge of the government. No Zamindar or landowner should maintain any police force.
ii. Magistrates of the districts were ordered to divide the jurisdictions, each under the charge of a "Darogah"[3] with appropriate establishment.
iii. Darogahs were empowered to receive reports of offences and arrest accused persons, sending them to a magistrate *within twenty-four hours of arrest. Once a person has been arrested, the "Darogah" has no power to release him, only a magistrate could do that.*
iv. Village police were made subject to the orders of the Darogahs.
v. Darogahs were given autonomy to pursue criminals into other jurisdictions, to keep peace in public places and to submit monthly report to their District Magistrates.

The system worked well initially but antagonised the powerful Zamindar lobby, which was the locus of real authority in a predominantly rural population. Coupled with this, the lack of supervision over the Darogahs made them and their subordinates corrupt and oppressive. The problems present inherently within the system required new solutions and various committees were instituted by the Directors of the East India Company. The system of policing which followed this could be consolidated into a list of various attempts featuring the centralised police organisation system or the local village police as a product of experimentation, till the solution was found in the province of Sind.

The annexation of Sind in 1843 followed the introduction of a regular police force by Sir Charles Napier. Sir Napier based his model of the police organisation along the lines of the Irish constabulary, as Sind required a force with a military character due to its recent annexation. The distinct nature of this system introduced by Sir Napier was present in the fact that the policing system was independent and self-contained, under the control of superior officers within the organisation who would place their focus only on the administration of the force and crime prevention (University of Calcutta 1913; Curry 1932). The success of this system attracted and grasped the attention of the Governor of Bombay, Sir George Clerk when he visited the province in 1847. He believed that the poor condition of the Bombay Police was due to inadequate supervisory mechanisms. In 1853, the Bombay Police was restructured based on the Sind model. Distinct characteristics of this system were the appointment of a Superintendent with complete and exhaustive control over the police in every district, and the appointment of a native officer in every Tahsil,[4] marking a shift in the control of police in government. In 1859, by an Act XXIV, Madras adopted this system and so did Bengal in 1860.

Thus, by the 1850s, the solution to the problem of policing was found and adopted in various parts of India (Curry 1932). The Police Commission of 1860 was instituted to examine systems of policing present in India then with the draft policies based on the following principles:

i. The Indian Police should have duties which are civil in nature and subsequently, they should be responsible to the civil government.
ii. The functions of the police should be to protect the public and repress the criminals.
iii. There should be a separation between judicial, police and detective functions.
iv. The police should be centralised and the discipline and organisation of the force should be akin to that of the Indian Army.
v. There would only be a singular police force in an area under the control of a police officer.
vi. The village police would see a shift in their role from an executive character to that of an information gatherer.

Another contemporary development, the Mutiny of 1857,[5] made the British realise the responsibilities of imperial domination over such a vast and diverse territory. It ushered in a period of hectic reassessment, the results of which set the seal on administrative development for a hundred years. "Reforms that had been maturing with pragmatic and bureaucratic thoroughness for many years were suddenly enshrined in law" (Bayley 1969). The Government of India Act 1858 transferred control of the Greater Indian territory to the British Government and major criminal codes such as the Indian Penal Code 1860 and Code of Criminal Procedure 1861 were enacted along with the Police Act 1861 based on the Police Commission's recommendations.

The Commission recommended the initiation of a civil police force across India. It was recommended that the policing powers of Commissioners should be rescinded, and the post of Inspector General of Police should be created provincially. The administration of the police in a district would lie under the purview of the District Superintendent of Police under the general control and the direction of the District Magistrate. The duties laid down for the police would include the prevention and detection of crime, intelligence management and collection, public order maintenance in general, roads and thoroughfares, and escort and guarding of prisoners among others.

Critics argue that the Police Act 1861 suffered from few inherent weaknesses that affected the fairness and credibility of the police in India, which continued even after India became independent. Bayley (1969) argues that principles of the Act were neither revolutionary nor particularly novel. They were an extension of arrangements which were being experimented in bits and pieces across British India. Arnold (1986) discerns a deeper trend that spans India's history from early colonialism to post-independence period that saw "creation, evolution and consolidation of a powerful state apparatus with police as one of the primary agencies". He argues that the proliferation of the centrally controlled armed forces and intelligence agencies since Independence has "built upon and elaborated a colonial police structure already well established by 1920s and 1930s. In this heavy reliance upon police, the rulers of India since Independence have been no more than faithful to their colonial inheritance". Joshi (2013) points out that the provisions of the Act made India inherit a police organisation that was totally subservient to the executive, whose managerial philosophy was based on distrust to lower ranks, was militaristic and authoritarian in design and whose charter of function was too narrow and limited with disproportionate emphasis on maintenance of law and order rather than citizen's protection. The National Police Commission (Ch XIV, Second Report 1979) observed that the insistence on "prompt obedience to all orders lawfully issued by any competent authority underlines the total submission of police to executive authority and provides immense scope for the executive to use police for implementing decisions which may not be spelt out in any law, rule or regulation". Further, in its Fifth Report, the National Police Commission observes that "the evolution of police system in India was closely linked with the objectives of government in power and the need for maintaining a tight control over the people of this country so that the stability and growth of British rule was not threatened".

Good or bad, the Police Act of 1861, and the criminal major Acts which were legislated contemporaneously ingrained the concept of "rule of law" into the fabric of governance. A state-owned and centralised police structure was developed out of expediency and it is highly doubtful whether the typical British model[6] could have been successfully implanted in a society without any tradition of self-government and in a country as varied as a continent.

3.2 The Legacy of Police Act 1861

The British till the independence of India in 1947 made no structural reforms in police administration. "It was a time of consolidation, of trying to work more successfully the machine already developed" (Bayley 1969). The Police Commission set up in 1902 by Lord Curzon enquired into the functioning of the police and was critical of its performance. Some of the recommendations resulted in the subsequent setting up of specialised units such as criminal investigation division, railway police, river police and chemical examiners' department (precursor to modern forensic laboratories). An Inspector General of Police, Sir Edward Henry, developed the world-renowned fingerprint system in India. Among other changes, the Commission recommended the posting of a Sub-Inspector of Police as the officer-in-charge of a police station, and the creation of Circle Inspectors of Police as supervisory officers of a group of police stations. One of the most pathbreaking recommendations of the Commission was to induct educated Indians at officer levels.

Bayley (ibid.) argues that the British influenced the system of policing in India in a major way through the reforms of 1861, a system which is still in place today. The independence struggle pitted the police against the national movement, and Indian policemen against Indian freedom fighters. These memories were implanted in the minds of people, which still fundamentally affect the relations between the two. The second legacy relates to this phenomenon. The perceptions, attitudes and predispositions towards the police on the part of public and policymakers still remain rooted in this mindset. Thirdly, they underlined the role that the police should play in Indian society; "that 'proper' police duties today are very much what were considered 'proper' duties under the British".

3.3 Development After Independence

Indian independence brought to life a representative democracy with a parliamentary system and federalism. It consolidated the concept that the parliament and the state legislatures would be the sole law-making bodies in the country. "Independence brought revolutionary changes in the political structure of the government, but none of any consequence to the structure of police administration" (Bayley 1969). An analysis of the Constitution of India would reveal that the police in India are state subjects under the strict control and regulation of those states itself.[7] States in India have retained control over the maintenance and direction of their police forces. The Union government has federal investigative agencies such as the Central Bureau of

Investigation[8] and National Investigation Agency, which investigate federal crimes. Besides, as part of its internal security responsibilities,[9] the Union government has raised Central Armed Police Forces (CAPF), such as the Central Reserve Police Force, Border Security Force, Indo-Tibetan Border Police, Sashastra Seema Bal, Central Industrial Security Force, National Security Guard and Railway Protection Force. The members of the Indian Police Service, or superior officer cadre, are recruited and their service conditions are regulated by the Union government although most of these officers are posted at the top leadership positions of the State police organisations.

The strength of each State police organisation and that of the Central Armed Police Forces have increased manifold since India's independence. India is a union of twenty-eight States and eight Union Territories[10] with a total strength of more than 1.67 million police personnel.[11] The strength in the top ten states varies from 81,145 (Madhya Pradesh) to 327,540 (Uttar Pradesh). The total strength of the Central Armed Police Force as of January 2020 was more than 1.1 million.[12] The growth in the strength of police organisations in India in the post-independence period is commensurate with the vast array of duties and responsibilities that need to be carried out by the police: from crime prevention and investigation to order maintenance, from internal security to security of protected persons, from traffic regulation to disaster management and from collection of intelligence to organising special operations.

The post-independence period saw a plethora of new legislations including criminal legislations created to address specialised crimes, legislations focused on creating social reform such as the prevention of regressive social practices such as "dowry" as well as environmental legislations to protect the environment.[13] The core substantive criminal legislation, that is, the Indian Penal Code of 1860 continued its primacy with periodic amendments to address new forms of crimes. The procedural law, that is, the CrPC was overhauled in 1973 with the primary objective being the separation of powers of executive and judiciary in true constitutional spirit.

3.4 Constitution of India

The Constitution of India was framed by the Constituent Assembly set up under the Cabinet Mission Plan of 1946.[14] After about three years of studying the best features of the Constitutions of several other countries and intense debate, a draft Constitution was finally adopted in November 1949 and its major parts came into force on January 26, 1950. The Constitutions which profoundly influenced the Indian Constitution are those of Britain, USA, Ireland and Canada. The Indian Constitution is the largest written Constitution in the world, premised on a parliamentary system of government and a federal system with a unitary bias.

The highest court of the land, the Supreme Court, through various judgements has laid down the "basic features" of the Constitution, which include the rule of law,[15] the rule of equality,[16] an independent and efficient judicial system,[17] republican and democratic form of government,[18] equality clauses contained in Articles 14, 15 and 16[19] and judicial review.[20]

Two of the Articles assume critical importance and serve as the conscience keeper of the procedural laws that the police are required to observe while arresting a person. Article 21 states that "no person shall be deprived of his life or personal liberty except according to the procedure established by law". The scheme of Article 21which includes under its broad sweep the right to personal liberty, right to live with human dignity holds a pivotal position in the life of any citizen, and act as a guarantee for the citizens against repression by the state.[21] Article 21 of the Constitution (before the 1976 judgement in the Maneka Gandhi case[22]), was conceptualised quite narrowly. It served only to protect rights that were leftover after adjudication under Articles 14 and 19, against the acts of the executive lacking the sanction of law. However, the judgement of Maneka Gandhi opened up the way in which Article 21 was interpreted and laid down that any procedure by the state depriving its citizens of their Article 21 rights must be "reasonable, fair and just".[23] The 177th Report of Law Commission of India (2001),[24] based its argument on this broad interpretation of Article 21, suggests that the procedure and language of Section 41 CrPC on arrest by the police without a warrant do not pass the muster of "reasonableness" as required by the Supreme Court. Therefore, the Commission argues that the pre-constitutional position of law on arrest must change and confirm to constitutional requirements.

Subclauses (1) and (2) of Article 22 are more specific to arrest. They provide that a person arrested shall be informed about the grounds of arrest and shall not be denied their right to consult or be defended by a legal practitioner of their choice. Clause (2) states that a person if arrested and detained in custody shall be produced before the nearest magistrate within a period of twenty-four hours of such arrest. The constitutional mandates applicable here have been captured in the CrPC, 1973 under Section 50 (1), which states that police officer shall communicate the grounds of arrest and all the particulars of the offence to a person upon arrest and Section 57 of the CrPC which mandates that no police officer shall detain a person in custody for more than twenty-four hours from the time of arrest. Section 41D provides the rights of an arrested person to meet an advocate of his choice during interrogation.

Further, Article 142 of the Constitution grants the Supreme Court discretionary powers to grant reliefs to citizens when the existing law is found to be inadequate in granting the required relief.[25] Some of the directives of the Supreme Court on arrest and police custody in seminal cases such as Joginder Kumar[26] and D.K. Basu[27] later became part of CrPC (e.g. the service of notice or the preparation of the arrest memo) through legislative amendments. The preparation of a "check list" that justified an arrest made in case of a "noticeable offence" was first pronounced in the Arnesh Kumar[28] case and still awaits to be part of the law.

3.5 The National Police Commission (1977–1981)

Joshi (2013) remarks that while "independent India adopted a new system of democratic governance marked by a prominent bill of rights, guaranteeing liberties and justice to all citizens without any discrimination, unfortunately no attempt was made to change or reform the institution of police which would have fulfilled the constitutional aspirations. India persisted with a colonial regime system of policing and made it work in a democratic environment". To address the lacunae in the incumbent policing system, many state governments, along with their various Police Commissions, began to examine the existing system and initiated attempts to create and legislate new Acts for the police. However, the slew of solutions in the form of legislations and recommendations failed to improve the state of Indian policing and there were no discernible signs of improvement. Joshi (2013) believed that the reason for this failure could be ascribed to the fact that the reforms which came out of these enactments were all based on the Police Act 1861. Further, various states tightened the noose of executive control over the police and did not take any steps to safeguard misuse and render accountable the *malafide* actions of the police. No initiatives were taken as well towards the concept of democratic policing, missing in earlier legislations.

During the "emergency of 1975–77"[29] the police committed excesses on a massive scale. Post the emergency, and with the formation of a new government, the Shah Commission of inquiry was instituted to investigate these excesses. In its report, the Shah Commission observed that "employing the police to the advantage of any political party is a sure source of subverting the rule of law" and recommended that the government take measures to insulate the police from illegitimate political and executive interference. The government appointed the first National Police Commission (NPC) of independent India in 1977. The Commission produced eight reports between 1979 and 1981, suggesting wide-ranging reforms and structural changes in the existing set-up, including a draft model Police Act. The scope of the discussion for the purpose of this book is limited to the recommendations of the NPC on provisions of arrest, which were referred by the 177th Report of the Law Commission of India and on police functional autonomy and accountability that laid the foundation of the famous Prakash Singh case.[30]

In its Second Report, the NPC[31] acknowledged the existence of discretion in police work. Some examples of discretion that have been cited include, "whether or not to make preventive arrests in any situation", "whether or not to arrest a person during investigation" and "whether or not to pursue minor infractions of law like traffic rule and regulation, etc.". It was believed that discretion as to whether to make an arrest or not should be vested in the judgement of the police and its functionaries. However, broad guidelines covering a wide array of unpredictable situations, that were clear in terms of language and accessible by the public, were considered necessary. NPC was further of the view that "in the absence of a guideline, the matter should be left to the sole discretion of the police officer directly involved in the situation and should not be subject to direction from above, except where it falls within the legitimate supervisory responsibility of a higher functionary under the law". The recognition of discretion in policing by the NPC is significant because study or research on police discretion in India was virtually unknown hitherto.

In its third Report the National Police Comission (1981) under Chapter XXII, while dealing with corruption in police, has observed that police powers which require the exercise of considerable discretion in the day-to-day working of police give rise to corruption and harassment of people, if such discretion is not exercised properly. The NPC recognised that the "power of arrest is the most important in this category and deserved a close look from the angle of reducing the scope for several attendant malpractices".

The NPC suggested three amendments to the CrPC which are directly or indirectly related to arrest discretion of police. Firstly, citing and analysing the arrest figures from 1969 to 1977, the NPC argued that the provisions of Section 41 CrPC (pre-amended position) create the room for subjectivity in the decision of whether to arrest or not, either on the basis of the complaint itself or on the receipt of credible information. The NPC also remarked that an unjustifiably large number of arrests are made for minor offences and can be avoided, if arrests in cognisable cases are considered justified in any of these circumstances:

i. The case involves a grave offence such as murder where arrest becomes necessary to wipe fear and uncertainty from the minds of the terror-stricken public.
ii. The accused may abscond or avoid the process of law.
iii. The person accused is likely to be dangerous with the possibility of committing further offences if not restrained.
iv. The accused is a habitual offender and likely to commit similar offences unless kept under custody.

Secondly, the NPC suggests amendments to the definition of a cognisable case, a definition which had remained unchanged since 1898. Cognisable cases have been defined under Section 2 (c) as a case in which the police officer may, in accordance with the First Schedule or under any other law for the time being force, arrest without warrant (equivalent of Section 4(f) of the 1898 CrPC). The NPC argues that "whether an offence should be deemed cognisable or not has to be determined on consideration whether or not it is desirable to make it investigable by police without orders from a Magistrate. The emphasis should be on police competence to investigate not on power of arrest". The irrationality continued even after the CrPC was amended in 1973. Therefore, the NPC was of the view that Section 2 (c) of CrPC needed to be amended to give clarity to the definition of cognisable offence as being investigable by police, not on arrestable criteria.

Thirdly, the NPC is of the view that Section 170 of the CrPC is another provision that induces a belief that the accused must be arrested in every non-bailable case and should be forwarded in custody to a competent magistrate. In fact, while interviewing IPS officers at the National Police Academy in the course of researching for this book, it came to light that magistrates in some States insist on the production of accused persons along with the charge sheet filed by the police even if the accused persons had already been arrested during investigation. Whether it amounts to a second arrest for the same offence is debatable. But the NPC argues that the rationale of the process of arrest during the investigation of a case is only necessary to bring about a restraint in movement of the accused person to secure his continued presence for the entire legal proceedings connected with investigation. Citing the example of the Central Bureau of Investigation, the NPC argues that premier federal investigation agency does not insist on arrest in certain categories of cases during investigation, and only after charge sheets are filed the accused is summoned by the court to take part in the subsequent proceeding. In addition to the arrest and forward of the accused under custody in non-bailable cases and taking security for appearance in bailable cases, an option may be given to the investigating officer to take security from the person for his appearance in the court.

3.6 Recommendations on Structural Changes

The NPC, following a period of analysis and study from 1978 to 1981 with a broad scope and strenuous examination of the role and performance of the police in its dual nature as an enforcement agency and protector of rights laid down in the Constitution, recommended a new Police Act. The draft Act recommended among other things the criminalisation of custodial violence.[32]

The NPC examined and dealt with the misuse of police and extraneous interference in police affairs in its Second Report.[33] It recommended fixed tenure of the Chief of Police in every state so as to remove any fear of indiscriminate removals. Once appointed, he could not be removed from his office unless he renders himself unfit under certain circumstances.

The NPC also suggested the constitution of a State Security Commission which would be headed by an ex officio chairman in the form of a minister in charge of police affairs, and various other members of which two would be from the state assembly, including one from the opposition party in the assembly. The Commission would lay down policy guidelines and directions so as to make the performance of the police accountable. The mechanism of the state assembly within the Commission in the opinion of the NPC would "help the State government to discharge the superintending responsibility in an open manner under the framework of law, with due regard to healthy norms that may develop in due course".

3.7 Prakash Singh Case on Police Reforms

In 1996, Prakash Singh, a former police DGP and two others, petitioned the Supreme Court in a writ petition[34] urging the Supreme Court to issue directives to the government for immediate police reforms. The contentions in the petition inter alia stated that the

> violations of fundamental and human rights of the citizens are generally in the nature of non-enforcement and discriminatory application of the laws so that those having clout are not held accountable for blatant violation of laws like unauthorised detention, torture, harassment, fabrication of evidence, malicious prosecution etc.

The petitioners argued that the problems faced in the effective operation of the Indian police were rooted in the Police Act 1861 and urged the Supreme Court to give directions for implementations of the recommendations provided by the NPC, to redefine and re-examine the functions and role of the police and to frame a new Police Act in line with the ideas and suggestions of the NPC. After a period of ten years, the Supreme Court in 2006 delivered a pivotal judgement expressing that "given the gravity of the problem" and the "total uncertainty as to when the police reforms be introduced" it felt compelled to issue "appropriate directions for immediate compliance". The following constitutes the core recommendations:

i. Formation of State Security Commission
ii. Procedure for appointment of State Police Chief and fixity of tenure
iii. Minimum tenure of field functionaries from the level of officer-in-charge of a police station to Inspector General of Police
iv. Separation of investigation and law and order wing of police
v. Formation of Police Establishment Boards at the District and State levels for transfer and posting of field functionaries
vi. Establishment of Police Complaint Authority at the District and State levels to inquire into allegations of police misconduct
vii. National Security Commission for selection and appointment of Chiefs of Central Police Organisations
viii. Legislation of the new Police Act[35]

3.8 National Human Rights Commission

The National Human Rights Commission (NHRC) and individual State Human Rights Commissions across India were established by the Protection of Human Rights Act, 1993. The functions of the Commission covered, inter alia, inquiry into the violations of human rights which were reported across their jurisdiction. It was also within the Commission's ambit to suggest solutions for the effective enforcement of human rights guaranteed by the Constitution or any other law in force.

In 1999, the NHRC issued a set of guidelines on "arrest" with a request to make them available to all police stations for compliance, across all the states and union territories of India. The NHRC observed that "arrest involves restriction of liberty of a person arrested and therefore, infringes the basic human rights of liberty. Nevertheless, the Constitution of India as well as international human rights laws recognise the powers of the State to arrest any person as part of its primary role of maintaining order. The Constitution requires a just, fair, and reasonable procedure established by law under which alone such deprivation of liberty is permissible". The guidelines for pre-arrest, arrest and post-arrest have been clearly delineated by the NHRC. Though the guidelines do not offer anything new, it is nevertheless a good compilation of the provisions contained in the procedural law of India and the directives of the Supreme Court of India regarding arrest, and is placed in *Appendix B*.

3.9 The Supreme Court and High Courts of India on Police Discretion

Despite certain legislative guidelines as well as policy discussions, the courts of India continued to grapple with the adjudication of cases that involved the actual exercise of discretion in arrest and investigation by the police. Several judgements have either contributed to the doctrine of judicial rule-making for the guidance of law enforcement officials or shed light on the complex question of law fact in the interpretation of discretion. Some of the judicial decisions in this regard have been discussed in subsequent sections to highlight the judicial interpretation of the issues and concerns regarding the exercise of discretion.

3.9.1 Madras High Court

One of the earliest decisions on arrest discretion came from the Madras High Court, In Re Om Prakash Gupta.[36] Section 151 of CrPC lays down the authority of a police officer to arrest a person concerned if the officer had knowledge that the person arrested had entertained a design to commit a cognisable offence and if it appears to the police officer that the commission of the cognisable offence cannot be averted otherwise. The court observed that both "knowledge" and "appearance" are that of the police officer concerned and are not capable of independent investigation. "The discretion is vested solely in the police officer and that discretion cannot be questioned in a proceeding under Section 491 CrPC.[37] It is not open to the High Court exercising its jurisdiction under Section 491 to go into the question whether, in fact, the police officer was justified in concluding that the person sought to be arrested was about to commit a cognizable offence and whether the police officer was equally justified in concluding that there were no other means by which the perpetration of the offence could have been prevented. The object of the section is to prevent the commission of an offence which a person designs or intends to commit. The facts would not be capable of investigation in order to find out whether, in fact, a cognizable offence was intended to be committed or not, as the offence would still be at the stage of an intention and not passed into the region of facts". There would be nothing therefore on the face of the record to show that the arrest was illegal or improper within the meaning of Section 491 CrPC. The High Court, while upholding the letters of the law, did not question the highly subjective phrase, "appears to the officer", which could not be applied unfettered and held above questioning. The officer while explaining the legality of arrest under Section 151 CrPC must account for the reason of his belief, a stand the Courts would take much later.

3.9.2 Kerala High Court

Questioning the legality of arrest, the Kerala High Court in the landmark A.K. Gopalan case[38] decided whether the powers under Section 151 CrPC are within the exclusive discretion of the police officer. The petitioner, Shri A. K. Gopalan, was a sitting member of the Parliament and the president of the Indian Kishan Sabha. He was arrested by the Circle Inspector of Police, Ernakulam under Section 151 CrPC. The circumstances which led up to the arrest as disclosed in the reply affidavit filed by the Circle Inspector are as follows: The Circle Inspector had information that the petitioner and the ten others who were arrested along with him were organising a mass of volunteers under the auspices of the Kerala Karshaka Sangh and were instigating and inciting them to form themselves into unlawful assemblies and to cause obstruction to public servants in the discharge of their official duties by forcibly blocking all entrances to government offices. The High Court relying on Prakash Gupta decided that the question "whether the police officer had the requisite knowledge and whether the commission of the designed offence could have been prevented otherwise than by an immediate arrest are matters essentially within the discretion of the police officer and are not capable of an independent investigation and this court cannot substitute its own opinion as to whether the commission of the offence could have been prevented by some means other than the arrest of the person or whether the arrest was in fact premature. The discretion is mainly with the police officer and unless there is clear evidence that it is a *fraudulent exercise* of the power vested in the officer, his discretion cannot be questioned in proceeding under Sec 491 of the CrPC". The Court here delved into the spirit of the law by stating that the exercise of arrest power must be free from mala fide.

3.9.3 Allahabad High Court

The Allahabad High Court in Mohammad Ali v. Sri Ram Swarup[39] was ahead of its time. Ram Swarup was the Head Constable while the remaining three respondents were constables posted at the Police Station Kairana, district Muzaffarnagar. The complainant Mohammad Ali was a Homoeopath, practising at Kairana. His case was that on 15–10–1961 at about 1 pm the respondents unlawfully arrested him after which he was taken to the police station where he was detained till 7 am on the next day when he was sent to the District Jail, Muzaffarnagar, and was released on bail on the evening of 16–10–1961. Proceedings under Section 107/117 CrPC[40] were taken against him which remained pending till 8–12–1961 when they were dropped for want of evidence. Twenty-three days later, the complainant lodged a complaint on 1–1–1962 with the allegations that he had been put under arrest and detained under unlawful custody without any rhyme or reason. The respondents were acquitted by the lower court. The appellant went to the High Court on appeal. The plea of the respondents was that the appellant was publicly inciting communal feelings. The High Court, differing from Prakash Gupta and relying on the dissenting views in A.K. Gopalan, observed that "discretion was mainly with the police officer, and unless there was clear evidence that it was fraudulent exercise of the power vested in the officer, his discretion could not be questioned by the court". Thus, the jurisdiction of the court to go into the matter in a proper lease had not been held to be barred altogether. The High Court, quoting Article 21 of the Constitution of India, observed that there is no arbitrary power in the executive or police authority to either detain or punish a person except for the violation of law. The court found abuse of discretion by the respondent Head Constable in dictating the FIR immediately after arrest, and held that apprehension of breach of peace could not be said to be a design to commit a cognisable offence. The order of acquittal of the lower court under Section 342/109 IPC was set aside. The case of Mohammad Ali v. Sri Ram Swarup laid down a precedent for judicial review of executive actions before the same was laid down in Maneka Gandhi.[41]

3.10 The Supreme Court of India

Two Supreme Court judgements in the late seventies laid the foundation of judicial review of executive action and changed the landscape of the Constitution of India – one, Nandini Satpathy v. P.L. Dani[42] and, the other, Maneka Gandhi v. Union of India (ibid.). Nandini Satpathy, a former Chief Minister of Odisha was called to appear in questioning for a disproportionate assets case against her in the Vigilance Police Station of Cuttack. She was presented with a long list of questions alleging her incrimination, when by refusing to answer the questions put forward, she exercised her rights under Article 20 (3) of the Constitution of India which guarantees that a person accused of an offence shall not be compelled to be a witness against himself/herself. Subsequently, a complaint under Section 179 of Indian Penal Code[43] was filed against her before the Sub-Divisional Judicial Magistrate, Cuttack by the Deputy Superintendent of Police, Vigilance in Cuttack. When summons were issued by the Sub-Divisional Judicial Magistrate, it was challenged by Nandini Satpathy by contending that the ambit of Article 20 (3) and Section 161 of the CrPC (which protects a person from having to answer questions which may incriminate him/her) were wide enough to allow her to refuse answering the questions. After the rejection of the appeal by the High Court, Nandini Satpathy moved to the Supreme Court. Justice VR Krishna Iyer while allowing her appeal quashed the Magistrate's proceedings and laid down that the scope of Article 20 (3) extended to police investigations as well. Justice Iyer held that an "accused person was entitled to keep his or her mouth shut if the answer had a reasonable prospect of exposing him or her to guilt in some other accusation, actual or imminent, even though the investigation underway was not with reference to that". This landmark judgement can be considered as the Indian equivalent of Miranda v. Arizona (384 U.S. 436, 1966).

The case of Maneka Gandhi widened the ambit of Article 21 to integrate the concept of due process into the term "procedure established by law", a concept erstwhile rejected by the Constituent Assembly during the drafting of the Constitution. Article 21, often dubbed as the bedrock of the Constitution, states that "no person shall be deprived of his life or personal liberty except according to procedure established by law". The Court held that the "procedure established by law must be fair, right and just, not arbitrary, fanciful and oppressive". Such law can be struck down by the Court for being unconstitutional. An element of natural justice is core to any legislation and cannot be lost sight of by the lawmakers.

The Law Commission of India in its 177th Report on arrest law (2001) questions if the provisions of arrest existing in the procedural law (Section 41 CrPC; pre-amendment position) could be construed to be a reasonable law or a law laying down reasonable procedure within the meaning of Article 21 as constructed in Maneka Gandhi. It was also argued in that Report that the provisions of arrest within Section 41 (1) (a) of the CrPC provide for a scope of "subjective satisfaction of the police officer" and laid down that it could be considered unreasonable to subject the liberty of a citizen to the "subjective satisfaction of the police officer". The Commission strongly contended that "even if Maneka Gandhi was rendered long after the enactment of the provisions of arrest in the CrPC, yet that circumstances is no excuse nor a ground for not testing the said provisions on the touchstone of Article 21 as interpreted and adumbrated in Maneka Gandhi".

3.10.1 Joginder Kumar

In Joginder Kumar v. State of UP,[44] the Supreme Court paved the way for the amendments to the laws of arrest that would eventually take place after fifteen years of the judgement. In this case, the petitioner Joginder Kumar, a lawyer, was told to appear before the Senior Superintendent of Police (SSP), Ghaziabad for certain inquiries. His accompanying friends and brother were told that he would be released in the evening, however, the petitioner was taken to the police station with the assurance of release the next day. Non-release on the second day compelled his family to visit the police station on the third day where they found that he was taken to an undisclosed location to be illegally detained for a total of five days. A Habeas Corpus petition was filed before the Supreme Court to extract his whereabouts, on which the Supreme Court issued notices to the government of Uttar Pradesh and the SSP to answer why Joginder Kumar was detained for five days without a valid reason and why his detention was not recorded in the police diary, and also why he was not produced before a magistrate.

The Court discussed various provisions and reports to lay down that no arrest can be made solely on the basis that it is legal for the officer to do so, and there is a separation between the "existence of the power to arrest" and "justification for its exercise". It was laid down that the police officer should be able to justify his arrest bereft of any justification on the grounds of the "existence of the power to arrest". It held that

> Arrest and detention in police lock-up of a person can cause incalculable harm to the reputation and self-esteem of a person. No arrest can be made in a routine manner on a mere allegation of commission of an offence made against a person. It would be prudent for a police officer in the interest of protection of the constitutional rights of a citizen and perhaps in his own interest that no arrest should be made without a reasonable satisfaction reached after some investigation as to the genuineness and bona fides of a complaint and a reasonable belief both as to the person's complicity and even so as to the need to effect arrest. Denying a person of his liberty is a serious matter.

Quoting from the Royal Commission Report on Criminal Procedure by Sir Cyril Philips, Police and the Criminal Evidence Act 1984 of England, and from the Third Report of National Police Commission of India (1980), the Supreme Court held that "a person is not liable to arrest merely on the suspicion of complicity in an offence. There must be some reasonable justification in the opinion of the officer effecting the arrest that such arrest is necessary and justified. Except in heinous offences, an arrest must be avoided if a police officer *issues notice* to person to attend the Station House and not to leave the Station without permission would do" (emphasis added).

For effective enforcement of these fundamental rights, Court issued the following guidelines:

1. "An arrested person being held in custody is entitled, if he so requests to have one friend, relative or other person who is known to him or likely to take an interest in his welfare told as far as is practicable that he has been arrested and where he is being detained.
2. The police officer shall inform the arrested person when he is brought to the police station of this right.
3. An entry shall be required to be made in the diary as to who was informed of the arrest. These protections from power must be held to flow from Articles 21 and 22(1) and enforced strictly".

The decision in Joginder Kumar is the first judicial pronouncement to suggest the issue of notice to the accused persons in offences other than the heinous offences. It directed the police officer making the arrest to inform the relatives of the arrestee about the place of lodging, keep a record of who was given such information in the station diary and to inform the arrestee of his rights. These directives became part of the D.K. Basu judgement[45] later in 1997. The 117th Law Commission Report on arrest law, while recommending the amendments of arrest provisions in CrPC, heavily relied on Joginder Kumar's judgement.

3.10.2 D.K. Basu

The Supreme Court in the case of D.K. Basu believed that structuring the administrative machinery for prompt recording and notification of arrests and detentions would promote a culture of transparency and accountability and hence issued twelve guidelines which were to be followed in cases of arrest and detention on top of constitutional safeguards and statutory safeguards. The following six guidelines are among the twelve laid down in the D.K. Basu case:

"(1) The police personnel carrying out the arrest and handling the interrogation of the arrestee should bear accurate, visible and clear identification and name tags with their designations.

(2) That the police officer carrying out the arrest shall prepare a memo of arrest at the time of arrest and such memo shall be attested by at least one witness, who may be either a member of the family of the arrestee or a respectable person of the locality from where the arrest is made. It shall also be countersigned by the arrestee and shall contain the time and date of arrest.

(3) A person who has been arrested or detained and is being held in custody in a police station or interrogation centre or other lock-up, shall be entitled to have one friend or relative or other person known to him or having interest in his welfare being informed, as soon as practicable, that he has been arrested and is being detained at the particular place.

(4) The person arrested must be made aware of this right to have someone informed of his arrest or detention as soon as he is put under arrest or is detained.

(5) The arrestee should, where he so requests, be also examined at the time of his arrest and major and minor injuries, if any present on his/her body, must be recorded at that time. The 'Inspection Memo' must be signed both by the arrestee and by the police officer effecting the arrest and its copy provided to the arrestee.

(6) A police control room should be provided at all district and State headquarters, where information regarding the arrest and the place of custody of the arrestee shall be communicated by the officer causing the

> arrest, within 12 hours of effecting the arrest and at the police control room it should be displayed on a conspicuous notice board".

The directives laid down in the D.K. Basu case were inserted into the CrPC by introducing a new section – Section 50A – through an amendment in 2005, which cast an obligation on the police officer to inform the person arrested or to a nominated person about the arrest and place of lodging. Besides, in the light of the judgement, a set of amendments was brought in the CrPC in 2009 by introducing new sections, including Sections 41B, 41C, 41D, 55A and 60A which broadly redefined the procedures of arrest, right to an advocate during interrogation, examination by medical practitioner, health and safety of an arrested person etc.

3.11 Police Manual

Police Manual provides rules guiding the role, responsibility, discipline and punishment, service matters, promotion etc. of a police organisation. Every state police and central police organisation in India has its own police manual. Let us consider an illustration from the Police Manual rules of Odisha Police prior to the Arnesh Kumar guidelines, way back in 1996 when Rule 221 of Police Manual Rules of Odisha Police concerning arrest was substituted by Home Department Notification No. 299/PIA-3/99, dated January 3, 1996. Though it has not been expressly mentioned what prompted the substitution, this was obviously in response to the directives of the Supreme Court in Joginder Kumar as the language appears to be imported straightaway from the judgement. It goes as follows:

> 221. (b) No arrest can be made only because it is lawful for the police officer to do so. The existence of power of arrest is one thing. The justification for the exercise of it is quite another. The police officer must be able to justify the arrest apart from his power to do so . . . Except in heinous offences an arrest must be avoided. If a police officer issued notice to a person to attend the station house and not to leave the station without permission it would do. (paragraph 20 of the judgement)
>
> . . .
>
> (d) An arrested person being held in custody is entitled, if he so requests, to have a friend, relative or other person who is known to him or likely to take an interest in his welfare told as far as is practicable that he has been arrested and where he is being detained.
> (e) The police officer shall inform the arrested person when he is brought to the police station of his right.
> (f) An entry shall be required to be made in the diary as to who was informed of the arrest. These protections (from power) must be

> held to flow from Articles 21 and 22(1) of the Constitution of India and enforced strictly. (paragraph 21 of the judgement)

The substitution in the Police Manual Rules consequent to the Joginder Kumar ruling was brought in the year 1996, much before the 2009 amendment of Section 41 CrPC. This is just an illustration of one state police organisation to establish the fact that a liberal arrest policy was part of the police manual even before the amendment of the CrPC.

3.12 Law Commission of India: 177th Report on Law Relating to Arrest[46]

The task of examining the century-old arrest laws of India was taken up by the Law Commission suo motu with a view to "clearly delineate and regulate the powers of arrest without warrant vested in the police by Sec 41 of CrPC". The provisions of Section 41 had been a part of the CrPC since 1898, long before India became a constitutional democracy and the landmark judgement of the Supreme Court in Maneka Gandhi (1978).[47] The law laid down in the said judgement "casts a cloud upon the validity of some of the provisions of Sec 41 and allied provision". In the language of Justice Jeevan Reddy, the Chairperson, "the theme of the report is to maintain a balance between the liberty of the citizen (the most precious of the fundamental rights) and societal interest in maintenance of peace and law and order".

The 177th Law Commission Report is an exhaustive study on arrest laws in India. The Law Commission has examined the field arrest figures compiled by National Human Rights Commission, collected stakeholders' perspective on the existing law and proposed amendments, analysed its own 152nd Report on Custodial Crime and 154th Report on Code of Criminal Procedure, took due note of recommendations of National Police Commission Reports (1978–1981), and pronouncements made by the Supreme Court in a catena of judgements including that of Joginder Kumar v. State of UP[48] and D.K. Basu v. State of West Bengal.[49]

While proposing sweeping changes in the arrest provisions under Section 41 CrPC, the Law Commission relied on the following premises and recommendations:

1. "Procedures prescribed by Sec 41(1)(a) fall short of reasonableness as constructed in Maneka Gandhi and left entirely to the sole and absolute discretion of the police officer making arrest.
2. Regulate the power of arrest to make it reasonable so as to ensure that power is not exercised whimsically or for oblique purposes and for extortion and harassment.
3. Restrictions on the power of arrest on the basis of the 'principle of necessity'- two main objectives of this principle are that police can exercise powers only in those cases in which it is genuinely necessary to enable

them to execute their duty to prevent commission of offence, to investigate crime. Such restrictions would diminish the use of arrest and produce more uniform use of power.

4. The criminal procedure devised by any country should aim at resolving state-citizens' dispute in a manner that commands society's respect for fairness of its process and reliability of its outcomes. This is referred to as 'principle of restraint'. The 'principle of restraint' means that liberty of an individual and his freedom should be interfered only where circumstances necessitate the same.
5. Arrest and detention in police lock-up of a person can cause incalculable harm to the reputation and self-esteem of a person. No arrest can be made on a mere routine manner on a mere allegation of commission of an offence made against a person. Police officer must be able to justify the arrest apart from his power to do so.
6. A person is not liable to arrest merely on the suspicion of complicity in an offence. There must be some reasonable justification in the opinion of the of the officer effecting arrest that such arrest is necessary and justified.
7. Except in heinous offences, an arrest must be avoided if a police officer issues notice to a person to make himself available for purpose of investigation or trial- in the line of the recommendations of Royal Commission of UK to issue appearance notice as was the practice of Ontario police to help reduce the use of arrest.[50]
8. Every police officer while making arrest shall bear an accurate, visible and clear identification of his name and inform the person arrested the offence for which he is being arrested.
9. Preparation of a memorandum of arrest which shall be attested by one witness or relative and inform the friend or relative of the person arrested the place where he is detained in custody.
10. State and District level Control Room displaying details of arrest on the notice board or maintain a database for the information of the general public.
11. When a person arrested is interrogated by the police, he shall be entitled to have an advocate of his choice present during such interrogation in order to ensure that his rights are not infringed".

Based on such recommendations, a number of amendments were brought to the CrPC in the year 2005 (by Act 25 of 2005). However, the most crucial set of recommendations of the Law Commission on the amendment of Section 41 CrPC (arrest by police without warrant) would wait until 2009 to become part of the statute by the Code of Criminal Procedure (Amendment) Act 2008 (5 of 2009). It is highly relevant to quote the amended provisions of Section 41 CrPC and compare and contrast them with the old provisions as this is the crux of this study. Table 3.1 contains the old provision and proposed amendment.

Table 3.1 Comparative study of Section 41 (pre- and post-amendments)

Sec 41 CrPC in its pre-2009 form	*Sec 41 CrPC as it stands after amendment in 2009*	*Remarks*
41. When police may arrest without warrant (1) Any police officer may without an order from a Magistrate and without a warrant, arrest a person – (a) who has been concerned in any cognizable offence, or against whom a reasonable complaint has been made, or credible information has been received, or reasonable suspicion exists, or having been so concerned; or	**41. When police may arrest without warrant** (1) Any police officer may without an order from a Magistrate and without a warrant, arrest any person – (a) who commits, in the presence of a police officer, a cognizable offence; (b) against whom a reasonable complaint has been made, or credible information has been received, or a reasonable suspicion exists that he has committed a cognizable offence punishable with imprisonment for a term which may be less than seven years or which may extend to seven years whether with or without fine, if the following conditions are satisfied, namely: (i) the police officer has reason to believe on the basis of such complaint, information, or suspicion that such person has committed the said offence; (ii) the police officer is satisfied that such arrest is necessary- (a) to prevent such person from committing any further offence; or (b) for proper investigation of the offence; or (c) to prevent such person from causing the evidence of the offence to disappear or tampering with such evidence in any manner; or (d) to prevent such person from making any inducement, threat or promise to any person acquainted with the facts of the case so as to dissuade him from disclosing such facts to the Court or to the police officer; or (e) as unless such person is arrested, his presence in the Court whenever required cannot be ensured; and the police officer shall record while making such arrest, his reasons in writing.	1. 177th Law Commission Report on Arrest rejected the provisions of Section 41 CrPC as it stood in its pre-2009 for being arbitrary, susceptible to subjective interpretation of the officer making arrest and more importantly could not pass the "reasonableness" test of *Maneka Gandhi*. 2. The ambiguity and vagueness of the phrase "having been so concerned" in pre-2009 position was replaced with words and phrases in Clause 41(1)(b)(i) to ensure that the power of arrest is exercised only after the police officer has the reason to believe on the basis of the complaint, information and suspicion that such person has committed the said offence. It has been held by the Law Commission that the only check upon the subjective power is the existence of circumstances or material or information; in case it is established that there was no material or information or factual basis, the exercise of power becomes illegal. 3. The law does not distinguish two types of cognisable offences, one which is punishable with imprisonment for a term which may be less than or extend up to seven years; the other beyond seven years.

	(ba) against whom credible information has been received that he has committed a cognizable offence punishable with imprisonment for a term which may extend to more than seven years whether with or without fine or with death sentence and the police officer has reason to believe on the basis of that information that such person has committed the said offence;	In the first category of cognisable offences (imprisonment for a term which may extend up to seven years), arrest is necessary only if the police officer is satisfied that one of five conditions under (b)(ii) forms the ground of such arrest. Reasons for arrest as well as non-arrest are to be recorded by the police officer.
No old equivalent; new insertion	**41-A. Notice of appearance before police officer:** (1) The police officer may, in all cases where the arrest of a person is not required under the provisions of subsection (1) of Section 41, issue a notice directing the person against whom a reasonable complaint has been made, or credible information has been received, or a reasonable suspicion exists that he has committed a cognizable offence, to appear before him or at such other place as may be specified in the notice. (2) Where such a notice is issued to any person, it shall be the duty of that person to comply with the terms of the notice. (3) Where such person complies and continues to comply with the notice, he shall not be arrested in respect of the offence referred to in the notice unless, for reasons to be recorded, the police officer is of the opinion that he ought to be arrested. (4) Where such person, at any time, fails to comply with the terms of the notice, it shall be lawful for the police officer to arrest him for the offence mentioned in the notice, subject to such orders as may have been passed in this behalf by a competent Court.	This is in line with recommendations of the Law Commission based on the principle of "necessity" and "restraint". "Appearance Notice" was dealt in *Joginder Singh* by the Supreme Court citing the recommendations of Royal Commission, UK (practice of Ontario police). This category of arrest will be dealt as "noticeable offences" hereinafter for brevity and to refer to the provisions of the section.

(*Continued*)

Table 3.1 (Continued)

Sec 41 CrPC in its pre-2009 form	*Sec 41 CrPC as it stands after amendment in 2009*	*Remarks*
No old equivalent; new insertion	**41C. Control room at districts.** – (1) The State Government shall establish a police control room – (a) in every district; and (b) at State level. (2) The State Government shall cause to be displayed on the notice board kept outside the control rooms at every district, the names and addresses of the persons arrested and the name and designation of the police officers who made the arrests. (3) The control room at the Police Headquarters at the State level shall collect from time to time, details about the persons arrested, nature of the offence with which they are charged and maintain a database for the information of the general public.	Recommendations of Law Commission on the basis of rulings in *D.K. Basu*
No old equivalent; new insertion	**41D. Right of arrested person to meet an advocate of his choice during interrogation.** – When any person is arrested and interrogated by the police, he shall be entitled to meet an advocate of his choice during interrogation, though not throughout interrogation.	Recommendations of Law Commission on the basis of rulings in *D.K. Basu*

The amendments introduced in the form of the Code of Criminal Procedure (Amendment Bill) 2006 were placed in the Parliament in the year 2008 and notified in the year 2009. The rulings of the apex court in *Joginder Kumar* and *D.K. Basu* cases as well as the recommendations of the Law Commission of India in its 177th Report thus became part of procedural law of India.

The amended provisions of Section 41 CrPC on arrest surprisingly agitated the lawyers' community throughout India that forced the government to refer the matter to the Departmentally Related Parliamentary Standing Committee (DPSC) in 2010.

The agitation of lawyers was addressed by the Union Home Minister in referring it to the Chairman of the Law Commission and a few members of the Bar Association to bring about a consensus on the issues. After a series of deliberations, the meeting came to the following general consensus:

i. "That in Section 41A, the word 'may' be substituted by the word 'shall'.
ii. That in case of issuance of notice under Section 41A, if a person who is not arrested and to whom a notice will be issued is unwilling to identify himself, that could be a ground for his arrest.
iii. The police officer be obliged to record his reasons not only for making an arrest under Section 41, but also for not making an arrest under that Section".

The 146th DPSC on Home Affairs accepted the suggestion offered by the Law Commission and recommended relevant amendments to the provisions of Section 41 CrPC which were inserted or substituted into the statute by the Code of Criminal Procedure (Amendment) Act 2010. The relevant portions before and after the amendments are quoted for comparison in Table 3.2.

The lawmakers during the debate welcomed these amendments and intended that by bringing these amendments police discretion in arrest will be considerably restricted, a higher level of accountability will be ensured against arbitrary arrests, and the constitutional safeguards for personal liberty enshrined under Article 21 of the Constitution will be secured.

3.13 Arnesh Kumar

The amendments made at the behest of the recommendations of the Law Commission to the century-old arrest laws of India based on the constitutional principles of "reasonableness" cut no ice with field law enforcement. It failed to bring about the desired decline in arrest figures in India following the amendment. To address this issue, the Supreme Court came out with additional directives in Arnesh Kumar.[51]

The Supreme Court in this case laid down that a police officer should arrest the concerned person only after he satisfies himself of the fulfilment of the parameters laid down in Section 41 of the CrPC. The Court also

Table 3.2 Pre- v. post-amendment (2010) position of Section 41 CrPC

Pre-amendment position	*Post-amendment position*	*Remarks*
No old equivalent, new insertion	After 41(1)(b)(ii)(e), the following clause was inserted: Provided that a police officer shall, in all cases where arrest of a person is not required under the provisions of this subsection, record the reasons in writing for not making the arrest	The police are required to record the reason of non-arrest in noticeable offences. However, the pre-amendment requirement was to record the reason of arrest in noticeable offences mandatory. Now, for both the possibilities, recording of reason has become mandatory.
41-A Notice for appearance before police officer- (1) The police officer may, in all cases . . .	41-A Notice for appearance before police officer- (1) The police officer shall, in all cases . . .	Discretion to serve notice in noticeable offences, if arrest is not resorted to, taken away from the police by substituting "may" with "shall".
41-A(4)Where such person, at any time, fails to comply with the terms of the notice, it shall be lawful for the police officer to arrest him for the offence mentioned in the notice, subject to such orders as may have been passed in this regard by a competent Court	41-A(4) Where such person, at any time, fails to comply with the terms of the notice or is unwilling to identify himself, the police officer may, subject to such orders as may have been passed by a competent Court in this behalf, arrest him for the offence mentioned in the notice.	Discretion of arrest by police was restored for non-compliance to the conditions of notice in noticeable offence by substituting "shall" with "may".

recommended the provision of a "Check List" which contained certain sub-clauses present in Section 41 (1) (b) (ii), and that it should accompany every arrest where there is an eventuality of production before the Magistrate. The "Check List" should, inter alia, furnish the reasons and materials which necessitated the arrest. Some of the directives are as follows:

(1) "The police officer shall forward the check list duly filed and furnish the reasons and materials which necessitated the arrest, while forwarding/producing the accused before the Magistrate for further detention;
(2) The Magistrate while authorising detention of the accused shall peruse the report furnished by the police officer in terms aforesaid and only after recording its satisfaction, the Magistrate will authorise detention;

(3) The decision not to arrest an accused, be forwarded to the Magistrate within two weeks from the date of the institution of the case with a copy to the Magistrate which may be extended by the Superintendent of police of the district for the reasons to be recorded in writing;
(4) Notice of appearance in terms of Section 41A of CrPC be served on the accused within two weeks from the date of institution of the case, which may be extended by the Superintendent of Police of the District for the reasons to be recorded in writing;
(5) Failure to comply with the directions aforesaid shall apart from rendering the police officers concerned liable for departmental action, they shall also be liable to be punished for contempt of court to be instituted before High Court having territorial jurisdiction;
(6) Authorising detention without recording reasons as aforesaid by the judicial Magistrate concerned shall be liable for departmental action by the appropriate High Court".

The judgement, while lamenting that the true spirit of the amended Section 41CrPC is not being followed by the police officers, sought to put strict accountability mechanisms in place for ensuring compliance to the letter and spirit of law. However, a study of secondary data from the National Crime Records Bureau (refer Table 1.1), while identifying the research problem, shows that despite the strict liability directives of the apex court in Arnesh Kumar, the situation in the field remained unchanged. The legislative intent to reduce the number of avoidable arrests remains confined to the debates in the Parliament.

3.14 Rajesh Sharma

In Rajesh Sharma,[52] the Supreme Court has gone a step ahead of its directives issued in Arnesh Kumar. The Apex Court has expressed concern that "certain safeguards against uncalled for arrest or insensitive investigation have been addressed by this Court. Still, the problem continues to a great extent". It observes that at times matrimonial harassment complaints lead to uncalled for harassment to the relatives of the accused persons who are roped in the allegation. Uncalled for arrest may ruin the chances of settlement. The Court has cited the Standing Order of Delhi police directing the investing officers in dowry harassment cases to arrest of main accused only after thorough investigation has been conducted and with the prior approval of the Assistant or Deputy Commissioner of Police. Arrest of the collateral accused, such as father-in-law, mother-in-law, brother-in-law or sister-in-law, should only be made after prior approval of Deputy Commissioner of Police on file. The Court concluded, inter alia, that in every district one or more Family Welfare Committees be constituted by the District Legal Services Authorities, preferably comprising three members. Every complaint under Section 498A IPC received by the police or the Magistrate be referred to and looked into by such committee. Till the report of the committee is received, no arrest should normally be resorted.

The judicial intervention of the Apex Court in Rajesh Sharma in limiting the power of arrest of the investigating officer in domestic harassment cases has a parallel with Jacob Mathew[53] in dealing with medical negligence. In Jacob Mathew, the Apex Court held that "the investigating officer should, before proceeding against the doctor accused of rash or negligent act or omission, obtain an independent and competent medical opinion preferably from a doctor in government service qualified in that branch of medical practice who can normally be expected to give an impartial and unbiased opinion. A doctor, accused of rashness or negligence, may not be arrested in a routine manner (simply because a charge has been levelled against him). Unless his arrest is necessary for furthering the investigation or for collecting evidence or unless the investigation officer feels satisfied that the doctor proceeded against would not make himself available to face the prosecution unless arrested, the arrest may be withheld".

Arrests remained routine and the norms and rulings were glossed over by the police using various justifications, resulting in the abuse of arrest discretion often being clothed as a legitimate exercise of policing. This clearly shows that there exists an eternal conflict between the letter and spirit of the law. Richard (2016) explains the two sides of the law as the letter of the law being the literal word of the law while the spirit of the law being less literal and less concrete. It is in and from the spirit of the law that different interpretations emerge and because of this imprecision that emerges from the spirit, those charged with maintenance and administration of law must often use discretion in the course of their duties. While the spirit of the amended arrest law in India is more of a rights-based approach, the letter still provides wide discretionary latitude to bypass its core ethos.

The foremost challenge when it comes to evaluating these factors is the task of effectively measuring the influences of different determinants of discretion and their interplay in arrest decisions. There is no dearth of anecdotal and experiential accounts of abuse of arrest discretion by the police, but empirical studies are non-existent in the context of the Indian police. To do so, the first task is to operationalise the factors that have a bearing on the arrest discretion behaviour of the police and devise a suitable methodology to measure the discretionary determinants. The next chapter deals with these issues and formulates a workable solution in this regard.

Notes

1 The "Foujdar" can be defined as a person who was primarily responsible for the maintenance of peace and security in the province under his charge aided by military troops by which way the will of the Emperor would be enforced.
2 The class of landowners
3 A government-appointed police official of subordinate rank
4 Territorial revenue units

5 The Mutiny, variously known as the Sepoy (soldier) mutiny, Indian Revolt or Rebellion of 1857, was an unsuccessful violent and bloody uprising against British Rule.
6 The explicit consent of policing is an inherent feature of British policing, known as "policing by consent" and is based on the principles of transparency about the powers of the police, a sense of integrity in the exercise of those powers and accountability for the exercise of this power.
7 Government of India, Constitution, Seventh Schedule, List II, item 2
8 Ibid., List I, item 2
9 Ibid., List I, item 2-A
10 Union Territories are federal territories governed directly by the union government, though Delhi and Puducherry have their own legislatures.
11 Data on Police Organisation as on January 2020, BPR&D, Government of India
12 Ibid.
13 The wide range of such legislations could be appreciated from their titles itself. Some of these legislations are Essential Commodities Act, 1955; Copy Right Act, 1957; Arms Act,1959; Dowry Prohibition Act, 1961; Medical Termination of Pregnancy Act, 1971; National Security Act, 1980; Environment Protection Act, 1986; Prevention of Corruption Act, 1988; Narcotic Drugs and Psychotropic Substance Act, 1988; Scheduled Caste and Scheduled Tribe (Prevention of Atrocities) Act, 1989; Juvenile Justice (Care and Protection of Children) Act, 2000 and Information and Technology Act, 2000.
14 The Cabinet Mission came to India with the objective to discuss the transfer of power from the British government to the Indian leadership.
15 High Court of Judicature at Bombay v. SKR Patil, (1997) 6 SCC 339
16 Indira Sawhney v. Union of India, (2000) 1 SCC 168
17 All India Judges Association v. Union of India (2002) 4 SCC 247
18 Union of India v. Association of Democratic Reforms, AIR 2002 SC 1752
19 RP Garg v. State of UP, AIR 2006 SC 2912
20 Indira Nehru Gandhi v. Raj Narain, AIR 1975 SC 2299
21 Munshi Singh Goutam v. State of M.P. AIR 2005 SC 402
22 Maneka Gandhi v. Union of India AIR 1978 SC 597
23 Francis Coralie Mullin v. Union Territory of Delhi, Administrator, AIR 1981 SC 746
24 The 177th Report of Law Commission of India recommended sweeping changes in law of arrest
25 Vishaka v. State of Rajasthan AIR 1997 SC 3011
26 Joginder Kumar v. State of UP, 1994, 2 Crimes 106 SC
27 DK Basu v. State of West Bengal, A.I.R. 1997 SC 610
28 Arnesh Kumar v. State of Bihar, (2014) 8SCC 283
29 The Emergency proclaimed under Article 352 of the Indian Constitution on June 26, 1975 and lifted on March 21, 1977 saw the suspension of fundamental rights of citizens along with the right to move to court for enforcement of fundamental rights, wrongful detention of opposition political leaders under regressive laws and censorship.
30 Civil Writ Petition No 316 of 1996 Prakash Singh & others v. Union of India & others
31 Paragraph 14.45, Chapter XIV, Police Role, Duties, Power and Responsibilities, Second Report
32 Section 129 of the draft Act provides that any police officer who vexatiously and unnecessarily detains, searches or arrests a person shall upon conviction be punished with imprisonment for a term which may extend to one year and with fine which may extend to five hundred rupees or both.
33 Chapter XV, Second Report, 1979, para 15.43
34 Civil Writ Petition No 316 of 1996 Prakash Singh & others v. Union of India & others

35 The Government of India set up a "Police Act Drafting Committee" (PADC) – commonly known as Soli Sorabjee Committee – tasked to draft a new model Police Act. The PADC submitted the Model Police Act, 2006 on October 30, 2006.
36 AIR 1949 Mad 744
37 This Section empowered the High Courts to issue writs in cases of illegal or unlawful detention in a public or private custody.
38 AK Gopalan v. State of Kerala AIR 1962 Ker 215
39 AIR 1965 All 161
40 Sec 107 CrPC empowers an Executive Magistrate to require an individual to show cause for security for keeping peace.
41 AIR 1978 SC 597
42 AIR 1978 SC 1025
43 Offence for refusing to answer a public servant authorised to question
44 1994 AIR 1349
45 DK Basu v. State of WB A.I.R. 1997 SC 610
46 The Law Commission chaired by Justice B.P. Jeevan Reddy submitted its report on Law relating to Arrest in 2001.
47 AIR 1978 SC 597
48 Joginder Kumar v. State of UP, 1994(2) Crimes 106 SC
49 DK Basu v. State of West Bengal, A.I.R. 1997 SC 610
50 The Royal Commission on Criminal Procedure: report/Chairman: Sir Cyril Philips, London [H.M.S.O.], 1981
51 2014, 8 SCC 273
52 Rajesh Sharma & Ors. v. State of U.P. & Anr Criminal Appeal No. 1265 of 2017
53 Jacob Mathew v. State of Punjab AIR 2005 SC 3180

4 Measuring the Factors Influencing Arrest Discretion

As already discussed in the preceding chapters, the arrest figures in cognisable offences in India do not show any appreciable decline as was expected in the post-2009 period following the amendment of the CrPC. The legislative intent, rulings of the courts and departmental guidelines have not resulted in any desirable reduction in the number of avoidable arrests in which the offences punishable up to seven years of imprisonment are to be treated "noticeable" in the post-amendment period. The questions that logically follow such observations guide the inquiry further to explore if there are factors that act as impediments to the legislative intents and the rulings of courts and departmental guidelines. Is the exercise of arrest discretion enjoined in the amended arrest law too wide to negate the legislative intent? What are the factors that influence arrest discretion behaviour of the police? What are the legal and extra-legal factors of arrest discretion behaviour? Which are the factors that exert more influence on the arrest discretion behaviour as compared to the others?

To effectively tackle these questions that are complex and highly subjective in equal measures, the key determinants or factors influencing the arrest discretion behaviour of police have been identified from the literature. A broad overview of these drivers – categorised into organisational, environmental, situational and individual factors – has been undertaken to translate these factors into their operational manifestations.

4.1 Distilling the Drivers of Arrest Discretion

Organisational factors include the official departmental policy, processes and values on one hand and informal organisational culture on the other. "Departmental policies and constraints of law exert quite a powerful influence over police discretion. This is because, they set forth certain written guidelines or legal directives that stipulate what the officer can or cannot do concerning accountability actions among other things" (Halliday 2009). For example, when an officer arrests and forwards an offender in an offence that prescribes not more than seven years of imprisonment, instead of issuing notice of appearance, s/he needs to satisfy the Court with the reasons for her/his action. The organisational accountability mechanism, training, and role

DOI: 10.4324/9781003406679-4

of the supervisory officers in a hierarchical organisation like police etc. play an important role in discretionary behaviour of police.

When it comes to informal organisational culture, it has been said that "the informal organisational culture, a subset of organisational factors, refers to the unwritten organisational subculture comprised of individual values and traditions that are communicated informally across from officer to officer" (Walker and Katz 2005). Research has established that the members of the police organisation are guided by their own set of beliefs, attitudes and behaviour, factors that can together be termed as police subculture. The works of William Westley (1970) explain that "police subculture is a crucial concept in the explanation of police behaviour and attitudes". For the purpose of this study, informal organisational factors or police subculture has been taken as a distinct and separate determinant of discretion. This is because the influence of subculture on individual discretion is an area of least research though the literature review strongly suggests the subculture has a significant effect on the decision-making process in the realm of arrests (Ingram, Paoline and Terrill 2013).

Environmental and situational factors have a key role to play in the exercise of arrest discretion as well. "Research on police discretion suggests that even when organisational and informal organisational characteristics are very similar, policing practices differ depending on the operational environment and community characteristics. Police officers develop behaviour models that are acceptable in the community where policing is practiced" (Hidayet 2011). The environment in which the police operate shapes decision-making processes. Under the environmental determinants, the literatures have generally emphasised on crime rate, the minority status, demography, lower level of social control, political culture, media etc. as the variables that influence the arrest decision of the police (Groeneveld 2005; Halliday 2009; Hidayet 2011). Having regard to the Indian context and the macro external environment in which the organisation is embedded, factors like political culture, pressure groups and media are taken as environmental determinants influencing the decision-making processes.

Studies conducted in a variety of settings underscore the importance of situational/offender factors in the arrest discretion behaviour of the police. (Hidayet 2011). "Since legal factors affect discretion, it is not surprising that officers make more arrests when crimes are serious, when weapons are used, when suspects are intoxicated, and so on, compared to situations involving extra-legal factors" (Klinger 1996). Hostility of the offender, disrespectful behaviour and race of the offender are some of the extralegal factors that influence the arrest decisions of the officers. Black (1971) argues that police officers are more inclined to arrest hostile offenders. "Disrespectful behaviours of offenders increase the likelihood of an officer making an arrest and using force toward those suspects" (Hidayet 2011). "One variable found to be related to officer behaviour is seriousness of offence. Scholars investigating the seriousness of offence operationalized it as felony versus misdemeanour"

(Smith 1987). Existing research and literature indicate that there is a nexus between the demeanour of the offenders in question and the decisions made by the police. In the Indian context, where no such previous empirical study has been attempted on the subject, the socio-economic status of offenders has been surveyed to find out if there is a correlation between poor and marginal and their being more likely to be arrested than their more affluent counterparts in a similar situation. The procedural laws of India provide a number of rights to an arrested person including the right to be informed about the grounds of arrest, right to be released on bail in bailable offences and the right to not be detained for more than twenty-four hours by the police following arrest. The awareness about legal rights or the lack of it depends upon the socio-economic condition of the individual. Members of poor and marginal sections of society are more likely to be at the receiving end of discretionary abuse as opposed to their affluent counterparts. Relevant variables from situational/offender's determinants in the Indian context have been studied by devising a suitable survey methodology.

Studies on individual factors examining the relationship between officer characteristics, such as gender, age, race, educational level, social class and experience, and police behaviour have produced mixed results concerning the influence of individual characteristics on officer decision-making (Hidayet 2011). Available literature indicates that studies based on individual determinants of police officers such as educational qualification or gender tend to produce a mixture of strong and weak relationships among attitude and behaviour which fails to judge whether a certain set of values guarantee an exact kind of behaviour. Walker, Spohn and DeLone (1996) argue that "male officers are more likely to arrest than their female counterparts". Terrill and Mastrofski (2002), on the other hand, suggested that "gender has no influence on discretionary decisions". Fyfe (1981) reported that "officers with higher levels of education tend to use less force than others", while others argued that "there is a weak relationship between education and officer behaviour" (Worden 1990). Further, work experience of officers is an important factor in decision-making. Stalans and Finn (1995) concluded that "years of experience reduces the likelihood of an arrest". "Overall, studies on individual characteristics of officers do not produce consistence findings and don't reveal a strong impact on behaviour. Empirical evidence on individual determinant's effects on officer decisions is not strong" (Hidayet 2011). However, this study aims at collecting officer's gender, experience etc. for any possible co-relation with arrest discretion behaviour in the Indian context. In the following section, these drivers have been translated into their operational manifestations.

4.2 Operationalisation of Organisational Determinants

Organisational influences refer to the system of administrative rules, policies and managerial controls designed to ensure conformity with departmental directives and the law (Groeneveld 2005). Literature indicates that the structure of an organisation for arrest discretion originates from the four sources of values, training, process and official policy. These dimensions capture the channel through which the departmental supervisory officers can influence or constrain the arrest discretion behaviour of the officers.

4.2.1 Policy Dimension

The policy dimension includes aspects such as the extensiveness of the arrest policies circulated by the department, and awareness of the officers about the directives of the Supreme Court and High Courts on arrest. Extensive and wide awareness of such directives are indicators of the keenness of the organisation to ensure that officers make decisions on arrest objectively and uniformly. Police departments in India have their own Police Manual Rules, a set of rules that guide the duties, responsibilities, discipline and control of the personnel of the organisation. Besides, the department issues important guidelines or advisories in the form of Police Circular Orders. The directives of the Supreme Court and High Courts are circulated by the State Police Crime Branch to all field functionaries. Clearly, the written guidelines described in the operation manuals or the circulars or the court directives covering the elements of arrest establish a foundation for valid arrests and the rights guaranteed by the Constitution. Another aspect of the policy dimension focuses upon the department's internal review mechanism on compliance with arrest procedures. Such reviews are important in that they formalise the policy process for developing guidelines that set standards, shape the inevitable use of discretion and can influence control over the proper exercise of police discretion. The preceding discussion has specified four specific indicators to the policy dimension of organisational attempts to influence arrest discretion. Those could be operationalised as follows:

Indicators of Policy Dimensions

a) *Specific Statutory Guidelines*
b) *Court Pronouncement, for example, Arnesh Kumar guidelines of the Supreme Court*
c) *Extensiveness of arrest policy, for example, Crime Branch Circular and provisions of Police Manual Rules*
d) *Internal Review mechanism of the organisation*

In addressing these four dimensions, the respondent police officers are asked to respond to the claim that

- "*The amended provisions of Sec 41 Cr PC (arrest in cognisable offences) are very specific and provides detailed guidelines on arrest in cognisable cases*".

- *"Guidelines of the Supreme Court in Arnesh Kumar case made the compliance to the amended provisions of arrest more specific and accountable".*
- *"Department Arrest Policy circulated in Crime Branch Circular 350/2014 gives clear guidelines for decision on arrest in cognisable offences".*
- *"The department has strong internal review mechanism of compliance to arrest procedures".*

4.2.2 Process Dimension

A second important dimension of the way the department attempts to influence the officer's discretion in arrests can be found in the process or procedural requirements associated with making arrests (Groeneveld 2005). The process dimension includes organisational imposition of procedures that must be followed while making arrests and puts accountability mechanism in place for exercise of unwarranted discretion. Use of such procedures allows the organisation to exercise influence over arrest discretion through supervisory scrutiny and imposition of sanction against non-compliance.

Investigation of offences by officers is often overseen by their superiors. The power of such supervisory officers has been defined in the procedural law. Section 36 of the CrPC spells out that the police officers who are senior in rank to an officer in charge of a police station can exercise the same powers in their respective charge as being exercised by the officer-in-charge within the limit of his jurisdiction. The directions of the supervisory officer on whether to arrest and when to arrest the accused take precedence over the personal judgement of the investigating officer, thereby limiting the latter's discretionary latitude. The third and fourth indicators of the process dimension measure the extent to which the detection of procedural violations exists, and the presence of departmental actions on officers for violating the norms or procedures. In a way, the sanctions against wrongdoing or intentional violations of procedures pave way for accountability. Individual accountability is a key factor against abuse of discretion. The process dimensions thus can be represented by the following four indicators.

Indicators of Process Dimensions

a. *Supervisory monitoring*
b. *Weightage to supervisory instructions over personal judgement*
c. *Discovery of procedural violations*
d. *Departmental/legal actions*

These four dimensions can be operationalised by noting the responses of the respondent police officers on the following statements:

- *"Supervisory officers like IIC or SDPO/ACP or SP/DCP often take decision on arrest procedures in specific cases".*

- *"Supervisory officers' opinions or instructions on arrest decision take precedence over personal judgement".*
  "The department has organisational mechanism in place to detect violations of arrest procedures".
- *"The department places strong emphasis on formal disciplinary action for any officer who intentionally violates arrest procedures".*

4.2.3 Value Dimension

Another dimension of the organisational determinant through which the organisation attempts to influence the arrest decision addresses the notion of departmental values. According to Groeneveld (2005), the professional ethos of the organisation sets the tone for its members. As the police organisations start working with the community, the field officers increasingly rely on values instead of the departmental norms or procedures. Indicators such as operational independence, discretionary choices and effect of community policing have been included under this dimension. However, training, which could have been categorised as an exclusive dimension, has been clubbed with value dimension for the purpose of this study. With respect to functional independence, the concern is whether the departmental norms or expectations are still respected while the officer takes a decision independently. The more the operational independence, one would expect higher level of tolerance towards discretion. One may operationalise this indicator by asking a response that *"it is acknowledged that officers have to make arrest decisions sometimes on criteria not covered by written policy or standard procedure"* or *"arrest in many instances precedes formalities like collection of prima facie evidences"*. In addressing discretionary choices, the concern is whether the officer's preference of one among several options is just, fair and in public interest. The amended provisions of arrest under CrPC, however, have provided wide discretionary latitude to the police officer whether to arrest in "noticeable" offences. Although the amended Section 41 CrPC provides for issuance of notice to a person who commits an offence for which maximum punishment extends up to seven years, the investigating officer may arrest the person, if he has the reason to believe that arrest is necessary, (i) to prevent such person from committing further crime, or (ii) for proper investigation, or (iii) prevent the person from tampering with the evidence, or (iv) to prevent threat to the witnesses or (v) to ensure his presence in the court. All these five choices provide enough scope to the investigating officer whether to arrest or serve notice.

One of the important indicators under this dimension is the role of training. In all organisations, training represents the chief way in which policy and procedures are translated into behaviour expectation for employees. Training also ensures that employees have the elemental ability to execute the organisational expectations (Groeneveld 2005). Interestingly, only in the mid-twentieth century, legal scholars and academics "discovered" that wide decisional latitude is at the heart of police functioning. Kenneth Culp Davis, in his seminal study of Chicago Police Department, argues that about half of the discretionary decisions made by criminal justice agencies were made by police. He added, "the police are among the most important policy makers of our entire society. And they make far more discretionary determinations in individual cases than any other class of administrators; I know of no close second." Most of police academies in India have not included "police discretion" as a subject in their course curriculum while SVP National Police Academy, Hyderabad has a passing reference on discretion under the "Ethics" curriculum. The study intends to explore the critical aspect of training through empirical studies.

The fourth indicator under the aforementioned dimension is community policing, which can be defined as a strategy revolving around the principle of "pro-active policing", implemented through "people-friendly policing practices", participation in the community and problem-solving. "The community police officer plays the role of the 'linking pin' between the community and the police station. The new 'linking pin' organisational structure will make the police more accountable to the people it is meant to serve" (Mohanty and Mohanty 2014). This accountability mechanism is expected to ensure better exercise of the police discretion including in cases of arrest. The value dimensions can be represented by the following four indicators.

Indicators of Value Dimensions

a. *Independence*
b. *Discretionary Choices*
c. *Training*
d. *Community Policing*

These dimensions may be operationalised by asking the police respondents to react to the respective statements:

- "*It is acknowledged that officers will sometimes make arrest decisions on criteria not covered by written policy or standard procedure*".
- "*Arrest in many instances precedes formalities like collection of prima facie evidences*".
- "*Department training specifically addresses the use of officer's discretion in arrest decision*".
- "*Community policing practices will substantially constrain the arrest discretion of the officers*".

4.3 Operationalisation of Subculture Determinants

The police are often forced to work in a potentially hostile environment with an objective to maintain order in the society for long hours amidst resource constraints. Research has established that members of the police organisation are guided by their own set of beliefs, attitudes and behaviour, what can be termed as "police subculture". According to the seminal work of William Westley (1970), "the police subculture is a crucial concept in the explanation of police behaviour and attitudes. The subculture, in his view, characterizes public as hostile, not to be trusted, and potentially violent; this outlook requires secrecy, mutual support, and unity on the part of the police". Manning (1977) suggested that the "inherent uncertainty of the police work, combined with the need for information control, leads to police team work, which in turn generates collective ties and mutual dependency". "Police officers are influenced by the formal organisational structures and expressed organisational values and also by informal values, beliefs, norms, rituals, and expectations of the other police officers that are passed through the organisational culture and from one generation of police officers to another" (Scaramella, Cox and McCamey 2011). "Its influence begins early in the new officer's career when he is told by more experienced officers that training given in the police academies is irrelevant to 'real' police work" (Bayley and Bittner 1989). Sparrow, Moore and Kennedy (1990) argued that the police subculture creates a set of truth, according to which the officers are expected to live. It may be noted that there is some basis for each of these subcultural truths and each alienates police from the citizens.

- "It is impossible to win the war on crimes without bending the rules
- Public are potentially hostile and untrustworthy.
- Citizens are unsupportive and make unreasonable demands.
- The police are the only real crime fighters.
- Loyalty to colleague counts more than anything else.
- No one understands the nature of police work but fellow officers".

Researchers have gone into the details of these subcultural truths and arrived at interesting findings and phenomena. The first of these perceived truths is what sociologist Carl B Klockers terms as "Dirty Harry" dilemma which rationalises vigilante justice. The impact of this dilemma in everyday police operations including in arrests is significant. Police officers generally perceive the criminal justice system as too liberal or ineffectual to deal with the hardened criminals. It is common that the police apply graver sections of law than actually committed by a "hardened and habitual offender" with an objective to ensure extended judicial custody and make the relief of bail difficult. This dimension can be operationalised by asking for a reaction to a claim that

- "*Arrest and judicial custody during investigation is the only punishment meted out to antisocials as they are most likely to get acquitted*".

"The dangers associated with policing often prompt officers to distance themselves from the chief source of danger- other citizens. Thus, the police officers, who are socially isolated from public, and rely on each other for protection from a hostile and dangerous work setting, tend to develop an '*us versus them*' attitude towards public and a strong sense loyalty towards fellow officers" (Terril, Paolin and Manning 2003). The amended provisions of arrest in the CrPC in the post-2009 era make it incumbent on the part of the officer to issue notice instead of formally arresting a person accused of an offence(s) that prescribes punishment of less than or up to seven years. But in many such instances, when an officer issues a notice to the accused person in accordance with the provisions of the law, he becomes the subject of public criticism with the victim of crime often attributing motive to police for being soft with the accused person. The public either don't appreciate the nuances of the law or paint police with their world view of being corrupt and letting the accused person go with lighter penalty (Mohanty 2019). The "us versus them" dilemma thus shapes the arrest decision of the police. This may be operationalised by asking the police respondents to react to the statement that

- "*The legal choice of serving notice to an accused person involved in an offence for which the punishment is less than seven years is likely to be attributed motive by the public*".

Yet another distinct subculture that perpetuates in the organisation is the feeling and belief that police are the real crime fighters. The thin line between order and chaos is held by them. Once police withdraw from the scene, disorder will descend and chaos will prevail. In the 1950s, Bill Parker, the Chief of LAPD, coined the term "thin blue line" to reinforce the role of LAPD in fighting crime and maintaining order in Los Angeles. The sentiments are echoed by the police organisations in India during the study of the Law Commission of India for its 177th Report (2001) on "Law relating to arrest". The Law Commission conducted three seminars and invited written suggestions on its Consultation Paper to assess the responses of the police organisations, human rights organisations, eminent jurists, legal academia etc. on the proposed amendments to the arrest law. According to the Law Commission, "two diverging and sharply opposing viewpoints emerged. One was the view espoused by the police officers and other by the members of the Bar and the representatives of the Human Rights' organisations". One former Union Home Secretary opined that "arrest is one of the most immediate preventive actions that can be taken by the police and this power should not be curtailed. Today, only the fear of arrest is there among the criminals but not the fear of conviction because of the undue delays in the courts". The state police organisations too expressed grave concern on the proposed amendment. For example, Inspector General of Police, Haryana stated in his written response that "the proposal to limit the power to arrest an accused in bailable offences, if implemented, would cause tremendous damage to maintenance of public order in the society". Odisha police justified the power of arrest arguing that "the aggrieved public see the arrest of the culprits by the police as a first step in their yearning for justice. Any curtailment of this power will result in the loss of public faith in the criminal justice system". Meghalaya police submitted that any further curtailment of the powers of the police would disable them from fighting the militancy effectively. These strong sentiments of police organisations in India against liberal arrest laws betray the deep-seated ethos of this subculture across the police organisations. However, the term in the Indian context may be rephrased as "thin khaki line", having regard to the shade of the uniforms donned by the Indian police (Mohanty 2019). This can be operationalised by responding to the statement that

- *"Formal police arrest, not service of notice for appearance, is essential to maintain order in the society".*

"Code of silence" is a strong subcultural ethos in policing signifying the informal rule of secrecy that exists among the police officers not to report on colleague's errors, misconduct or brutality. "Secrecy is a set of working tenets that loosely couple the police to accountability, that allow them to do their work and protect each other in the face of oversight interference" (Crank 2004).

This ethos compliments the "us versus them" mindset and "Dirty Harry" dilemma. Because police perceive the public as non-cooperative, unappreciative and are critical of their work, and because the "rules are to be bent" for espousing a greater social cause, the loyalty to a fellow colleague acts as a premium against the professional hazards one encounters in career advancement. The perceived feeling of protection from colleagues against the abuse of power, particularly against illegal arrests or excesses during arrest, gives a sense of immunity to the officer and influences his discretionary determinations. This can be operationalised by eliciting response to a statement that

- *"Department and officers should protect each other on the face of allegation of malafide arrest by an officer as arrest is made for larger public interest".*

From the foregoing discussions, the subculture dimensions thus can be represented by the following four indicators.

Indicators of Subculture Determinants

a. *Dirty Harry Dilemma (criminal justice system is ineffectual)*
b. *"Us versus them" (public potentially hostile and untrustworthy)*
c. *"Thin Blue (khaki) Line" (thin line between order and chaos)*
d. *"Code of Silence" (to maintain solidarity and protect each other)*

4.4 Operationalisation of Environmental Determinants

The literature has generally emphasised on crime rate, minority status, demography, lower level of social control, political culture, media etc. being the variables that influence the arrest decision of the police (Groeneveld 2005; Halliday 2009; Hidayet 2011). But having regard to the Indian context, and the macro external environment in which the organisation is embedded factors, such as, the political dispensation, pressure groups and media have been identified as they have considerable influence on the decision-making processes.

Police in India are denoted as a "state subject" under a collective reading of Article 246 of the Constitution and List II of Seventh Schedule. State governments within the Union of India frame rules and regulations governing police forces and ensuring accountability for maintaining law and order. The working of the police in general is governed by respective State Police Acts and in the absence of the same by the central Police Act of 1861. The Act provides that the supervision and control of the police in a particular district is to be done by the State government which effectively means that the Minister in charge of the portfolio of police is legally authorised to undertake the supervision and control over police. And it is within the limits of these powers of superintendence that the administration of the police within a State is vested in the Director General of Police, his deputies and assistants. "The executives, comprising the Chief Minister or the Home Minister, who are also political bosses, are accordingly the controllers of the police – the big bosses of the police" (Singhvi 1994). Singhvi (ibid.) argues that from the Chief Minister and police Minister of the State government, who are big bosses of the state police, the Members of Parliament, Members of the Legislative Assemblies, Zilla Parishad and Municipal Corporation Chairmen, members of the Panchayati Raj Institutions, and political workers belonging to political party in power, draw clout, power and influences over the police. Singhvi observes that "an individual's capacity to generate political pressure on police is not linked to his formal association with a political party. He can operate through several links that are forged by considerations of money, caste, community, regional affinity etc.".

The National Police Commission (1979) in its Second Report, while highlighting the misuse of police by illegal or improper orders or pressures from political, executive or other extraneous sources, observes that "the unhealthy influences and pressures that are brought to bear on the police don't always originate from political sources alone. Capitalists, industrialists, businessmen, landlords and such others who form the richer and more influential sections of the society have immense capacity to generate such pressure to operate at different levels of the police, either directly or indirectly through political sources, and influence the course of police action".

As regards arrests, the NPC enlists typical situations or matters in which pressure is brought to bear on the police by the political, executive or other extraneous sources as follows:

1. "Arrest or non-arrest of a person against whom a case is taken up for investigation by the police
2. Release or non-release on bail after arrest

3. Taking persons into preventive custody to immobilise them from legitimate political activity in opposition to the party in power
4. Discretionary enforcement of law while dealing with public order situations, with emphasis on severity or ruthlessness in regard to persons opposed to the ruling party
5. Manoeuvring police intervention by exaggerating a non-cognisable offence to gain advantage over another party".

Media considerably influences the police functions. Media and police world over have an ambiguous relationship. Rarely does a major piece of police work receive the accolade of general approval. "Literature on the subject of police and media relations reaches a consensus that there is an extreme amount of animosity between these two groups. The literature also bears out the fact that this animosity had perpetuated itself over a long period of time and may even be the result of built-in biases that solidify in the morals of the officers and reporters before they ever even begin their jobs" (Bellew 2001). A study conducted by Selke and Bartoszek (1984) reveals that apparently "the animosity between journalists and police officers may have its seeds in the backgrounds and personal orientations of those who choose these professions". They further point out that "the majority of recruits also believed that the media is not generally objective and is more concerned with printing what sells papers rather than merely covering new events". Skolnick and Fyfe (1993) argue that not a single instance of police action has ever been "wholly satisfactory" to all the stakeholders involved, particularly due to a negative perception of an otherwise perfect piece of police work by the offender in question. The environment in which police must do their work is therefore certain to be unfavourable. Good immediate results are difficult to secure and may bring new and unexpected favours into the operation. The chain of circumstances thus forged proves a burden to even the best police organisation. Ghosh and Rustamji (1994), two distinguished police scholars, argue that the public and their mouthpiece – the press – are interested in every aspect of police work and the tone of press reporting and comments profoundly influences the public opinion.

The public opinion adds a layer of accountability to police functions. It is argued in earlier chapter that accountability and exercise of discretion are interrelated. Strong criticism by the media of mishandling a grave crime or police excesses or inaction brings the organisation under the scanner. There are numerous instances of political leadership seeking immediate remedial measures, often in the form of disciplinary action against the delinquent officer or instituting judicial or magisterial inquiries to fix accountability, in order to counter the public criticism. The field functionaries in the organisation are therefore weary of undue media interest in police works. Besides, most of the police organisations, at the level of district Superintendent of Police, maintain a system of collection of daily clippings of the newspaper reports that relate to their jurisdictions. In so far as the reports are critical of police functions, the concerned field functionary is asked to explain, and in some instances, inquiry is ordered. Prompt arrests in the face of media criticism often save the police from further embarrassment. But in the process the procedural and legal formalities may become a casualty.

Thus, the media, public opinion, public reaction and political influences create a complex maze within which the police take decisions. Each of these components either independently or in combination influences decision-making processes of police. From the foregoing discussions, the environmental dimension thus can be represented by the following four indicators.

Indicators of Environmental Determinants

a. *Fall out of action*
b. *Public perception*
c. *Media and civil society*
d. *Politics*

This study intends to measure the extent to which these variables affect the arrest discretion of the officer. These dimensions under environmental determinant were operationalised by asking the police respondents to react to the following statements:

- "*Arrest decisions are often taken having regard to the fall out or outcome of such decisions in maintaining public order*".
- "*Public perception of police action on specific cases considerably influences arrest decision*".
- "*Media and response of the civil society to a specific offence weigh on the officer's arrest decision*".
- "*Arrest decisions are sometimes taken on political consideration or influence*".

4.5 Operationalisation of Individual Determinants

Individual determinants refer to the influences of police officers' own characteristics over their behaviour. Studies on individual factors examine the characteristics like gender, experience, educational level, race and social class and their influences on officers' response to a situation including discretionary behaviour. The assumption here is that female, more experienced and better educated officers will react differently to arrest discretion determinants than their male, rookie and less educated counterparts, respectively. Research has attempted to find out if these assumptions are accurate. Contrary to the suggestions, barring few exceptions, the empirical studies do not produce consistent findings and do not reveal a strong impact on behaviour (Hidayet 2011; Terril and Mastrofski 2002; Stalans and Finn 1995). However, this study intends to examine these assumptions on three variables, such as officer's gender, experience and position in the hierarchy. The police in India are State subject according to the Eighth Schedule of the Constitution of India, which authorises the constituent States of the Union to recruit, train and regulate their respective police forces. The reservation for women in police recruitments across the States varies from ten to thirty-three percent. The minimum educational qualification for lower subordinate ranks, that is, Sub-Inspector of Police to senior supervisory posts, that is, Assistant Superintendent of Police is graduation though postgraduates or aspirants with higher educational qualifications apply for the job and get recruited. Since the minimum educational qualification of the police respondents is a graduate degree, this has not been considered as a variable in this study. However, the senior supervisory officers join the organisation at a higher level than the lower subordinates, who actually conduct the arrests in the course of investigation.

This study has examined the responses of these two categories of officers from among the respondents. Experience of the officers as a key variable has also been considered for the purpose of this study. Police officers are career civil servants in India with an average of more than thirty years of service rendered before retirement. Therefore, experience of twenty years in the organisation has been taken as the interval scale for this study.

4.6 Operationalisation of Situational/Offender Determinants

"Empirical research has provided overwhelming support to the notion that police have a great deal of discretion in how they address a citizen's conduct and that both legal and extra-legal criteria can influence the outcomes of police – citizen encounters" (Smith and Visher 1981). Although decision-making by police officers when encountering with citizens is expected to be centred on legal factors, for example, the gravity of conduct or evidence against the suspect, empirical research finds support for arguments of discrimination centring around race or gender in arrest outcomes, which are not strictly legal considerations. While the empirical research leaves little doubt about the influence of legal factors on arrest outcomes, Worden (1989) notes in his assessment of the discretionary context of policing that "officer behaviour is not solely influenced by the law" and "policing is for the most part extra-legal, for while officers (often) work within the constraints of the law, they seldom invoke the law in performing police work". "There is a strong relationship between the demeanour of the offender and police decisions" (Black 1971). "For example, disrespectful behaviours of offenders increase the likelihood of an officer making an arrest and using force toward those suspects" (Hidayet 2011).

In this study, having regard to the Indian context, the socio-economic status of the offenders has been surveyed to find out if there is a correlation between poor and marginal and their being more likely to be arrested. The awareness about the legal rights or lack of it depends upon the socio-economic condition of the individual. Members of poor and marginal sections of the society are more likely to be at the receiving end of discretionary abuse than their affluent counterparts. The procedural law of India, the Criminal Procedure Code (CrPC), provides certain rights to the arrestee and casts obligations on the officer while making an arrest. The officer making an arrest should prepare an arrest memo which shall be attested by at least one family member of the person arrested or a respectable member of the locality (Sections 41B, 50A of CrPC); communicate to the arrestee the grounds of arrest and whether the person is involved in a bailable offence, and his right to be released on bail (Section 50 CrPC); inform a relative, or friend, or acquaintance about the arrest and place of lodging (Section 50A CrPC); arrange for a medical examination of the arrestee (Section 54 CrPC); shall not detain a person in custody for a period exceeding twenty-four hours (Section 57 CrPC); inform the arrestee of his right to meet an advocate of his choice during interrogation (Section 41D CrPC) etc. Knowledge of these legal rights is the prerequisite to assert them. However, offenders from poor and marginalised sections of the society are neither legally literate nor can they afford a lawyer during arrest to assert these legal rights on their behalf. Therefore, they are more likely to be at the receiving end of the discretionary abuse of police officers making arrest. Empirical study of these variables, like socio-economic status of the accused person, his level of awareness of the legal rights, the extent of legal assistance sought during arrest and his treatment during arrest required a well-thought-out written interview schedule for administration to the purposive sample offenders selected for the study.

Despite the constitutional guarantee of equality before law (Art 14) and non-discrimination on the ground of caste and race (Art 15), the fact remains that the deep-rooted caste system in India has placed the Dalits, tribesmen and backward class people at a disadvantage in accessing justice. Prevalence of relatively higher level of poverty and illiteracy among this class of people are some of the contributing factors for lack of assertiveness of legal rights. The study intends to capture these variables by conducting a socio-economic survey of the sample offenders. Some of the variables selected for the study are "category" (scheduled caste, scheduled tribe and other backward class), "occupation" (cultivation, wage earner, trading and government job), "level of education", "land ownership", "annual income" etc. of the offender *(Appendix E)*. The sample offenders are asked to respond to the level of their legal awareness to simple statements such as

- "Police normally should not arrest but issue appearance notice, if the punishment for the offence involved is not more than seven years".
- "Getting bail at the police station is a matter of right of the accused person involved in a bailable offence".
- "Upon arrest the police should inform the arrested person about the ground of arrest and inform the relatives about the arrest".

4.7 Variables or Indicators of Discretion

From the preceding discussion, twenty items representing indicators of the dimensions under organisational, informal organisational or subcultural, and environmental determinants are enumerated as follows. Three indicators each under situational and individual determinants are taken for the purpose of this study.

A. Organisational Determinants

1. ***Policy Dimensions***
   a. *Specific Statutory Guidelines*
   b. *Court Pronouncement, for example, Arnesh Kumar guidelines*
   c. *Extensiveness of arrest policy, for example, Crime Branch Circular*
   d. *Internal Review*
2. ***Process Dimensions***
   a. *Supervisory monitoring*
   b. *Weightage to supervisory instructions over personal judgement*
   c. *Discovery of procedural violations*
   d. *Departmental/legal actions*
3. ***Value Dimensions***
   a. *Independence*
   b. *Discretionary Choices*
   c. *Training*
   d. *Community Policing*

B. Subculture Determinants

a. *"Dirty Harry Dilemma" (criminal justice system is ineffectual)*
b. *"Us versus them" (public potentially hostile and untrustworthy)*
c. *"Thin Blue Line" (thin line between order and chaos)*
d. *"Code of Silence" (to maintain solidarity and protect each other)*

C. Environmental Determinants

a. *Fall out of action*
b. *Public perception*
c. *Media and civil society*
d. *Politics*

D. Individual Determinants

a. *Gender*
b. *Work experience*
c. *Length of service*

E. Situational/Offender Determinants

a. Socio-economic status
b. Awareness of rights
c. Legal assistance

A diagrammatic summary of the framework established for operationalisation of the determinants is shown in Figure 4.1.

Each indicator under organisational, subcultural and environmental determinants needs to be distinct and different from other indicators in that each measures a specific aspect of the given dimension. This is consistent with the statistical notion that indicators should be additive, such that the accumulation of the indicators individually captures different aspects of the dimension and collectively they represent the conceptual space defined by the dimension (Groeneveld 2005). But, the indicators under situational and individual determinants are mutually exclusive enough to need any statistical validation to prove that they are different from one another, whereas the indicators under the rest of the three determinants may require such validation.

4.8 Translating Indicators to Response Statements

The next step is to translate these twenty indicators under organisational, subcultural and environmental determinants into meaningful response statements that can be used to measure the perception under each head. However, this presents a challenge in terms of measurement. Since the determinants and indicators developed in this study are constructed to be additive, the appropriate scaling technique is that of Summated Ratings and scale is "Likert scales". It assumes that each scale item is a statement, either positive or negative, related to the concept of interest, that the statements are additive in nature and that the respondents will be asked to express their degree of agreement or disagreement with each item. The process of scoring the scale is achieved by assigning numeric value to the response format. The classical Likert scales with five choices, starting from "Strongly Agree" to "Strongly Disagree" have been chosen for this study. The response format is worded such that strong agreement or disagreement with the item indicates higher degree of influence with respect to the indicator. Accordingly, a value of five has been assigned to "strongly agree" and each item choice after is numerically smaller until a "strongly disagree" receives a value of one.

Each variable under a major determinant or concept needs to be qualified with a statement which should be meaningful to the "world of experience" and collectively they must represent the concept. To take the example of influence of subculture on arrest discretion behaviour, the conceptual space of "subculture" is intended to be represented collectively by (i) "Dirty Harry dilemma" (criminal justice system is ineffectual), (ii) "us versus them" (public potentially hostile and untrustworthy), (iii) "thin blue line" (thin line

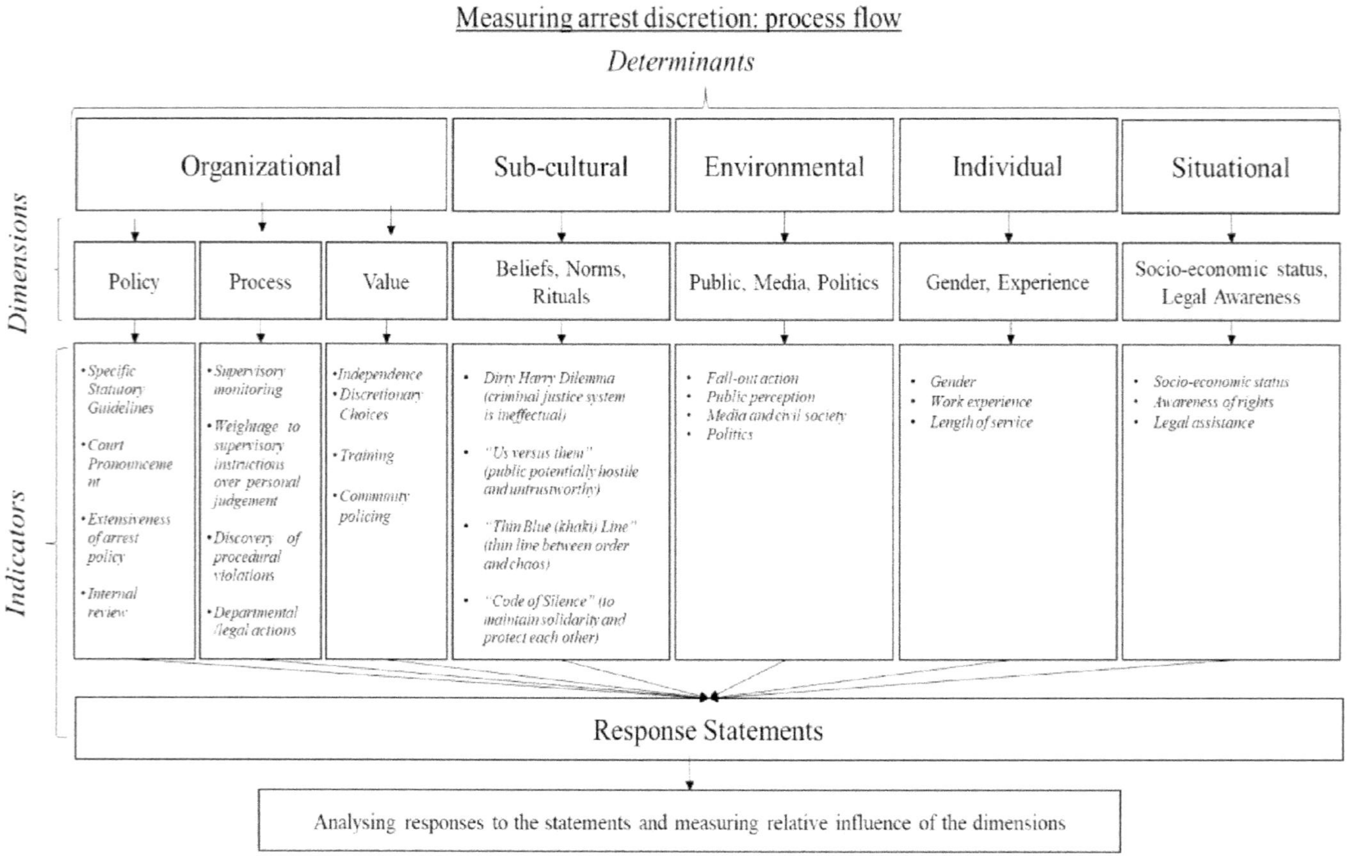

Figure 4.1 Diagrammatic summary of operational framework

Table 4.1 Response format example

Strongly Agree	*Agree*	*Cannot Say*	*Disagree*	*Strongly Disagree*
5	4	3	2	1

between order and chaos) and (iv) "code of silence" (to maintain solidarity and protect each other). Each necessarily needs to be qualified with a statement which the respondent must be able to relate to the "world of experience" and when responded must indicate the degree of his/her agreement or disagreement. The following is an example of Likert scales used for this study to operationalise "Dirty Harry dilemma".

The response format with 24 five-answer choices on Likert rating scale is enclosed in *Appendix C*. Statements 1 to 6 relate to policy dimensions, 7 to 10 process dimensions, 11 to 16 value dimensions under organisational determinants, 17 to 20 represent subculture determinants and 21 to 24 environmental determinants. More than one response statement has been used for certain response predictors to get more accurate response but the statistical averaging of the summated values has been done for comparative study. In the case of IPS officers of other States, one out of three response statements under response predictor, extensiveness of arrest policy, has been used as rest two are specific to the state police. Therefore, the number of response statements for IPS officers (rest of Odisha) comes to 22, which is placed in *Appendix D*.

The socio-economic and legal awareness survey form is placed in *Appendix E* which is designed to be filled up after interacting with the respondents.

4.9 Sampling Technique

The study has been undertaken in the context of the Indian police. Article 246 of the Constitution of India read with List II of Seventh Schedule essentially designates the police as a state subject which means that the state governments of the union of India shall remain responsible for the maintenance of law and order and frame the rules and regulations that govern each police force. These rules and regulations are contained in the police manuals of each state force. As of 2020, there are twenty-eight State and eight Union Territory police organisations in India. It has been argued earlier in Chapter 1 (please refer section 1.5) that despite multiple police organisations there is quite some commonality among them. There are four main reasons for these premises. First, the police organisations are governed either by the Police Act of 1861 or by their own State Police Act modelled mostly on a draft Act prepared under the supervision of the Supreme Court of India.[1] Secondly, major criminal laws, such as the Indian Penal Code, the Code of Criminal Procedure and the Indian Evidence Act are uniformly applicable to almost all the States. Thirdly, the uniformity in the functioning of the higher judiciary and the applicability of the rulings of the Supreme Court throughout the country in all civil and criminal matters including those on police have shaped the police procedures through the process of judicial reviews. And finally, the leadership of the police organisations has been held by the members of Indian Police Service (IPS), who are recruited, trained and governed by uniform rules and procedures.

In this study, the state of Odisha is taken as a universe. Besides, random selection of senior officers from Indian Police Service from across different States and Union Territory police organisations of the country on training course at SVP National Police Academy, Hyderabad have been taken as respondents. Therefore, inductively, the research findings are expected to mirror pan Indian characteristics of police discretion behaviour.

Odisha has thirty revenue districts and thirty-four police districts. From the various types of available sampling methods, multi-stage sampling procedure has been adopted. Considering the feasibility of the study, the steps followed to draw the samples are placed in *Appendix F*

The list of the districts, police subdivisions and police stations thus selected by adopting the simple random method is placed in *Appendix G*. In all, a total of 178 (Sub-Inspector – 102, Officer-in-charge – 51 and Deputy Superintendent of Police – 25) respondents were scheduled to be covered and their responses would be analysed using various statistical methods. Besides, purposive sample of senior police officers from rest of Indian states were proposed to be collected preferably from the National Police Academy, Hyderabad which conducts training programme for IPS officers of State and UT police organisations.

For the purpose of selecting samples for Situational/Offenders' determinants, twelve Districts have been selected by simple random method from three Revenue Divisions of the state of Odisha. From each of the Districts, three police stations have been selected purposively – one urban and two rural. From each police station, six persons (purposive) have been selected out of which four have been arrested by police in "noticeable offences" and two have been served with notice in similar offences. Thus, the total number of respondents comes to 216.

4.10 Data Collection

Interactive sessions were arranged with the respondents at the respective district headquarters to explain them the concepts of arrest discretion before they filled up the response format. After briefing on the context and purpose of study, the respondents were given a brief write-up to recapitulate what they have been explained and to appreciate how the responses are to be made in the classical Likert scales with five choices. The brief explanatory note given to the respondent is placed in *Appendix H*. A total of 222 respondents participated in the study. The district-wise break-up is placed in *Appendix I*. Similar procedure was adopted for the respondents from the Indian Police Service. On two occasions, the author visited the SVP National Police Academy, Hyderabad which offers various training courses for officers from Indian Police Service and interacted with two batches of IPS officers, one batch doing the Mid-Career Training Programme and the other doing the Induction Course. The officers belong to different state and union territory cadres of India. The respondents are random samples fairly representing the state and union territory police organisations. A total of 138 respondents participated in the study. The states and union territories-wise break-up is placed in *Appendix J*.

A total of 360 respondents, from both Odisha State Police and Indian Police Service officers from different state and union territory police organisations, have participated in this study.

In order to study the situational/offender's determinants on arrest discretion behaviour, a separate socio-economic survey was undertaken with offenders in criminal offences as respondents. The socio-economic survey form is placed in *Appendix E*. A local language version of the survey form was supplied to the respondents. A total of 195 respondents were surveyed and participated in this study. *(Appendix K)*

4.11 Data Analysis Techniques

There are several analytical goals in this study. The first one is to characterise and examine how far and to what extent the organisational, informal organisational/subcultural and environmental determinants influence arrest discretion behaviour. The average values of the response statements, standard deviations and correlation coefficient (Pearson's "r") values have been analysed to arrive at the findings.

Correlation coefficients are traditionally defined in such a way as to take values extending from –1 to +1. A negative value indicates a negative relation, that is, X decreases as Y increases. The main purpose of the study is to find out the relationship between the predictors and to see if they suffer from multicollinearity. The values of "r" for weak, moderate, good and strong relationships are as follows:

"r" from 0.00 to ±0.20 denotes negligible relationship (weak)
"r" from ±0.20 to ±0.40 denotes low correlation (moderate)
"r" from ±0.40 to ±0.70 denotes substantial or marked relationship (good)
"r" from ±0.70 to ±1.00 denotes high or very high relationship (strong) (Garrett 1926)

Weak or moderate value of "r" indicates a lack of multicollinearity, required for meaningful regression analysis. This is consistent with the statistical notion that predictors should be additive, such that the accumulation of the predictors individually captures different aspects of the dimension and collectively they represent the conceptual space defined by the dimension.

The second objective is to study the influence of individual determinants on arrest discretion behaviour. Three variables have been chosen for this study – gender, work experience and length of service. Out of 360 respondents, sixty are women, comprising 16.7 percent of the population. Operationalisation of work experience has been done by splitting the population into two groups – the senior supervisory officers which include the members of Indian Police Service and officers of and above the rank of Additional Superintendent of Police and the other one being non-supervisory officers from the rank of Sub-Inspector to Deputy Superintendent of Police. The number is fairly well distributed with 158 senior supervisory officers and 202 non-supervisory officers. The third variable is service experience. For this study, the population has been divided into two categories, the first category being those with work experience of up to twenty years and the second one being those with more than twenty years of work experience. The responses have been grouped according to the study variables and compared with data generated from the cross-tables to find out if the gender or work experience or years of service rendered have any relationship with arrest decision.

The third objective is to find out if the groups in the individual determinant, for example, male and female or supervisory officers and subordinates, impact the arrest discretion behaviour comprising the organisational, subcultural and environmental factors differently. In situation like this, where the research focuses on examining the impact of several independent variables (gender, position and experience) on a single dependent variable (organisation or subculture or environment), multiple regression is the appropriate analysis technique. This approach is used as a means of quantifying the amount of variance explained by relative importance of each independent variable. The relative importance of independent variables is assessed using the standardised regression coefficient, also known as beta (β) coefficient. It is interpreted as the amount of change in the dependent variable associated with a standardised one-unit change in the focal independent variable, controlling for the effects of all other independent variables. Beta coefficients vary between a lower anchor value of –1.0 and an upper limit of +1.0. The higher the coefficient value, the greater the amount of unique change caused in the dependent variable by the focal predictor (independent variable). Consequently, greater is the relative importance of that independent variable (Groeneveld 2005).

And finally, a combination of simple frequency and cross-tabulation comparative analysis has been attempted to study the situational/offenders' characteristics. Multiple regression analysis, combination of simple frequency table and cross-tabulation, has been employed for data analysis by adopting SPSS[2] software.

The major approach in this study is quantitative which seeks to deduce cause and effect relationships to predict patterns of behaviour by confirming theories and hypotheses through a deductive process of reasoning. This study is a maiden attempt to empirically test if the determinants of arrest discretion (empirically validated in the Western world) are valid in the context of the police in India. The results are expected to shed light on some of the queries raised in Chapter 1 (please refer section 1.7) and to test the validity of the hypotheses listed out in Chapter 2 (please refer section 2.6). The next chapter deals with data analysis and findings. It is expected that the study would ultimately contribute to evaluation of policies, programmes and interventions.

Notes

1 Soli Sorabjee Committee
2 Statistical Package for Social Science is a software package used for interactive or batched statistical analysis. In the present study, SPSS 16.0 has been used for correlation and multiple regression analysis.

5 The Interplay of Legal and Extralegal Factors in Police Discretion

5.1 Data Analysis and Findings

This chapter presents the findings and results of the data analysis. For the purpose of this study, Arrest Discretion Response Statements have been designed by adopting the classical five-point Likert scales (*Appendix C*). Twenty-four statements reflecting the twenty dimensions of interest (for three dimensions more than one statement is chosen) under three determinants, namely, organisational, subcultural and environmental variables, have been carefully prepared having relevance to the context of policing in India. Response statements are coded such that the lowest level of discretion control corresponds with lower numerical anchor of the scale (1), and the highest levels are represented by upper numerical anchor point (5). The intensity of agreement of the respondent to one of the five categories – Strongly Agree, Agree, Don't Know, Disagree and Strongly Disagree – indicates that the procedures, protocols, guidelines, subcultural and environmental determinants do exist in the organisation to shape or influence the arrest discretion behaviour of the officer.

While there exists intuitive support for the connection between police discretion and organisational, subcultural, environmental, situational and individual dispositions, no empirical research has been conducted to examine this issue in the Indian context. This study is intended to fill that gap. Several empirical tasks were undertaken on the basis of response statements and their summated values. The first one is to characterise and examine how far and to what extent the organisational, subcultural and environmental determinants influence arrest discretion behaviour. The second goal is to find out from among the dimensions which have significant contribution towards influencing the determinants – that is, organisational, subcultural and environmental – and which among the determinants has maximum contribution towards influencing arrest discretion behaviour of police. The study examines each response format on the basis of frequency tables to find out the degree of agreement or disagreement as a measure of discretionary control.

As regards the individual determinants, a cross-table comparative study of the responses based on variables, such as gender, work experience and length of service, has been conducted to find out if these factors influence

DOI: 10.4324/9781003406679-5

the discretionary determinations differently. Besides, the socio-economic and legal awareness survey of 195 offenders was undertaken separately to examine if the variables, such as the socio-economic status or degree of legal awareness of the offenders, have any bearing on the arrest discretion behaviour of the police. Are the poor and marginal people of the society on the receiving end of the discretionary abused by the police? Findings and analysis of these two determinants are dealt in a separate chapter (Chapter 6) for two reasons. Firstly, the variables under the organisational, subcultural and environmental determinants have been measured, compared and analysed through a uniform methodology as opposed to those under individual and situational determinants. Secondly, the data analysis of the first three determinants has challenged the popular narratives on arrest discretion and deserves to be treated exclusively.

Table 5.1 shows the major determinants, corresponding dimensions and code given to each response statement in a matrix.

Table 5.1 Determinants-dimensions-predictors-code matrix

Serial no.	*Determinants*	*Dimensions*	*Response predictors*	*Code (Odisha)*	*Code (Others)*
1.	**Organisational**	Policy	*Specific Statutory Guidelines*	R-1	R-1
			Court Pronouncement, for example, Arnesh Kumar Guidelines	R-2	R-2
			Extensiveness of arrest	R-3,	R-3,
			Policy, for example, Crime	R-4,	N/A,
			Branch Circular, police	R-5	N/A
			Internal Review	R-6	R-4
		Process	*Supervisory monitoring*	R-7	R-5
			Weightage to supervisory instructions over personal Judgement	R-8	R-6
			Discovery of procedural Violations	R-9	R-7
			Departmental/legal actions	R-10	R-8
		Value	*Independence*	R-11	R-9
			Discretionary choices	R-12, R-13	R-10, R-11
			Training	R-14	R-12
			Community Policing	R-15, R-16	R-13, R-14

(*Continued*)

Table 5.1 (Continued)

Serial no.	*Determinants*	*Dimensions*	*Response predictors*	*Code (Odisha)*	*Code (Others)*
2.	**Informal Organisational/ Sub cultural**		*Dirty Harry Dilemma (criminal justice system is ineffectual)*	R-17	R-15
			"Us versus them" (public potentially hostile and untrustworthy)	R-18	R-16
			"Thin Blue Line" (thin line between order and chaos)	R-19	R-17
			"Code of Silence" (to maintain solidarity and protect each other)	R-20	R-18
3.	**Environmental**		*Fall out of action*	R-21	R-19
			Public perception	R-22	R-20
			Media and civil society	R-23	R-21
			Politics	R-24	R-22
4.	**Individual**		*Gender*	N/A	N/A
			Work experience	N/A	N/A
			Length of service	N/A	N/A
5.	**Situational (offenders' perspective)**		*Socio-economic status*	N/A	N/A
			Awareness of rights	N/A	N/A
			Legal assistance	N/A	N/A

NB: N/A – Not Applicable. More than one response statement has been used for certain response predictors – 24 as against 20 – to get more accurate response but the statistical averaging of the summated values has been calculated for comparative study. In the case of IPS officers, one out of three response statements under response predictor, extensiveness of arrest policy, has been used as rest two are specific to the Odisha State Police. Therefore, the number of response statements for IPS officers (rest of Odisha) comes to 22. Refer *Appendices C and D*

5.2 Sample Area for the Study

In this study, the state of Odisha is taken as the universe. Besides, random selection of senior officers from Indian Police Service from across different States and Union Territory police organisations of the country on training course at National Police Academy, Hyderabad have been taken as respondents. In the previous chapter, it has been argued that the constitutional provisions, uniformity of the procedural and substantial laws and of the functions of judiciary in the country inductively establish the sample area to be representative of the Indian police.

Odisha has thirty revenue districts and thirty-four police districts. From the various types of available sampling methods, multi-stage random sampling procedure for the present study has been adopted with the selection of seventeen districts. In all, a total of 178 (Sub-Inspector – 102, Officer-in-charge – 51,

Table 5.2 Rank of respondents

Code no.	*Designation*	*Frequency*	*Percentage*
1	IPS Officers (All India)	138	38.3
2	IG & above	2	0.6
3	DIG	2	0.6
4	SP	14	3.9
5	Addl SP	2	0.6
6	DySP	44	12.2
7	Inspector	54	15.0
8	Sub-Inspector	104	28.9
Total		**360**	**100.0**

NB: Codes 2 to 8 are from Odisha Police

Deputy Superintendent of Police – 25) respondents were scheduled to be covered for the study. But 222 respondents with few senior officers from Indian Police Service participated in the study. This is statistically valid in that the sample areas come from the randomly selected districts.

Purposive sample of senior police officers from the rest of the Indian states was proposed to be collected preferably from the National Police Academy, Hyderabad which conducts training programme for IPS officers of State and union territory polices. The respondents are random samples fairly representing the country. A total of 138 respondents from Indian Police Service rest of Odisha participated in the study.

A total of 222 officers from Odisha police including fourteen IPS officers of the cadre participated as study respondents. They were asked to record the degree of their agreement or disagreement on the twenty-four responses *(Appendix C)*. All together, 138 IPS officers from the rest of India on the other hand responded to twenty-two responses *(Appendix D)* as two of the response statements under response predictor "extensiveness of arrest policy" are specific to Odisha Police Manual (Ratho 2000) and Crime Branch Circular of Odisha Police. The rank-wise break-up of the respondents is shown in Table 5.2.

Codes 2 to 8 are the respondents of the Odisha Police, from the rank of Sub-Inspector to Inspector General of Police. They represent 61.7 percent of the study population. Code 1 represents the respondent Indian Police Officers who were undergoing mid-career or induction training course at SVP National Police Academy, Hyderabad. Most of them have put in more than twenty-five years of service in the senior supervisory rank, representing 38.3 percent of the study population that was studied.

5.3 Analysis of Frequency Distribution

A well-constructed frequency distribution makes it possible for a detailed analysis of population structure with respect to a given characteristic. A list of frequency tables is presented in this section in respect of each response statement to analyse how the respondents have reacted to the predictors or the variables on the Arrest Discretion Response Statement. On the basis of the frequency of agreement to a response statement, a general proposition can be drawn to find out how much the population agrees to the existence of response predictors that influence the arrest discretion behaviour.

5.3.1 Organisational Determinants

As discussed in the preceding chapter, organisational influences refer to the system of administrative rules, policies and managerial controls designed to ensure conformity to the departmental directives and to the statute. "The research literature clearly indicates that the organisation creates a structure for arrest discretion, flows from four primary sources; official policy, process, training and values" (Groeneveld 2005). These dimensions capture the channel through which the departmental supervisory officers can influence or constraint the discretionary behaviour of the officers in arrests. For the purpose of this study, training has been included under value dimensions. Therefore, for operationalisation of these three broad dimensions – policy, process and value – a set of response predictors has been selected from the literature review and for each predictor a response statement has been prepared so that the respondent can relate it with the "world of experience" and express his degree of agreement or disagreement on the Arrest Discretion Response Statement.

5.3.1.1 Policy Dimensions

Under policy dimension, the extensiveness of the arrest policy circulated by the department, and awareness of the officers about the statutory guidelines of the Supreme Court and High Courts on arrest are some of the measures put in place by the organisation to make the decisions on arrests objectively and to maintain uniformity in decision-making. The directives of the Supreme Court and High Courts are circulated by the Crime Branch of the State police to all field functionaries. Clearly, the written guidelines described in the operation manuals or circulars or court directives covering the elements of arrest establish a foundation for valid arrests and ensure the rights guaranteed by the Constitution. Another aspect of the policy dimension focuses upon the department's internal review mechanism on compliance to arrest procedures. Such reviews are essential to ensure that the departmental and court guidelines are followed within the acceptable limits of discretion and to regulate proper exercise of discretion. The six indicators or response predictor variables for policy dimensions are enlisted in Table 5.3. Two of the response predictors, coded R-4 and R-5, are specific to internal guidelines of Odisha police and hence not included in the Arrest Discretion Response Statement for IPS officers from other states. As a result, the total number of response statements for IPS officers from other states has been two less than that for

Table 5.3 Indicators or response predictor variables for policy dimensions

Indicators or response predictor variables	*Code (Odisha)*	*Code (others)*
Specific Statutory Guidelines; Sec 41 of Cr PC is very specific and provides detailed guidelines	R-1	R-1
Court Pronouncement, for example, Arnesh Kumar guidelines is more specific and ensures accountability	R-2	R-2
Extensiveness of arrest policy, for example, department's arrest policy following Arnesh Kumar gives clear guidelines on arrest	R-3	R-3
The Crime Branch Circular 350/2014 provides more clarity on arrest decision	R-4	N/A
The Odisha Police Manual Rule 221 stipulates about issue of notice in offences punishable up to 7 years	R-5	N/A
Adequate internal review mechanism exists in the department to ensure compliance to arrest procedures	R-6	R-4

Odisha police respondents. Response statement coded R-6 for respondents of Odisha police and its equivalent R-4 for IPS officers of other States is one and the same.

5.3.1.2 Frequency Table Analysis for Policy Dimensions

The six response statements (R-1, R-2, R-3, R-4, R-5 and R-6) corresponding to four indicators or response predictors have been carefully prepared. The respondents were asked to note the degree of their agreement or disagreement to the statements on a five-point Likert scale, the Arrest Discretion Scale. Two of the response statements (R-4 and R-5) are not relevant to the officer respondents from cadres other than Odisha. However, this may not pose any statistical problem of summated values as the four response statements are sufficient for calculating the frequency. The response format is worded such that strong agreement or disagreement with the item indicates higher degree of influence with respect to the indicator. Accordingly, a value of five has been assigned to "strongly agree" and each item choice after is numerically smaller until a "strongly disagree" receives a value of one. The combined frequency chart of summated ratings with a range of scale values corresponding to the category descriptors used for the response format is shown in Table 5.4.

R-1 is designed to elicit response if the amended provisions of Section 41 of Criminal Procedure Code (2009), that provide statutory guidelines on arrest including the circumstances when notice is to be served to an offender and when to arrest, are detailed and specific enough for the officer intending to arrest. More than ninety-two percent of respondents have either agreed or strongly agreed, which validates the hypothesis that detailed and unambiguous statutory guidelines limit the boundary of discretion and influence control over its proper exercise. But one of the research questions doubts the

Table 5.4 Policy dimensions

Code	*Response*	*Frequency and percentage*					
		R-1	*R-2*	*R-3*	*R-4/NA*	*R-5/NA*	*R-6/R-4*
1.	Strongly Disagree	5 (1.4)	4 (1.1)	3 (0.8)	1 (0.4)	4 (1.8)	4 (1.1)
2.	Disagree	20 (5.6)	13 (3.6)	23 (6.4)	11 (4.9)	21 (9.5)	59 (16.4)
3.	Cannot Say	3 (0.8)	48 (13.3)	41 (11.4)	23 (10.4)	24 (10.8)	32 (8.9)
4.	Agree	236 (65.5)	210 (58.3)	206 (57.2)	146 (65.8)	101 (45.5)	210 (58.3)
5.	Strongly Agree	96 (26.7)	85 (23.6)	87 (24.7)	41 (18.5)	72 (32.4)	55 (15.3)
Total		360 (100.0)	360 (100.0)	360 (100.0)	222 (100.0)	222 (100.0)	360 (100.0)

NB: The figures in the parenthesis represent the percentage share. N/A is not applicable for IPS officers of other states

validity of this hypothesis and raises the fundamental question that in spite of detailed statutory guidelines on arrest in the amended provisions of Section 41 CrPC, why it is that the arrest per offence in India has not shown any significant decline (1.18 as against 1.19 in the pre-amended period). Theoretically, it should have been reduced by two-thirds as similar proportion of the offences in the substantive laws in India prescribes imprisonment up to or less than seven years and therefore the offenders could have been served with notice instead of being arrested. Do the amended provisions, while being liberal, still have enough discretionary latitude for police to manoeuvre in a manner that could negate the legislative intents? This question will be dealt in the subsequent section.

R-2, R-3 and R-4 are key predictor variables which intend to elicit the response whether the directives of the Supreme Court in Arnesh Kumar[1] are specific enough on arrest procedures and whether they could ensure accountability against irregular arrest. In the year 2014, the Supreme Court in a landmark judgement deliberated on the arrest procedures followed by the police in the light of amended provisions of Section 41 of the CrPC. It expressed displeasure over non-application of mind while making arrests, and non-compliance to the statutory provisions enjoined in the amended CrPC.

After the observation, the Court pronounced a series of guidelines that could be termed as classic examples of court pronounced directives to regulate or control the arrest discretion behaviour. The directives include issuance of instructions from the state government to the police officers not to automatically make an arrest when a case is registered but to satisfy themselves first about the necessity of an arrest under the provisions of Section 41 of the CrPC, and that the checklist complied with stating the reasons and materials which made it necessary to make an arrest while producing the accused before the Judicial Magistrate for further detention. With regard to accountability, the judgement in the same breath directed that failure of compliance would make the police officer liable for the departmental action and for the contempt of court proceedings. The Crime Branch of Odisha Police issued a circular in compliance to the directives of the Supreme Court in the form of CB Circular 350/2014 in the year 2014, which is a check list requiring the investigating officer intending to arrest an offender in a "noticeable" offence to record his grounds of belief in order to justify the arrest as enjoined in Section 41(1)(b)(ii) CrPC. *(Appendix L)*

The present study seeks to test the hypothesis that the "organisation through issue of guidelines and the Court through its judgment shapes the inevitable use of discretion and can influence its proper exercise". A higher value on the Arrest Discretion Response Statement for these three response predictors, R-2, R-3 and R-4, will validate the hypothesis. For all three responses, the summated "agree" and "strongly agree" responses come to 81.9, 81.9 and 84.3 percent, which validate this hypothesis.

R-5 relates to the provision of Odisha Police Manual Rules 221, which was inserted in the Manual in the year 1996 following the directives of the Supreme Court in Joginder Kumar.[2]

The service of notice to an offender in offences except in heinous ones was suggested by the Supreme Court of India way back in 1994.[3] This served as the prelude to the 177th Report of the Law Commission on laws relating to arrests. Interestingly, in the year 1996, the police manual of Odisha incorporated the directive much before it became part of the procedural law of India in the year 2009. But there was not a single instance of service of notice following the insertion of this provision in the Odisha Police Manual till the amendment of the CrPC in 2009. It means that either the police officers did not take note of this significant amendment in the police manual rules or the department did not make the officers accountable for non-compliance. The compliance, howsoever little, came only after the provisions became part of the amended CrPC in 2009 and more so after the Supreme Court took note of the non-compliance and put an accountability mechanism in place in the year 2014.[4] This throws light on yet another hypothesis that statute and court monitored accountability mechanism ensures more procedural compliance than that of the organisation, though both are intended to influence arrest discretion behaviour. R-5 validates this observation with about 77.9 percent respondents of the Odisha police agreeing or strongly agreeing with the response predictor.

An important aspect of the policy dimension emphasises upon the department's internal review mechanism on compliance to the arrest procedures. Such review mechanisms are important as they formalise the policy process for developing the guidelines that set particular standards, shape the inevitable use of discretion by the police officers and can influence control over proper exercise of police discretion (Groeneveld 2005). R-6 captures this aspect with a suitable response statement. While 73.6 percent of the respondents have either agreed or strongly agreed that the police departments have robust internal review mechanisms to ensure compliance to arrest procedures, 17.5 percent of the respondents disagree to any such strong mechanism. The high percentage response of "agree" and "strongly agree" denotes the fact that strong internal review mechanism of arrest procedures in the organisation regulates exercise of discretion.

To sum up, a significantly higher percentage of agreement for all the dimensions under policy determinants shows that departmental policies play a significant role in regulating arrest discretion control, though each with different degrees.

5.3.2 Process Dimensions

The process dimensions focus mainly on organisational procedures and protocols such as supervisory review and the disciplinary procedures for intentional violation of arrest policy (Groeneveld 2005). The process dimension includes organisational imposition of procedures that must be followed while making arrests and puts accountability mechanism in place for exercise of unwarranted discretion. Use of such procedures allows the organisation to exercise influence over arrest discretion through supervisory scrutiny and imposition of sanctions against non-compliance. The dimension has been captured by four response predictors, broadly falling under two categories. Firstly, the weightage or the say of the senior supervisory officers in arrest decision; the powers of supervisory officers have been defined under Section 36 CrPC, which is equivalent to that of a station house officer (officer-in-charge of a police station). In a hierarchical organisation like police, the directions of the supervisory officer on whether to arrest and when to arrest the accused take precedence over the personal judgement of the investigating officer, thereby limiting the latter's discretionary latitude. R-7 and R-8 (R-5 and R-6 for IPS officers of rest of Odisha) capture these aspects by devising suitable response statement. Secondly, the existence of disciplinary procedures for intentional violation of arrest policies ensures accountability. In a way, the sanctions against wrongdoing or intentional violations of procedures pave way for accountability. Individual accountability is a key factor against abuse of discretion. This aspect is intended to be captured by response statements coded, R-9 and R-10 (R-7 and R-8 for IPS officers of rest of Odisha). The four indicators or response predictor variables for process dimensions are enlisted in Table 5.5.

5.3.2.1 Frequency Table Analysis for Process Dimensions

Four response statements have been suitably prepared capturing each of the dimensions under this determinant – statement that is meaningful to the "world of experience" and collectively they must represent the conceptual

Table 5.5 Process dimension; response predictor variables

Indicators or response predictor variables	*Code (Odisha)*	*Code (others)*
Supervisory monitoring; IIC, SDPO/ACP, SP/DCP take decision on arrest procedure in specific cases	R-7	R-5
Weightage to supervisory instructions over personal judgement; it takes precedence over personal judgement	R-8	R-6
Discovery of procedural violations; department has mechanism in place to detect violations of arrest procedure	R-9	R-7
Departmental/legal actions; the department places strong emphasis on departmental action for intentional violation of arrest guidelines	R-10	R-8

Table 5.6 Frequency table for process dimension

Code No.	*Response*	*Frequency and percentage*			
		R-7/R-5	*R-8/R-6*	*R-9/R-7*	*R-10/R-8*
1	Strongly Disagree	6 (1.7)	8 (2.2)	7 (1.9)	15 (4.2)
2	Disagree	43 (11.9)	74 (20.6)	108 (30.0)	101 (28.1)
3	Cannot Say	10 (2.8)	32 (8.9)	61 (16.9)	39 (10.8)
4	Agree	189 (52.5)	176 (48.9)	155 (43.1)	143 (39.7)
5	Strongly Agree	112 (31.1)	70 (19.4)	29 (8.1)	62 (17.2)
	Total	360 (100)	360 (100)	360 (100)	360 (100)

NB: The figures in the parenthesis represent the percentage share.

space. The frequency of agreement and disagreement of the respondents have been calculated on the basis of their responses to the indicators or predictor variables to study the degree of influence the process dimension exerts on the arrest discretion behaviour. Table 5.6 shows the combined frequency chart of summated ratings corresponding to the category descriptors used for this response format.

Statements coded R-7/R-5 and R-8/R-6 are meant to elicit response on influence of supervisory monitoring on arrest discretion behaviour. As discussed in the preceding section, the supervisory police officers enjoy statutory powers over the subordinate ranks and ordinarily their views take precedence over those of the juniors. So, it is expected that a higher percentage of population would either agree or strongly agree to the two predictor statements.

All together, 83.6 percent of the respondents either agree or strongly agree to the statement (R-7/R-5) that it is the supervisory officers who take decision on the matter of arrest in specific cases. But on the question of whether the instructions of supervisory officers take precedence over the personal judgement, 68.3 percent (R-8/R-6) of the population believes it to be so, while 22.8 percent don't agree to this proposition. It establishes that a statistically significant population endorses that the views or opinions of supervisory officers considerably influence the arrest decisions of the subordinates. Further, it validates the hypothesis that organisational dimension like supervisory monitoring and instructions is positively correlated to arrest decision behaviour.

5.3.3 Value Dimensions

The departmental values address the extent to which the organisation attempts to influence arrest processes. According to Groeneveld (2005), the professional character of the organisation sets the tone for the members. As the police organisations start working with the community, the field officers increasingly rely on values instead of the departmental norms or procedures. The indicators, such as the operational independence, discretionary choices and effect of community policing have been included under this dimension. However, training which could have been an exclusive dimension has been clubbed with value dimension for the purpose of this study. The conceptual space of the dimensions has been captured by four predictor variables with six statements, one each for operational independence and two each for discretionary choices and community policing. The six indicators or response predictor variables for value dimensions are enlisted in Table 5.7.

Table 5.7 Value dimension; response predictor variables

Indicators or response predictor variables	*Code (Odisha)*	*Code (others)*
Independence: Investigating officers sometimes have to make arrest decisions on their personal judgement as opposed to guidelines	R-11	R-9
Discretionary Choice: Arrests in some instances are carried out before formalities like collection of evidences	R-12	R-10
Discretionary Choices: the five conditions under Sec 41(1)(b)(ii) for arresting an offender in noticeable offence give enough discretionary choices to the police officer	R-13	R-11
Training: subject like "exercise of discretion" is not part of formal police training	R-14	R-12
Training: police training specifically addresses issues like officer's arrest decisions	R-15	R-13
Community Policing: community policing practices will help reduce abuse of arrest powers	R-16	R-14

5.3.3.1 Frequency Table Analysis for Value Dimensions

Six statements have been carefully chosen for operationalisation of the components under the value dimension. R-11/R-9 captures the operational independence, R-12/R-10, R-13/R-11 the discretionary choices, R-14/R-12, R-15/R-13 the training component and R-16/R-14 the community policing aspect. The frequency of agreement and disagreement of the respondents have been calculated on the basis of their response to the indicators or predictor variables on the Arrest Discretion Response Statement to study the degree of influence that value dimensions exert on arrest discretion behaviour. Table 5.8 shows the combined frequency chart of summated ratings corresponding to the category descriptors used for this response format.

Response statement R-11/R-9 is designed to elicit information on how much operational independence the officers enjoy to manoeuvre on a larger discretional latitude. The courts have been critical of the wide discretionary powers the police officers enjoy while effecting arrest and have been delivering judgements to regulate the unbridled powers. The directives of the Supreme Court in *Joginder Kumar*,[5] *D.K. Basu*[6] and *Arnesh Kumar*[7] have laid down guidelines to regulate the arrest discretion behaviour of police. The first two judgements served as a prelude to the amendment of a century-old arrest law in the CrPC. In spite of the statutory provisions and court pronouncements, 73.3 percent of the respondents either agree or strongly agree to the response statement that investigating officers sometimes have to make arrest decisions on their personal judgement as opposed to guidelines. This is revealing in that the larger proportion of population believes that scope for personal judgement exists within the boundary of statute.

Two very critical aspects of the study have been captured in the statements R-12/R-10 and R-13/R-11. Both are related to discretionary choices.

Table 5.8 Frequency table for value dimension

Code no.	*Response*	*Frequency and percentage*					
		R-11/ R-9	*R-12/ R-10*	*R-13/ R-11*	*R-14/ R-12*	*R-15/ R-13*	*R-16/ R-14*
1	Strongly Disagree	19 (5.3)	13 (3.6)	8 (2.2)	6 (1.7)	15 (4.2)	6 (1.7)
2	Disagree	80 (22.2)	65 (18.1)	25 (6.9)	62 (17.2)	123 (34.2)	47 (13.1)
3	Cannot Say	8 (2.2)	9 (2.5)	10 (2.8)	37 (10.3)	41 (11.4)	37 (10.3)
4	Agree	190 (52.8)	202 (56.1)	181 (50.3)	184 (51.1)	155 (43.1)	196 (54.4)
5	Strongly Agree	63 (17.5)	71 (19.7)	136 (37.8)	71 (19.7)	26 (7.2)	74 (20.6)
	Total	360 (100)	360 (100)	360 (100)	360 (100)	360 (100)	360 (100)

NB: The figures in the parenthesis represent the percentage share.

Statement, R-12/R-10 is intended to elicit response on the oft-criticised police practice to arrest an accused person before collection of evidences in spite of litany of court directives and requirements of the statute proscribes such practices. The respondents (75.8 percent) believe that arrests in some instances precede formalities like collection of evidences. This casts doubt on the efficacy of accountable mechanism of the department against intentional violation of arrest guidelines.

Statement R-13/R-11 intends to find out how do the officers react to the statutory discretionary choices provided under the amended provisions of Section 41 CrPC. The provisions under 41(1)(b)(ii) of CrPC are a rider or exception clause, which state that the police can arrest any person without warrant if such person has committed a cognisable offence punishable with imprisonment up to seven years provided that the police officer is satisfied that such arrest is necessary –

(a) to prevent such person from committing further crime, or
(b) for proper investigation, or
(c) to prevent such person from tampering with evidence, or
(d) to prevent such person from making any inducement and threat to any witness, or
(e) to ensure the presence of such person in the Court whenever required. Otherwise, the person can be served with notice under Section 41A.

An overwhelming 88 percent of respondents believe that the conditions under Section 41(1)(b)(ii) provide enough statutory scope for exercise of discretion whether to arrest an accused person involved in a "noticeable" offence and vests enough discretionary choices in the police officer. Interestingly, while on one hand, the lawmakers amended the century-old arrest law dubbing it as archaic being unable to pass the constitutional test of "reasonableness" and that allows too much of discretion and subjectivity at the hands of police, on the other, the five rider clauses to the amended provisions of arrest are but wide discretionary latitudes to the police officer which cannot be vouched for not being subject to potential misuse.

As discussed in the preceding chapters, Davis (1969) argues that the police make far more discretionary decisions in individual cases than any other class of administrators. Surprisingly, most of the training academies do not teach "discretion" as a discipline. Most of the police officers are not even aware of the discretionary decisions they routinely make in everyday policing. Training prepares a newcomer to the organisation to contribute to the organisational goal. Therefore, training is expected to play a vital role in making the police officers aware of the discretionary choices they make, the value of good judgement and the potential abuse of discretionary powers. Response statements R-14/R-12 and R-15/R-13 are designed to validate the fact that "exercise of discretion" is not part of police training. About 71 percent of the respondents agree to this statement validating the proposition. While responding to the statement that police training specifically addresses issues like officer's arrest decision, only about 50 percent of the respondents agree to it, validating the observation that most of the police training curricula do not place emphasis on this critical aspect of policing.

Within the broad ambit of the dimension predictor variable, community policing has been included. Community policing as a strategy revolves around the philosophy of people-centric policing, partnership with citizens for crime prevention and decentralisation of the organisational hierarchy with a view to providing more decision-making powers to the field officers. Simultaneously, it ensures a layer of accountability to the police functions that are expected to influence decision-making process. Police in India have introduced several tactical dimensions of community policing within the broad policing functions. Response statement R-16/R-14 is expected to explore whether the accountability mechanism that community policing brings into the broad police functions could be helpful in regulating abuse of arrest powers. An overwhelming 75 percent of the respondents have either agreed or strongly agreed to this proposition.

To sum up, the summated values of response predictors under organisational determinants – policy, process and value – have validated several propositions under each dimension and combinedly prove the hypothesis that organisation through its policies, rules, regulations, supervisory control, compliance to the directives of the court, training, tactics and strategies influence the arrest discretion behaviour of its officers.

5.4 Subcultural Determinants

Having analysed the response frequency of three different dimensions under organisational determinants, this section examines the frequency responses under subcultural determinants.

Study of literature establishes that the members of the police organisation are guided by their own set of beliefs, attitudes and behaviour, what can be termed as police subculture. Four universally accepted police subcultural ethos have been carefully chosen for this study. Those are as follows: "Dirty Harry dilemma" (criminal justice system is ineffectual and justification of street justice), "us versus them" (public potentially hostile and untrustworthy), "thin blue (khaki) line" (thin line between order and chaos) and "code of silence" (to maintain solidarity and protect each other). For each of these dimensions, a statement has been created so that the respondents could relate it to the world of experience. The four response predictor variables or indicators with corresponding statements and codes are shown in Table 5.9.

5.4.1 Frequency Table Analysis for Subcultural Determinants

Response statement R-17/R-15 captures the "Dirty Harry dilemma" that prompts the police to take law into its hands and justify the excesses in larger

Table 5.9 Subcultural dimensions

Indicators or response predictor variables	*Code (Odisha)*	*Code (others)*
Dirty Harry Dilemma (criminal justice system is ineffectual): Arrest and pre-trial custody during investigation is the only punishment to the antisocials as they are most likely to get acquitted.	R-17	R-15
"Us versus them" (public potentially hostile and untrustworthy): The choice of serving notice to an accused person involved in an offence for which the punishment is up to seven years is likely to be attributed motive by the public.	R-18	R-16
"Thin Blue(khaki) Line" (thin line between order and chaos): Formal police arrest, not service of notice for appearance, is essential to maintain order in the society.	R-19	R-17
"Code of Silence" (to maintain solidarity and protect each other): Department and officers should protect each other while there is allegation of illegal arrest by an officer as arrest is made for larger public interest.	R-20	R-18

societal interest. The breach of discretionary boundary is strenuously justified by the police as dispensation of street justice, an eye for an eye. Statement R-18/R-16 is related to the subcultural trait that makes police believe that public are unappreciative of their constraints and potentially hostile and untrustworthy. Public would attribute motive to the practice of serving notice to the accused person instead of formal arrest. The perception is likely to force an officer to resort to avoidable arrests. Yet another subcultural ethos is that police are the sole agency of the society to maintain order and that there is a thin line between order and chaos. This reinforces the perception among the police officers that the amended arrest law is less potent than its pre-amendment counterpart. This has been captured by the statement R-19/R-17. The last of the dimensions for this study has been taken as the quintessential "code of silence". It's an unwritten oath among the police camaraderie to protect each other in a potentially hostile working environment, and therefore an instance of abuse of discretion has slim chance of being brought to light. In spite of the responses on such a contentious predictor being affected by the "code of silence" itself, an attempt has been made in this study to elicit responses of the police officers through statement R-20/R-18. Table 5.10 shows the combined frequency chart of summated ratings corresponding to the category descriptors.

About 61 percent of the respondents either agree or strongly agree to the existence of the subcultural ethos, Dirty Harry dilemma, in the organisation. This means that more than half of the population endorses the view that police excesses are sometimes justified for larger societal interest. About 35 percent of respondents however disagree to this proposition. More than

Table 5.10 Frequency table for subcultural dimensions

Code no.	*Response*	*Frequency and percentage*			
		R-17/R-15	*R-18/R-16*	*R-19/R-17*	*R-20/R-18*
1	Strongly Disagree	26 (7.2)	5 (1.4)	13 (3.6)	31 (8.6)
2	Disagree	99 (27.5)	61 (16.9)	110 (30.6)	104 (28.9)
3	Cannot Say	17 (4.7)	47 (13.1)	28 (7.8)	27 (7.5)
4	Agree	127 (35.3)	204 (56.7)	162 (45.0)	140 (38.9)
5	Strongly Agree	19 (25.3)	43 (11.9)	47 (13.1)	58 (16.1)
	Total	360 (100)	360 (100)	360 (100)	360 (100)

NB: The figures in the parenthesis represent the percentage share.

68 percent of the population endorse the trait, “us versus them”, perceiving the public to be untrustworthy, hostile and unappreciative. This subcultural ethos is likely to force an officer to resort to unavoidable arrest with a view to attracting public approbation for his acts. About 58 percent of the respondents believe that formal arrest should be the norm, and service of notice should be an exception. This is a reflection of the subcultural trait – thin blue (khaki) line. As was anticipated, the code of silence has affected the predictor statement under the same heading. More than half of the respondents (55 percent) have endorsed the statement that “department and officers should protect each other while there is allegation of illegal arrest by an officer as arrest is made for larger public interest”. The fact remains that the majority of the respondents either agree or strongly agree to all four subcultural traits within the police organisation.

5.5 Environmental Determinants

Having regard to the Indian context, the macro external environment in which the police organisation is embedded and influenced by the political culture, pressure groups and media are taken as factors influencing the decision-making processes. The media, public opinion, public reaction and political influences create a complex maze within which the police operate. Each of these components either independently or in combination influences decision-making processes of the police. From the foregoing discussions, the environmental dimension thus has been represented by the following four indicators. The four response predictor variables or indicators with corresponding statements and codes are shown in Table 5.11.

Table 5.11 Indicators of environmental determinants

Indicators or response predictor variables	*Code (Odisha)*	*Code (others)*
Fall out of action: Arrest decisions are often taken having regard to the outcome of such decision in the law and order scenario	R-21	R-19
Public perception: Public perception of police action on specific cases considerably influences arrest decision	R-22	R-20
Media and civil society: Media and response of the civil society to a specific offence weighs on the officer's arrest decision	R-23	R-21
Politics: Arrest decisions are sometimes taken on political consideration or influence	R-24	R-22

5.5.1 Frequency Table Analysis for Environmental Determinants

Response statements coded R-21/R-19 intend to capture how much the officer is influenced by the fall out of his action before taking decision on arrest in certain instances. For example, irate mob demands immediate arrest and custody of an offending driver who is accused of a run over death of a local resident even though the punishment prescribed for the offence entitles him service of notice. Citing statute and releasing the accused driver with service of notice may not convince the irate mob. Such decision may be fraught with risk of road blockade and demonstration before the police station. Statement R-22/R-20 is a corollary to the first predictor variable. Public perception of police action in certain instances is gauged by the officer before making a decision on arrest. In instances of vandalism of government institutions or intimidation and assault to high political or government functionary prompt arrest saves the day for the police, even before conduct of basic formalities of investigation and collection of evidence. Arrest and long pretrial judicial custody are perceived by public as an alternate form of retributive justice. Public opinion is carried and shaped by the media and civil society. Therefore, media and civil society play a very critical role in influencing arrest decision of the police. Considerable amount of discretions are exercised by police when these two important constituents are expected to rake up any issue. Statement R-23/R-21 is designed to explore how much these two environmental factors influence the arrest decision. The National Police Commission in its Second Report in 1979, while highlighting the misuse of police by illegal or improper orders or pressures from political, executive or other extraneous sources, enlists typical situations or matters in which pressure is brought to bear on the police by political, executive and other extraneous sources. Statement R-24/R-22 seeks to explore this aspect from the respondents. Table 5.12 shows the combined frequency chart of summated ratings corresponding to the category descriptors used for this response format.

Table 5.12 Combined frequency chart of environmental determinants

Code no.	*Response*	*Frequency and percentage*			
		R-21/R-19	*R-22/R-20*	*R-23/R-21*	*R-24/R-22*
1	Strongly Disagree	5 (1.4)	5 (1.4)	6 (1.7)	16 (4.4)
2	Disagree	22 (6.1)	22 (6.1)	25 (6.9)	51 (14.2)
3	Cannot Say	27 (7.5)	14 (3.9)	16 (4.4)	23 (6.4)
4	Agree	227 (63.1)	243 (67.5)	217 (60.3)	208 (57.8)
5	Strongly Agree	79 (21.9)	76 (21.1)	96 (26.7)	62 (17.2)
	Total	360 (100)	360 (100)	360 (100)	360 (100)

NB: The figures in the parenthesis represent the percentage share.

About 85 percent of the respondents either agreed or strongly agreed to the proposition that arrest decisions are often taken after weighing the fall out or bearing of such decisions on the law and order scenario. On whether public perception of police action on specific cases considerably influences arrest decisions, an overwhelming 88.6 percent population endorse the proposition. This being a corollary to the earlier statement, the high endorsement is in the expected line. The influence of media and civil society in arrest decision is validated by 87 percent of the respondents. As regards political influence on arrest decisions, 75 percent of the population either agrees or strongly agrees to the proposition and about 18.6 percent disagrees. To sum up, each indicator or predictor variable under environmental determinants exerts considerable influence on arrest discretion behaviour of police, validating the hypothesis that predictors like public perception, media and civil society, and political elements influence the operating environment of the police.

5.6 Factors With Significant Contribution in Influencing Arrest Discretion

One of the objectives of this empirical task is to find out from among the dimensions which has significant contribution towards influencing the determinants – that is, organisational, subcultural and environmental – and which among the determinants has maximum contribution towards influencing arrest discretion behaviour of police. The perceived impact of each of these dimensions individually, as well as when compared and contrasted with each other, has been discussed in the following sections.

5.6.1 Policy, Process and Value Dimensions

Organisational influences over arrest discretion behaviour refer to the system of administrative rules, policies, compliance to court directives, training and supervisory controls designed to ensure conformity to the departmental directives and to the law. Literature establishes that the organisation controls the discretion through three principal sources: official policy, process and values. These dimensions capture the channel through which the organisation can influence or constraint the arrest discretion behaviour of the officers. One of the empirical tasks is to find out which among these three has maximum impact on arrest discretion in the presence of the other two. Table 5.13 shows the mean, standard deviation and correlation coefficients of the three variables coded, AX1, AX2 and AX3, respectively.

The empirical study of the organisational determinants with its three dimensions and several factors defining each dimension validate a number of hypotheses and presuppositions besides establishing the model developed in this study being a good fit to the data. Firstly, negligible to low relationship exists between the dimensions (correlation coefficient, r). This is consistent with the statistical notion that factors or dimensions should be additive, not cloning each other, such that the accumulation of the factors individually captures different aspects of the dimension and collectively they represent the conceptual space defined by the dimension. Secondly, positive value of correlation coefficients without large variance validates that the significance of each dimension is directionally similar to that of the others. Thirdly, the study gives empirical support to the hypothesis that "the way the organisation creates a structure for arrest discretion flows from three principal sources; official policy, process, and values". Fourthly, we find that although the policy dimension, which involves the letter of the law, is considered to be a more significant influence on the organisational determinant, the significance accorded to the process and value dimensions is no less.

Table 5.13 Organisational determinants

Dimensions (independent variables or predictors)	*Code*	*Mean*	*Correlation coefficient (r)*		
			AX_1	AX_2	AX_3
Policy Dimensions	**AX_1**	3.950 (±0.57)	1.00		
Process Dimensions	**AX_2**	3.563 (±0.63)	0.21	1.00	
Value Dimensions	**AX_3**	3.673 (±0.49)	0.10	0.10	1.00

NB: The values in the parenthesis represent the standard deviation.

5.6.2 Subcultural Determinants

Four dimensions under subcultural determinants have been carefully chosen for the study – "Dirty Harry dilemma", "us versus them", "thin blue (khaki) line" and "code of silence". Detailed interpretations of each connotation have been explained in the previous chapter (section 4.3) under the head operationalisation of the variables. Literature review establishes that police subcultural ethos plays an important role in shaping decision-making processes. The study intends to establish if it could be empirically established. In course of the data analysis of the frequency tables under subcultural determinants, it has been established that majority of the respondents either agree to or strongly agree to all the four strong subcultural traits within the police organisation with varying degrees of endorsement ranging from 55 to 68 percent. Also, existence of relatively large percentage of "disagrees" (34.7 percent for "Dirty Harry dilemma", 34.2 percent for "thin blue line" and 37.5 percent for "code of silence") is noted as compared to the dimensions under organisational determinants. It is to be found out whether the dimensions capture the essence of subcultural ethos and how they relate with one another to impact the core subcultural determinant. Table 5.14 shows the mean, standard deviation and correlation coefficient values of the four variables coded, BX1, BX2, BX3 and BX4, respectively.

The correlation coefficient ("r") values between any two factors vary from 0.13 (BX2&BX3) to 0.25 (BX1&BX4), which are low. The factor, "us versus them" has the highest mean of 3.61 among the four independent variables, indicating that it is considered a strong influence to arrest decisions. However, others perceived to be the strong subculture determinants including the "code of silence", "the thin blue/khaki line" and "Dirty Harry dilemma" do not fall far behind.

The empirical tests thus validate the study presupposition that the factors taken to represent the subcultural determinants are highly relevant, relatively independent of each other's sphere of influence and yet collectively define the conceptual space while the factor, "Dirty Harry dilemma" impacts the subcultural ethos relatively deeper than the other three factors.

5.6.3 Environmental Determinants

As in case of informal organisation/subcultural determinants, on the basis of literature review and having regard to Indian context, four dimensions have been chosen to represent the environmental determinants that influence arrest decisions. They are "fall out of the action", "public perception", "media and civil society" and "politics". One of the objectives of this empirical task is to prove if this presupposition is validated and which among the factors has most influence on the operating environment of the police. Table 5.15 shows the mean, standard deviation and correlation coefficient values of the four variables coded CX1, CX2, CX3 and CX4, respectively.

Table 5.14 Informal organisational/subcultural determinants

Factors (independent variables or predictors)	*Code*	*Mean*	*Correlation coefficient (r)*			
			BX_1	BX_2	BX_3	BX_4
Dirty Harry Dilemma	**BX_1**	3.44 (±1.32)	1.00			
Us versus them	**BX_2**	3.61 (±0.95)	0.21	1.00		
Thin Blue (khaki) line	**BX_3**	3.33 (±1.15)	0.14	0.13	1.00	
Code of silence	**BX_4**	3.25 (±1.27)	0.25	0.16	0.24	1.00

NB: The values in the parenthesis represent the standard deviation.

Table 5.15 Environmental determinants

Factors (independent variables or predictors)	*Code*	*Mean*	*Correlation coefficient (r)*			
			CX_1	CX_2	CX_3	CX_4
Fall out of action	**CX_1**	3.98 (±0.82)	1.00			
Public perception	**CX_2**	4.01 (±0.79)	0.42	1.00		
Media and civil society	**CX_3**	4.03 (±0.86)	0.32	0.51	1.00	
Politics	**CX_4**	3.69 (±1.05)	0.19	0.32	0.45	1.00

NB: The values in the parenthesis represent the standard deviation.

The correlation coefficient ("r") value between any two factors is low except in three instances:

0.42 between "fall out of action" and "public perception" (CX1&CX2), 0.45 between "media and civil society" and "politics" (CX3&CX4) and 0.51 between "public perception" and "media and civil society" (CX2&CX3) which are bordering between low and marked relationship ("r" from < ±0.20 is negligible, from ±0.20 to ±0.40 is low and from ±0.40 to ±0.70 is marked relationship). This could be explained by the fact that the police weigh the fall out of their actions on the basis of public perception. Both media and civil society shape the public opinion. Hence, it is not strange that both have shown marked correlation. Media and civil society on one hand and politics on other show marked correlation as police perceive them as external oversight agencies. But the relationships reflected through "r" value do not touch the midpoint value of marked relationship, that is, 0.55. The highest relationship coefficient is 0.51. Therefore, the factors cannot be said to have suffered multicollinearity.

The factors, "Media and civil society" and "public perception" have the highest means within the environmental determinants, although the difference in the means is almost marginal between these and the other two factors.

5.7 Degree of Influence of the Determinants on Arrest Discretion Behaviour

Having established the validity of the model developed in this study, the next task is to find out the relative importance of the three key variables, such as the organisational, subcultural environmental determinants in influencing the arrest discretion behaviour and to examine which among the three determinants has the maximum influence on the arrest discretion behaviour while controlling for the other determinants. Table 5.16 shows the mean, standard deviation and correlation coefficient values of the three determinants coded X1, X2, and X3, respectively.

The correlation coefficient ("r") value between any two factors varies from 0.19 (X1&X3) to 0.28 (X1&X3), which denotes low relationship. The environmental determinants with a mean of 3.928 seem to be considered extremely influential achieving more positive responses as compared to the other two dimensions. However, it must be noted that there are leaders and laggards on the factor level (discussed earlier) which results in a raising or lowering the overall mean at the determinant level.

The findings on the face of it appear to be counter-intuitive. What could be the intuitive support for environmental and subcultural factors impacting the arrest discretion behaviour almost similarly or even more than the organisational determinants which are well defined with rules, regulations, statutes, departmental sanctions etc. in influencing the arrest discretion behaviour? The variations may be explained by the degree of subjective interpretation of the concerned determinant. More the subjective interpretation, more would be the impact on arrest discretion behaviour. Organisational determinants are more objective with rules, regulations, court directives and organisational sanctions against violation being in place. This is an area receiving enormous attention by the police leaders, courts and the organisation itself. The discretionary latitude here is well defined and sanction awaits anyone against breach of discretionary boundary. On the other hand, the conceptual space within the subcultural ethos or environmental determinants is complex and intangible and therefore, likely to be more susceptible to subjective interpretation. Where there is more scope for subjective interpretation of a situation, the decision-making is more likely to be non-uniform. This is reflected in the values of standard deviation over the mean values of the response statements of the three determinants. Standard deviation represents a quantity expressing how much the members of a group differ from the mean value of the group. Table 5.16 shows the mean values and standard deviations of the response statements for the three determinants. It is noticed that the informal

Table 5.16 Determinants of arrest discretion behaviour

Determinants (independent variables or predictors)	*Code*	*Mean*	*Correlation coefficient (r)*		
			X_1	X_2	X_3
Organisational determinants	X_1	3.727 (±0.37)	1.00		
Subcultural determinants	X_2	3.408 (±0.74)	0.22	1.00	
Environmental determinants	X_3	3.928 (±0.64)	0.19	0.28	1.00

NB: The values in the parentheses represent the standard deviation.

subcultural determinants show highest standard deviation (±0.74), followed by environmental determinants (±0.64) and least being organisational determinants (±0.37).

What does it signify? The respondents, ranging from frontline to senior officers in managerial positions, have reacted to the predictor variables of subcultural and environmental determinants with large variations than the organisational factors guided by rules and policies. The responses on the former two determinants call for more subjective assessment in the absence of written policies and guidelines. Therefore, the value of standard deviation for the predictor variables under organisational determinants is lower than what is noticed for the other two determinants. The response to organisational determinants shows relatively more central tendency and less variation as the response statements are based on statutes, departmental circulars, police manual orders, departmental sanctions against procedural transgression etc. The responses mimic the way police respondents react to the three different determinants in the field situation. In other words, officers process the organisational determinants more objectively and the subcultural and the environmental determinants more subjectively.

Now, having empirically proved that the police subculture and the operating environment influence the arrest discretion behaviour almost similarly or even more than the organisational constraints comprising the statutes, rules, circulars, court directives etc., it is imperative to look at the legal–extralegal debate in decision-making processes. Worden (1989) argues that "policing is for the most part extra-legal, for while officers (often) work within the constraints of the law, they seldom invoke the law in performing police work". Extralegal is not synonymous with illegal. Extralegal factors are those factors in decision-making which are not regulated or sanctioned by law, yet have influence on shaping the final outcome of the decision. Subcultural ethos and environmental determinants of arrest are but extralegal factors that have stronger influence on arrest decisions than the statutes or law per se, comprising the legal factors (Figure 2.1). Arrest decisions are made within the complex maze of legal and extralegal factors. The extralegal determinants have the potential for discretionary abuse. The challenge with the police management lies on how to regulate the influence of extralegal factors, as there is no one-size-fits-all solution to address the concerns. This is elaborated in the final chapter.

Notes

1 Arnesh Kumar v. State of Bihar, 2014 8 SCC 283
2 Joginder Kumar versus State Of U.P 1994 AIR 1349
3 Ibid.
4 Arnesh Kumar v. State of Bihar (2014) 8 SCC 283
5 Joginder Kumar versus State Of U.P 1994 AIR 1349
6 D K Basu versus State of West Bengal 1997 AIR SC 610
7 Arnesh Kumar versus State of Bihar (2014 8 SCC 283)

6 The Effects of Individual and Situational Factors on Arrest Discretion

This chapter deals with the individual and situational determinants of arrest discretion behaviour. One of the reasons to separately deal with the data analysis of these two determinants is the difference in methodology adopted here than that for the study of the organisational, subcultural and environmental factors. The studies on individual factors examine the characteristics such as gender, experience and position and their influences on officers' response to a situation including discretionary behaviour. The analyses are based on the study of the variables from within the sample respondents itself. For the situational determinant, having regard to the Indian context, the socio-economic survey of the offenders has been conducted *(Appendix E)* to find out if there is any correlation between the poor and marginalised being as such and their more likelihood of being arrested in comparison to their affluent counterparts under similar circumstances and whether the former category of respondents is less likely to exert their legal rights.

6.1 Analysis of Individual Determinants

Table 6.1 contains the gender break-up and Table 6.2 shows the years of experience of the respondents. Out of the study population, 16.7 percent are women officers of different ranks and 58 percent have put in more than 20 years of service as career police officers.

6.2 Individual Determinants: Gender, Experience and Position as Variables

The assumption here is that female, more experienced and senior supervisory officers will react differently to the arrest discretion determinants than their male, rookie and non-supervisory counterparts, respectively. For the purpose of experience, twenty years of service experience has been taken as the base year to split the respondents into two categories for comparative study. Officers of and above the rank of the Additional Superintendent of Police including all senior IPS officer respondents are categorised as supervisory officers

DOI: 10.4324/9781003406679-6

Table 6.1 Gender break-up of the respondents

Code no.	*Designation*	*Frequency*	*Percentage*
1	Male	300	83.3
2	Female	60	16.7
Total		**360**	**100.0**

Table 6.2 Years of service of the respondents

Code no.	*Experience*	*Frequency*	*Percentage*
1	0 to 10 years	81	22.5
2	11 to 20 years	70	19.5
3	21 to 30 years	156	43.3
4	31 years & above	53	14.7
Total		**360**	**100.0**

Table 6.3 Frequency distribution of the samples

Category	*Gender*		*Years of experience*		*Supervisory level*	
	Male – 1	*Female – 2*	*Up to 20Yrs – 1*	*>20Yrs – 2*	*Add1 SP & above – 1*	*DySP & below – 2*
Frequency	300	60	151	209	158	202
%	83.3	16.7	41.9	58.1	43.9	56.1
Total	360(100%)		360(100%)		360(100%)	

and rest as non-supervisory category for this study. A consolidated frequency distribution of the samples is placed in Table 6.3.

6.2.1 Gender as Variable

Table 6.4 represents the cross-table analysis of organisational determinants with gender as variables in respect of the fourteen response statements (R-1 to R-16 without R-4 and R-5; please refer Table 5.1).

Two response statements specific to Odisha Police have not been included as the sample tested here is from across India. They are originally part of the policy dimensions under organisational determinants. As such, four out of six response statements under policy dimensions (R-1, R-2, R-3 and R-6) have been included in this analysis, which may not affect the study outcome. Moreover, the responses will be studied with respect to individual predictor variable instead of combinations of variables comprising the conceptual space of a dimension. Response on a predictor variable with more than fifteen to twenty percent variations has been taken significant for analysis.

In Table 6.4, out of sixteen variables (R-1 to R-16), significance variations are noticed under R-2 (specific statutory guidelines), R-9 (discovery of procedural violations), R-10 (departmental sanction against intentional violations) and R-12 (discretionary choices). All together, 84.7 percent male respondents endorse that Arnesh Kumar guidelines[1] make arrest compliance specific and accountable as against 68.3 percent female respondents. As regards process dimensions, 48.7 and 54.7 percent male respondents, respectively, either agree or strongly agree that department has mechanism in place to detect violations of arrest procedure (R-9) and has strong emphasis on disciplinary action against intentional violation of arrest procedure (R-10). As against it, 63.3 and 68.3 percent of the female counterparts among the respondents endorse R-9, and R-10, respectively. R-12 represents the discretionary choice under the value dimensions. The response statement is intended to elicit whether the arrest precedes formalities like collection of evidences. About 78.3 percent male respondents either agree or strongly agree to this proposition as against 63.3 percent of female counterparts.

The pattern of response on the organisational variables on gender differentiation does not reveal anything significant except for the two responses, R-9 and R-10, under the process dimension. More female officers than their male counterparts perceive that the organisation has mechanism in place to detect and place sanctions against intentional violation of arrest procedures.

Table 6.5 presents the cross-table comparative values of subcultural determinants with gender as a variable.

The female counterparts score higher percentage of "agree" and "strongly agree" taken together under all the four variables of subcultural determinants; R-17 "Dirty Harry dilemma" 68.4 v. 59.0, R-18 "us and them" 76.6 v. 67.0, R-19 "thin blue/khaki line" 70.0 v. 55.7 and R-20 "code of silence" 81.0 v. 51.0. This shows that the subcultural determinants affect the female officer more in decision-making than their male counterparts. One interesting finding that is worth highlighting from the data analysis is the "code of silence", where the women officers outscore the male counterparts by more than fifty percent, which literally means that the female officers are less likely to speak out against a colleague's misconduct than their male counterparts.

The response frequency of environmental determinants with gender as a variable is placed in Table 6.6.

The frequency responses of both male and female counterparts under environmental determinants for all four variables do not show much of a significant difference; R-21 Fall out of action – 84.7 percent of males agree or strongly agree as against 86.7 females, R-22 Public perception – 89.3 v. 85.0, R-23 Media 87.4 v. 85.0 and R-24 Politics 76.0 v. 70.0. Hence, it may be deduced that the irrespective of gender the environmental determinants have by and large uniform impact on the arrest decision-making of police officers.

Table 6.4 Cross-table analysis of organisational determinants; gender as variable

Sl no.	*Response Statements*	*SD (1)*		*D (2)*		*CS (3)*		*A (4)*		*SA (5)*	
		1	*2*	*1*	*2*	*1*	*2*	*1*	*2*	*1*	*2*
1	R-1	3	2	17	3	3	0	191	45	86	10
		(1.0)	(3.3)	(5.7)	(5.0)	(1.0)	(0.0)	(63.7)	(75.0)	(23.9)	(16.7)
2	R-2	3	1	12	1	31	17	177	33	77	8
		(1.0)	(1.7)	(4.0)	(1.7)	(10.3)	(28.3)	(59.0)	(55.0)	(25.7)	(13.3)
3	R-3	2	1	17	6	31	10	174	32	76	11
		(0.7)	(1.7)	(5.7)	(10.0)	(10.3)	(16.7)	(58.0)	(53.3)	(25.3)	(18.3)
4	R-6	3	1	49	10	23	9	177	33	48	7
		(1.0)	(1.7)	(16.3)	(16.7)	(7.7)	(15.0)	(59.0)	(55.0)	(16.0)	(11.7)
5	R-7	5	1	37	6	9	1	158	31	91	21
		(1.7)	(1.7)	(12.3)	(10.0)	(3.0)	(1.7)	(52.7)	(51.7)	(30.3)	(35.0)
6	R-8	5	3	59	15	27	5	147	29	62	8
		(1.7)	(5.0)	(19.7)	(25.0)	(9.0)	(8.3)	(49.0)	(48.3)	(20.7)	(13.3)
7	R-9	5	2	96	12	53	8	125	30	21	8
		(1.7)	(3.3)	(32.0)	(20.0)	(17.7)	(13.3)	(41.7)	(50.0)	(7.0)	(13.3)
8	R-10	10	5	93	8	33	6	116	27	48	14
		(3.3)	(8.3)	(31.0)	(13.3)	(11.0)	(10.0)	(38.7)	(45.0)	(16.0)	(23.3)
9	R-11	15	4	70	10	5	3	160	30	50	13
		(5.0)	(6.7)	(23.3)	(16.7)	(1.7)	(5.0)	(53.3)	(50.0)	(16.7)	(21.7)
10	R-12	12	1	47	18	6	3	172	30	63	8
		(4.0)	(1.7)	(15.7)	(30.0)	(2.0)	(5.0)	(57.3)	(50.0)	(21.0)	(13.3)
11	R-13	7	1	20	5	9	1	154	27	110	26
		(2.3)	(1.7)	(6.7)	(8.3)	(3.0)	(1.7)	(51.3)	(45.0)	(36.7)	(43.3)
12	R-14	5	1	49	13	29	8	156	28	61	10
		(1.7)	(1.7)	(16.3)	(21.7)	(9.7)	(13.3)	(52.0)	(46.7)	(20.3)	(16.7)
13	R-15	13	2	101	22	37	4	127	28	22	4
		(4.3)	(3.3)	(33.7)	(36.7)	(12.3)	(6.7)	(42.3)	(46.7)	(7.3)	(6.7)
14	R-16	2	4	40	7	32	5	162	34	64	10
		(.7)	(6.7)	(13.3)	(11.7)	(10.7)	(8.3)	(54.0)	(56.7)	(21.3)	(16.7)

NB: 1 – Male, 2 – Female: Figures in parenthesis show %. Total for each row comes to 360 (100%); SD – Strongly Disagree, D – Disagree, CS – Cannot Say, A – Agree, SA – Strongly Agree; Refer Table 5.1 for variables R-1 to R-16

Table 6.5 Subcultural determinants; gender as variable

Sl no.	*Response Statements*	*SD (1)*		*D (2)*		*CS (3)*		*A (4)*		*SA (5)*	
		1	2	*1*	2	*1*	2	*1*	2	*1*	2
1	R-17	23 (7.7)	3 (5.0)	88 (29.3)	11 (18.3)	12 (4.0)	5 (8.3)	99 (33.0)	28 (46.7)	78 (26.0)	13 (21.7)
2	R-18	4 (1.3)	1 (1.7)	53 (17.7)	8 (13.3)	42 (14.0)	5 (8.3)	166 (55.3)	38 (63.3)	35 (11.7)	8 (13.3)
3	R-19	10 (3.3)	3 (5.0)	96 (32.0)	14 (23.3)	27 (9.0)	1 (1.7)	128 (42.7)	34 (56.7)	39 (13.0)	8 (13.3)
4	R-20	25 (8.3)	6 (10.0)	98 (32.7)	6 (10.2)	24 (8.0)	3 (5.0)	108 (36.0)	32 (53.3)	45 (15.0)	13 (27.7)

NB: 1 – Male, 2 – Female: Figures in parenthesis show %. Total for each row comes to 360 (100%); SD – Strongly Disagree, D – Disagree, CS – Cannot Say, A – Agree, SA – Strongly Agree; R-17 Dirty Harry dilemma, R-18 Us and them, R-19 Thin blue/khaki line, R-20 Code of Silence

Table 6.6 Environmental determinants; gender as variable

Sl no.	*Response Statements*	*SD (1)*		*D (2)*		*CS (3)*		*A (4)*		*SA (5)*	
		1	*2*	*1*	*2*	*1*	*2*	*1*	*2*	*1*	*2*
1	R-21	5	0	20	2	21	6	191	36	63	16
		(1.7)	(.0)	(6.7)	(3.3)	(7.0)	(10.0)	(63.7)	(60.0)	(21.0)	(26.7)
2	R-22	5	0	16	6	11	3	202	41	66	10
		(1.7)	(.0)	(5.3)	(10.0)	(3.7)	(5.0)	(67.3)	(68.3)	(22.0)	(16.7)
3	R-23	5	1	21	4	12	4	182	35	80	16
		(1.7)	(1.7)	(7.0)	(6.7)	(4.0)	(6.7)	(60.7)	(58.3)	(26.7)	(26.7)
4	R-24	13	3	41	10	18	5	179	29	49	13
		(4.3)	(5.0)	(13.7)	(16.7)	(6.0)	(8.3)	(59.7)	(48.3)	(16.3)	(21.7)

NB: 1 – Male, 2 – Female: Figures in parenthesis show %. Total for each row comes to 360 (100%); SD – Strongly Disagree, D – Disagree, CS – Cannot Say, A – Agree, SA – Strongly Agree; R-21 Fall out of action, R-22 Public perception, R-23 Media, R-24 Politics

6.2.2 Experience as Variable

The police officers in India are career civil servants and serve till the age of sixty, the common age for superannuation. For the purpose of this study, respondents with job experience of up to twenty years and more than twenty years have been taken as variables to find out if the determinants have differential impact with years of experience in the job. Out of the 360 participants, 151 (around 42 percent) have job experience of up to twenty years and rest 209 (around 58 percent) have experience beyond twenty years. Cross-frequency tables on the basis of their responses to predictor variables under organisational, subcultural and environmental determinants have been prepared to study if both the classes of respondents, differentiated on number of years put in the service, react differently to the discretionary determinants.

Table 6.7 represents the cross-table analysis of organisational determinants with years of experience in service as variables.

Significant variations in response are noticed only under three variables under organisational determinants – R-2 (Supreme Court guidelines in Arnesh Kumar case more specific on arrest procedure and ensures accountability), R-6 (internal review mechanism of compliance to arrest procedure) and R-15 (training addresses the arrest discretion behaviour). About 72 percent of respondents with up to twenty years of job experience either agree or strongly agree to the statement R-2, as against 87.3 percent of the respondents above twenty years of experience. This shows that relatively less percentage of officers under 20 years of work experience believe that the guidelines of the Supreme Court are significant in regulating arrest discretion behaviour. Relatively more percentage of such respondents (R-6, 79.5 as against 65 percent) endorse that department has mechanism in place for compliance to arrest procedures and that training addresses arrest discretion behaviour (R-15, 54.2 as against 44.5 percent).

Table 6.8 presents the cross-table comparative study of informal subcultural determinants with years of work experience as a variable.

Analysis of frequency cross-table shows that respondents under both categories do not react too differently to the variables under subcultural determinants except the "code of silence", represented by R-20. Relatively larger percentage of respondents with up to 20 years of work experience (65.8 percent) are more likely to be influenced by this subcultural ethos in comparison to their experienced counterparts (47.6), showing that with more years of experience in the organisation this subcultural imprint gradually wanes.

Table 6.9 presents the cross-table comparison values of environmental determinants with years of work experience as a variable.

Figures in frequency cross-table show that respondents of both categories do not react differently to the variables under environmental determinants (percentage of agree and strongly agree for R-21: 86.3 v. 84.2, R-22: 89.0 v. 88.3, R-23: 89.8 v. 85.1, R-24: 78.0 v. 75). This shows that respondents irrespective of their years of experience in the organisation react uniformly to the variables under environmental determinants.

Table 6.7 Cross-table analysis of organisational determinants; experience as variable

Sl no.	*Response Statements*	*SD (1)*		*D (2)*		*CS (3)*		*A (4)*		*SA (5)*	
		1	*2*	*1*	*2*	*1*	*2*	*1*	*2*	*1*	*2*
1	R-1	2 (1.4)	3 (1.4)	7 (4.8)	13 (6.1)	2 (1.4)	1 (.5)	107 (73.3)	129 (60.3)	28 (19.2)	68 (31.8)
2	R-2	0 (.0)	4 (1.9)	5 (3.4)	8 (3.7)	33 (22.6)	15 (7.0)	80 (54.8)	130 (60.7)	28 (19.2)	57 (26.6)
3	R-3	0 (.0)	3 (1.4)	10 (6.8)	13 (6.1)	18 (12.3)	23 (10.7)	87 (59.6)	119 (55.6)	31 (21.2)	56 (26.2)
4	R-6	2 (1.4)	2 (.9)	34 (23.3)	25 (11.7)	15 (10.3)	17 (7.9)	81 (55.5)	129 (60.3)	14 (9.6)	41 (19.2)
5	R-7	2 (1.4)	4 (1.9)	18 (12.3)	25 (11.7)	1 (.7)	9 (4.2)	72 (49.3)	117 (54.7)	53 (36.3)	59 (27.6)
6	R-8	3 (2.1)	5 (2.3)	30 (20.5)	44 (20.6)	7 (4.8)	25 (11.7)	72 (49.3)	104 (48.6)	34 (23.3)	36 (16.8)
7	R-9	4 (2.7)	3 (1.4)	40 (27.4)	68 (31.8)	29 (19.9)	32 (15.0)	60 (41.1)	95 (44.4)	13 (8.9)	16 (7.5)
8	R-10	8 (5.5)	7 (3.3)	39 (26.7)	162 (29.0)	17 (11.6)	22 (10.3)	57 (39.0)	86 (40.2)	25 (17.1)	37 (17.3)
9	R-11	9 (6.2)	10 (4.7)	33 (22.6)	47 (22.0)	4 (2.7)	4 (1.9)	65 (44.5)	125 (58.4)	35 (24.0)	28 (13.1)
10	R-12	4 (2.7)	9 (4.2)	32 (21.9)	33 (15.4)	4 (2.7)	5 (2.3)	80 (54.8)	122 (57.0)	26 (17.8)	45 (21.0)
11	R-13	3 (2.1)	5 (2.3)	17 (11.6)	8 (3.7)	1 (.7)	9 (4.2)	66 (45.2)	115 (53.7)	59 (40.4)	77 (36.0)

(Continued)

Table 6.7 (Continued)

Sl no.	*Response Statements*	*SD (1)*		*D (2)*		*CS (3)*		*A (4)*		*SA (5)*	
		1	*2*	*1*	*2*	*1*	*2*	*1*	*2*	*1*	*2*
12	R-14	3 (2.1)	3 (1.4)	26 (17.8)	36 (16.8)	17 (11.6)	20 (9.3)	71 (48.6)	13 (52.8)	29 (19.9)	42 (19.6)
13	R-15	7 (4.8)	8 (3.7)	56 (38.4)	67 (31.3)	18 (12.3)	23 (10.7)	55 (37.7)	100 (46.7)	10 (6.8)	16 (7.5)
14	R-16	5 (3.4)	1 (.5)	23 (15.8)	24 (11.2)	10 (6.8)	27 (12.6)	85 (58.2)	111 (51.9)	23 (15.8)	51 (23.8)

NB: 1 – up to 20 years, 2 – > 20 years; Figures in parenthesis show %. Total for each row comes to 360 (100%); SD – Strongly Disagree, D – Disagree, CS – Cannot Say, A – Agree, SA – Strongly Agree; Refer Table 5.1 for variables R-1 to R-16

Table 6.8 Subcultural determinants; experience as variable

Sl no.	*Response Statements*	*SD (1)*		*D (2)*		*CS (3)*		*A (4)*		*SA (5)*	
		1	*2*	*1*	*2*	*1*	*2*	*1*	*2*	*1*	*2*
1	R-17	11 (7.5)	15 (7.0)	38 (26.0)	61 (28.5)	9 (6.2)	8 (3.7)	55 (37.7)	72 (33.6)	33 (22.6)	58 (27.1)
2	R-18	1 (.7)	4 (1.9)	28 (19.2)	33 (15.4)	18 (12.3)	29 (13.6)	78 (53.4)	126 (58.9)	21 (14.4)	22 (10.3)
3	R-19	3 (2.1)	10 (4.7)	42 (28.8)	68 (31.8)	11 (7.5)	17 (7.9)	70 (47.9)	92 (43.0)	30 (13.7)	27 (12.6)
4	R-20	9 (6.2)	22 (10.3)	30 (20.5)	74 (34.6)	11 (7.5)	16 (7.5)	61 (41.8)	79 (36.9)	35 (24.0)	23 (10.7)

NB: 1 – up to 20 years, 2 – > 20 years; Figures in parenthesis show %. Total for each row comes to 360 (100%); SD – Strongly Disagree, D – Disagree, CS – Cannot Say, A – Agree, SA – Strongly Agree; R-17 Dirty Harry dilemma, R-18 Us and them, R-19 Thin blue/khaki line, R-20 Code of Silence

Table 6.9 Environmental determinants; experience as variable

Sl no.	*Response Statements*	*SD (1)*		*D (2)*		*CS (3)*		*A (4)*		*SA (5)*	
		1	*2*	*1*	*2*	*1*	*2*	*1*	*2*	*1*	*2*
1	R-21	1	4	6	16	13	14	85	142	41	38
		(.7)	(1.9)	(4.1)	(7.5)	(8.9)	(6.5)	(58.2)	(66.4)	(28.1)	(17.8
2	R-22	0	5	8	14	8	6	90	153	40	36
		(.0)	(2.3)	(5.5)	(6.5)	(5.5)	(2.8)	(61.6)	(71.5)	(27.4)	(16.8)
3	R-23	1	5	7	18	7	9	88	129	43	53
		(.7)	(2.3)	(4.8)	(8.4)	(4.8)	(4.2)	(60.3)	(60.3)	(29.5)	(24.8)
4	R-24	4	12	21	30	7	16	84	124	30	32
		(2.7)	(5.6)	(14.4)	(14.0)	(4.8)	(7.5)	(57.5)	(57.9)	(20.5)	(15.0)

NB: 1 – up to 20 years, 2 – > 20 years; Figures in parenthesis show %. Total for each row comes to 360 (100%); SD – Strongly Disagree, D – Disagree, CS – Cannot Say, A – Agree, SA – Strongly Agree; R-21 Fall out of action, R-22 Public perception, R-23 Media, R-24 Politics

6.2.3 Position as Variable

The police organisation functions in a hierarchal set-up with distinct job specifications for each position. The population in this study is from the rank of Sub-Inspector of Police to IPS officers, who occupy very senior supervisory positions. For the purpose of this analysis, the population have been split into two groups, one from the rank of Sub-Inspector of Police to Deputy Superintendent of Police, numbering 202 (about 57 percent) and the other comprising respondents from the rank of Additional Superintendent of Police to senior IPS officers, numbering 158 (about 44 percent). The former category has been taken as non-supervisory and the latter as supervisory category.

Table 6.10 represents the cross-table analysis of organisational determinants with position of the respondents in the organisation (supervisory and non-supervisory rank).

Analysis of the figures in the table shows that significant variations in opinion are noticed in six out of fourteen predictor variables under organisational determinants – R-2, R-9, R-10, R-11 and R-12. Statement R-2 denotes that the directive of the Supreme Court in Arnesh Kumar[2] case is presumed to have provided clarity to the amended provision of Section 41 CrPC and has placed accountability for violations. Higher percentage of supervisory officers endorses this response statement (about 88 percent) than the non-supervisory ranks (about 77 percent). Senior supervisory officers believe that department has to do more for detecting procedural violations of arrest (R-9; 45 percent v. 56 percent) and stronger emphasis on disciplinary action for intentional violation of arrest procedures (R-10; 51 percent v. 61 percent). Relatively more percentage of supervisory officers endorses the statement that an officer has to make decisions on arrest which is not always based on written policies (R-11; 74.7 v. 66.9 percent) and that arrest in many instances precede formalities like collection of evidences (R-12; 85.4 v. 68.3 percent). This testifies that the supervisory officers are more concerned about the discretionary abuse than their junior colleagues.

Table 6.11 presents the cross-table comparison values of subcultural determinants with position in the organisation as a variable.

Taking into account the frequency of "agree" and "strongly agree" for both the categories of study population, one comes across significant variations in all the four response predictors – R-17: 53 v. 66.4 percent, R-18: 61.4 v. 74.2 percent, R-19: 46.8 v. 66.8 percent and R-20: 43.7 v. 63.9 percent. This empirically establishes that supervisory officers are less likely to be affected by the subcultural determinants than their junior colleagues in the police organisation.

Study of responses for the environmental determinants with position as a variable does not show any marked differences of opinion, from which it may be concluded that operating environment affects the population by and large uniformly irrespective of the position in the organisation.

Table 6.10 Cross-table analysis of organisational determinants; position as variable

Sl no.	*Response Statements*	*SD (1)*		*D (2)*		*CS (3)*		*A (4)*		*SA (5)*	
		1	*2*	*1*	*2*	*1*	*2*	*1*	*2*	*1*	*2*
1	R-1	2 (1.3)	3 (1.5)	8 (5.1)	12 (5.9)	3 (1.9)	0 (.0)	97 (61.4)	139 (68.8)	48 (30.4)	48 (23.8)
2	R-2	2 (1.3)	2 (1.0)	1 (.6)	12 (5.9)	16 (10.1)	32 (15.8)	95 (60.1)	115 (56.9)	44 (27.8)	41 (20.3)
3	R-3	2 (1.3)	1 (.5)	9 (5.7)	14 (6.9)	23 (14.6)	18 (8.9)	86 (54.4)	120 (59.4)	38 (24.1)	49 (24.3)
4	R-6	3 (1.9)	1 (.5)	24 (15.2)	35 (17.3)	16 (10.1)	16 (7.9)	88 (55.7)	122 (60.4)	27 (17.1)	28 (13.9)
5	R-7	4 (2.5)	2 (1.0)	22 (13.9)	21 (10.4)	9 (5.7)	1 (.5)	91 (57.6)	98 (48.5)	32 (20.3)	80 (39.6)
6	R-8	4 (2.5)	4 (2.0)	37 (23.4)	37 (18.3)	20 (12.7)	12 (5.9)	71 (44.9)	105 52.0)	26 (16.5)	44 (21.8)
7	R-9	4 (2.5)	3 (1.5)	54 (34.2	54 (26.7)	29 (18.4)	32 (15.8)	55 (34.8)	100 (49.5)	16 (10.1)	13 (6.4)
8	R-10	9 (5.7)	6 (3.0)	48 (30.4)	53 (26.2)	20 (12.7)	19 (9.4)	57 (36.1	86 (42,6)	24 (15.2)	38 (18.8)
9	R-11	6 (3.8)	13 (6.4)	28 (17.7)	52 (25.7)	6 (3.8)	2 (1.0)	104 (65.8)	86 (42.6)	14 (8.9)	49 (24.3)
10	R-12	1 (.6)	12 (5.9)	15 (9.5)	50 (24.8)	7 (4.4)	2 (1.0)	104 (65.8)	98 (48.5)	31 (19.6)	40 (19.8)
11	R-13	2 (1.3)	6 (3.0)	6 (3.8)	19 (9.4)	4 (2.5)	6 (3.0)	93 (58.9)	88 (43.6)	53 (33.5)	83 (41.1)
12	R-14	0 (.0)	6 (3.0)	18 (11.4)	44 (21.8)	17 (10.8)	20 9.9	93 (58.9)	91 (45.0)	30 19.0	41 (20.3)
13	R-15	8 (5.1)	7 (3.5)	48 (30.4)	75 (37.1)	25 (15.8)	16 (7.9)	68 (43.0)	87 (43.1)	9 (5.7)	17 (8.4)
14	R-16	1 (.6)	5 (2.5)	16 (10.1)	31 (15.3)	22 (13.9	15 (7.4)	81 (51.3)	115 (56.9)	38 (24.1)	36 (17.8)

NB: 1 – Supervisory rank, 2 – Non-supervisory rank; Figures in parenthesis show %. Total for each row comes to 360 (100%); SD – Strongly Disagree, D – Disagree, CS – Cannot Say, A – Agree, SA – Strongly Agree; Refer Table 3.1 for variables R-1 to R-16

Table 6.11 Subcultural determinants; position as variable

Sl no.	*Response Statements*	*SD (1)*		*D (2)*		*CS (3)*		*A (4)*		*SA (5)*	
		1	*2*	*1*	*2*	*1*	*2*	*1*	*2*	*1*	*2*
1	R-17	14 (8.9)	12 (5.9)	52 (32.9)	47 (23.9)	8 (5.1)	9 (4.5)	59 (37.3)	68 (33.7)	25 (15.8)	66 (32.7)
2	R-18	3 (1.9)	2 (1.0)	32 (20.3)	29 (14.4)	26 (16.5)	21 (10.4)	85 (53.8)	119 (58.9)	12 (7.6)	31 (15.3)
3	R-19	5 (3.2)	8 (4.0)	56 (35.4)	54 (26.7)	23 (14.6)	5 (2.5)	68 (43.0)	94 (46.5)	6 (3.8)	41 (20.3)
4	R-20	21 (13.3)	10 (5.0)	54 (34.2)	50 (24.8)	14 (8.9)	13 (6.4)	58 (36.7)	82 (40.6)	11 (7.0)	47 (23.3)

NB: 1 – Supervisory rank, 2 – Non-supervisory rank; Figures in parenthesis show %. Total for each row comes to 360 (100%); SD – Strongly Disagree, D – Disagree, CS – Cannot Say, A – Agree, SA – Strongly Agree; R-17 Dirty Harry dilemma, R-18 Us and them, R-19 Thin blue/khaki line, R-20 Code of Silence

6.3 Relative Impact of Individual Determinants

One of the key assumptions of the study is that individual determinants, such as gender, work experience and position in the organisation, impact differently to arrest discretion behaviours. In order to test it empirically, multiple regression analysis has been adopted with gender, position and experience as independent variables and organisation, subculture and environment as dependent variables (Y1, Y2 and Y3, respectively). Independent variables, such as gender, position and experience have been arranged in order of male (1) v. female (2), supervisory rank (1) v. subordinate rank (2) and more than 20 years of work experience (1) v. less than 20 years (2), respectively, for this analysis. Table 6.12 shows the unstandardised coefficient (B), beta coefficients (β) and p-values under each variable. The higher the beta coefficient value, the greater the amount of unique change caused in the dependent variables (organisation, subculture and environment) by the independent variables (gender, experience and position)..

It is seen from the table that the significant p-values at 95 Percent level are 0.0 and 0.023 (less than 0.05), representing the relationship between subculture – position, and environment – experience, respectively. In other words, it can be said that for every one-unit change of supervisory position to subordinate level, the dependent variable, subculture changes by thirty percent (beta value being 0.291). This can be interpreted by stating that subordinate officers are more likely to believe that the subculture has a significant impact on arrest discretion and that they are more likely to be influenced by the subculture than their senior counterparts. The analysis of frequency tables (Table 6.11) with position and subculture as variables presents a similar finding.

Another significant relationship is noticed when experience is regressed with environment. The p-value here is 0.023 (<0.5). Having considered the beta value (0.136) for this relationship, it may be interpreted that the officers with less than twenty years of experience are more likely to react to the

Table 6.12 Regression analysis for individual determinants

Independent variables	*Y1_Organisation*			*Y2_Subculture*			*Y3_Environment*		
	UC "B"	*beta*	*p-value*	*UC "B"*	*beta*	*p-value*	*UC "B"*	*beta*	*p-value*
Gender	–.033	–.034	.556	.175	.088	.111	–.122	–.071	.214
Position	–.035	.048	.391	.434	.291	.000	.107	.083	.132
Experience	–.072	–.096	.107	.023	–.015	.787	.177	.136	.023

NB: $p < 0.05$ is significant at 95 Percent and < 0.1 significant at 90 Percent; UC – Unstandardised Coefficient environment, comprising the societal, media and political factors, than their more experienced counterparts. Here, the findings from the frequency tables (refer Table 6.9) give a not-so-significant relationship than what comes out of the regression analysis. This is understandable considering the fact that in the analysis of frequency tables variations in opinion over twenty percent is presumed as a precondition for data analysis.

In analysing the significance of p-values at ninety percent ($p < 0.1$), one relationship, though less significant, emerges while gender has been regressed with subculture. Females are relatively more affected by the impact of subculture than their male counterparts to the extent of nine percent (beta value – 0.088). This finding goes with what is observed in analysing the frequency table (refer Table 6.5) – the subcultural determinants affect the female officer more in decision-making than their male counterparts.

This validates the study hypothesis that individual determinants, such as gender, position and experience, in the organisation impact in varying degrees to the arrest discretion behaviour comprising the organisation, subculture and environment.

6.4 Data Analysis of Situational/Offenders' Determinants

In the Indian context, where no such previous empirical study has been attempted on the subject, the socio-economic status of the offenders has been surveyed to find out if there is a correlation between the poor and marginalised being as such and their more likelihood of being arrested in "noticeable offences" in comparison to their affluent counterparts under similar circumstances. This comparison aims to probe empirically if "racial profiling" has an equivalent in Indian policing. Numerous studies in the US context have proved that "discretion offers the opportunity for police officers to misuse it by treating offenders of different race, class, ethnicity etc. inappropriately" (Pepinsky 1984; Kleinig 1996). Racial profiling is an example of police discretion concerning race disparities, particularly the African-American and Hispanic population being at the receiving end of such differential treatment. The procedural laws of India provide a number of rights to an arrested person including right to be informed about the ground of arrest, right to be released on bail in bailable offences and right not to be detained for more than twenty-four hours by the police following the arrest. The awareness about the legal rights or lack of it depends upon the socio-economic condition of the individual. Relevant variables from situational/offender determinants in the Indian context have been studied by devising a suitable survey methodology, explained in Chapter 4. The interview schedule for this purpose is placed in *Appendix E*. The presupposition here is that socially and economically marginal members of the society are more likely to be at the receiving end of the discretional abuse of the police as they are less likely to exert their legal rights and to afford legal assistance.

6.5 Samples

For the purpose of selecting samples, twelve Districts have been selected by simple random method from three Revenue Divisions of the State of Odisha. From each of the Districts, three police stations have been selected purposively – one urban and two rural. Six persons (purposive) have been selected from each police station, out of which four have been arrested by police in "noticeable offences" and two have been served with notice for similar (noticeable) offences. Thus, the total number of respondents should have been 216 in the ratio of 2:1. But during field survey, 195 respondents could be contacted out of which sixty-eight persons have been served notice and the rest 127 have been arrested in "noticeable offences", which means police exercised its discretion in arresting some among the accused persons while preferred to serve notice to others in similar circumstances. The objective of taking purposive sample is to study if the respondents, who all are entitled to be served with notice instead of formal arrest as per the provision of the amended Section 41 CrPC, are subject to discriminatory treatment by the police for being members of socially and economically marginal sections of the society. The presumption here is that either they may not be able to exert their legal rights or they are unable to afford legal assistance.

The sample details for the study are placed in *Appendix K*. All the offender respondents are involved in offences that are punishable with imprisonment not exceeding seven years, which means that all of them could have been served notice instead of being formally arrested. But the sample is purposive in the sense that some of them have been arrested in "noticeable" offences and the objective here if such offender respondents (those arrested) could not be able to exert their legal rights due to their relatively lower socio-economic status than those who were served notice. This would throw light on the "poor and marginal" bias of the Indian police, if there is any. The study is intended to find out whether the respondents arrested (127) are socio-economically relatively poorer than the ones served with notice (68), and whether the former category of respondents is less likely to exert their legal rights and with lesser extent of legal awareness.

6.6 Socio-Economic Status of Offenders as Variables

The variables under socio-economic status are taken as caste, occupation, level of education, house pattern, land ownership and monthly income, corresponding to the output from serial 5 to 11 of the interview schedules in *Appendix E*.

6.6.1 Caste and Tribe as Variables

The Scheduled Castes (SCs) and Scheduled Tribes (STs) are officially designated groups of historically disadvantaged people in India and have been so categorised in the Indian Constitution to be beneficiaries of certain schemes as positive discrimination. The SCs and the STs in India comprise about 16.2–8.2 percent of the population, respectively.[3] They have been given certain percentage of reservation in political representation and government jobs. The Indian Constitution has laid down the general principles for the positive discrimination of SCs and STs. Other Backward Classes (OBCs) is a term used by the Government of India to refer to the castes which are educationally or socially disadvantaged collectively. It is one of the several official classifications of the population of India, along with the Scheduled Castes (SCs) and the Scheduled Tribes (STs). The Mandal Commission Report[4] of 1980 stated that the OBC population of the country then comprised 52 Percent of the total population whereas according to a 2006 report of National Sample Survey[5] it is pegged at 41 Percent. However, the exact percentage of OBC population in the country is debatable. Rest of the population are considered upper caste and termed general category. Table 6.13 shows the percentage of offender respondents arrested or served notice under each of the four categories, viz., SC, ST, OBC and general category.

The study shows that the percentage of offenders served with notice in SC and ST categories is more than those arrested in noticeable offences. About 22 percent offender respondents have been arrested as against 26.5 percent served with notice. On the contrary, a higher percentage of offender respondents in the case of OBC and general category offenders have been arrested in "noticeable offences". The findings with respect to relatively well-off population do not support presupposition that caste or tribe status make the population more vulnerable to discretionary abuse.

6.6.2 *Occupations as Variables*

Table 6.14 shows the occupations as variables. Cultivation, wage earning, trade or business, government jobs etc. have been taken as variables of occupation.

Among the occupations, cultivation is considered to be the breadwinner for the poorer section of the society. About 41.2 percent of such offender

Table 6.13 Caste/tribe as variables

Sl	*Variables*	*Cross-tabulation*	
		Arrest	*Notice*
1	Scheduled Caste	28 (22.0)	18 (26.5)
2	Scheduled Tribe	18 (14.2)	13 (19.1)
3	OBC	40 (31.5)	19 (27.9)
4	General	41 (32.3)	18 (26.5)
Total		127 (100)	68 (100)

NB: Figures in parenthesis are the percentage values

Table 6.14 Occupations as variables

Sl	*Variables*	*Cross-tabulation*	
		Arrest	*Notice*
1	Cultivation	15 (11.8)	28 (41.2)
2	Wage earner	51 (40.2)	21 (30.9)
3	Trading/business	10 (7.9)	6 (8.8)
4	Govt. Service	5 (3.9)	3 (4.4)
5	Others	45 (35.4)	9 (13.2)
Total		127 (100)	68 (100)

NB: Figures in parenthesis are the percentage values

Table 6.15 Education as variable

Sl	*Variables*	*Cross-tabulation*	
		Arrest	*Notice*
1	Up to Std V	33 (26.0)	16 (23.5)
2	Std VI to VIII	47 (37.0)	27 (39.7)
3	High School	23 (18.1)	9 (13.2)
4	Higher Secondary	9 (7.1)	8 (11.8)
5	Graduation and above	15 (11.8)	8 (11.7)
Total		127 (100)	68 (100)

NB: Figures in parenthesis are the percentage values

respondents have been served notice as against 11.8 percent of such class arrested, three and half times than those arrested. This is a substantial proportion of the population. Though more percentage of offender respondents have been served notice in occupations like trade or business or government job, this is statistically insignificant. Here also, the presupposition of "poor and marginal bias" of police does not get validated.

6.6.3 Education as Variable

It is presupposed that lack or less of education is an indicator of lower socio-economic status. Five variables for educational level attained by the offender respondents have been taken; up to Std V, Std VI to VIII, high school, higher secondary, graduation and beyond. Table 6.15 shows levels of education as variables.

The cross-tabulation analysis shows that 63.2 percent of the offender respondents were served notices as against 63 percent arrested, who studied up to Standard VIII. With relatively higher educational level – high school and above – the figures for both "arrest" and "notice" categories are almost equal; 36.8 v. 37 percent. Higher level of education of the offenders does not show any positive correlation with mobilising law to their advantage.

6.6.4 *House Types as Variables*

Cross-tabulation of house types of the offender respondents served notice and arrested, placed in Table 6.16 however indicates that those with asbestos and RCC houses (relatively well off) have been able to mobilise law to protect their interests compared to those living in thatched houses.

6.6.5 *Landholdings as Variables*

Landholding is a strong social stratification indicator in the Indian context. People with larger landholdings are economically better off than those without land or with marginal holdings. Land is considered as an immovable asset. Analysis of landholding pattern of the offender respondent indicates that people without land and with marginal holdings are at a disadvantage to mobilise law to protect their interest. Table 6.17 shows landholdings as variables.

Table 6.16 House types as variables

Sl	*Variables*	*Cross-tabulation*	
		Arrest	*Notice*
1	Thatch	33 (26.0)	15 (22.1)
2	Asbestos	35 (27.6)	21 (30.9)
3	RCC	39 (30.7)	26 (38.2)
4	Any other	20 (15.7)	6 (8.8)
Total		127 (100)	68 (100)

NB: Figures in parenthesis are the percentage values

Table 6.17 Landholdings as variables

Sl	*Variables*	*Cross–tabulation*	
		Arrest	*Notice*
1	Landless	61 (48.0)	24 (35.3)
2	< 1 acre	37 (29.1)	21 (30.9)
3	> 1 acre < 2 acres	19 (15.0)	17(25.0)
4	> 2acres < 4 acres	9 (7.1)	1 (1.5)
5	> 4 acres	1 (0.8)	5 (7.4)
		127(100)	68 (100)

NB: Figures in parenthesis are the percentage values

Table 6.18 Income as variable

Sl	*Variables in Rs*	*Cross-tabulation*	
		Arrest	*Notice*
1	Up to 1000	14 (11.0)	9 (13.2)
2	>1000 < 2000	16 (12.6)	10 (14.7)
3	>2000 < 5000	43 (33.9)	32 (47.1)
4	>5000 < 10000	41 (32.3)	7 (10.3)
5	>10000 < 15000	6 (4.7)	4 (5.9)
6	>15000	7 (5.5)	6 (8.8)
Total		127 (100)	68 (100)

NB: Figures in parenthesis are the percentage values

6.6.6 *Income as Variable*

Income is a direct reflection of the economic status of an individual. The cross-tabulation shown in Table 6.18 brings out an interesting empirical finding. Offenders with income less than Rs 5000 have been able to mobilise law to their advantage. All together, 75 percent of such category of the offenders has been served notice as against 57 percent who have been arrested in noticeable offences. What is interesting to note is that offenders with higher income (more than Rs 5000 per month) have not been successful to mobilise law to their advantage. About 43 percent from the higher income group have been arrested as against 25 percent being served with notice.

The foregoing discussions show that caste, education, house type, landholding, income etc. as social stratifications do not have positive correlation with mobilisation of law to one's advantage.

6.7 Awareness of Legal Rights

The procedural law of India provides a number of legal rights to the offender. Some of the rights which are considered for the purpose of this survey are as follows: collection of evidence should precede arrest, notice instead of arrest in offences punishable less than seven years, bail is a matter of right in bailable offences, police custody is not extended beyond twenty-four hours and arrestee to be informed about the ground of arrest. The responses are analysed to study if the respondents (all offenders here) are aware of these rights with the presupposition that assertion of rights follows only after the awareness of their existence. Table 6.19 captures the response of the population.

The percentage of legal awareness of the respondent offenders served with notice is more under five response statements from Sl 2 to Sl 5. This validates the presupposition that offenders with higher degree of legal awareness are more likely to mobilise law to their advantage.

Table 6.19 Awareness of legal rights

Sl	*Legal rights*	*Cross-tabulation*			*Total*
	Awareness	*Yes*	*No*	*Can't say*	
1	Police should arrest only after collection of evidence	52 (40.9)^	30 (23.6)^	45 (23.1)^	127 (100)^
		22 (32.4)*	13 (19.1)*	33 (48.5)*	68 (100)*
2	Police should issue notice if offence is punishable within seven years	5 (3.9)^	55 (43.3)^	67 (52.8)^	127 (100)^
		9 (13.2)*	22 (32.4)*	37 (54.9)	68 (100)*
3	Bail at the police station is a matter of right	17 (13.4)^	48 (37.8)^	62 (48.8)^	127 (100)^
		12 (17.6)*	18 (26.5)*	38 (55.9)*	68 (100)*
4	Courts grant bails in non-bailable offences	36 (28.3)^	25 (19.7)^	66 (52.0)^	127 (100)^
		22 (32.4)*	13 (19.1)*	33 (48.5)*	68 (100)*
5	Police custody shall not exceed more than 24 hours	44 (34.6)^	37 (29.1)^	46 (36.2)^	127 (100)^
		29 (42.6)*	12 (17.6)*	27 (39.7)*	68 (100)*
6	Arrestee should be informed about the ground of arrest and relative to be informed	35 (27.6)^	52 (40.9)^	40 (31.5)^	127 (100)^
		25 (36.8)*	18 (26.5)*	25 (36.8)*	68 (100)*

NB: Figures in parenthesis show the percentage; ^ indicates respondents arrested; * indicates the respondents served notice

6.8 Legal Assistance

Legal assistance during pre-arrest or arrest period is an option for the offender respondents to assert their legal rights. The survey intends to examine if respondents consulted a lawyer or person acquainted with police procedures or known to the police before their arrest. The response is captured in Table 6.20.

It shows that higher percentage of respondents who were served notice consulted a lawyer or person acquainted with police procedures than those arrested, validating the presupposition that legal consultation increases the likelihood of offender to mobilise law to his own advantage.

To sum up, study establishes that both male and female respondents positively impact the arrest discretion behaviour through organisational, subcultural and environmental factors. Females are more likely to be influenced

Table 6.20 Legal assistance

SL no.	Response statement "Consulted the following before arrest"	Cross-tabulation	
		Arrest	Notice
1	Lawyer	18 (14.2)	13 (19.1)
2	Person who knows police procedure	6 (4.7)	7 (10.3)
3	Person who knows the police	8 (6.3)	3 (4.4)
4	None	95 (74.8)	45 (66.2)
Total		127 (100)	68 (100)

NB: Figures in parenthesis are the percentage values

by the subcultural and environmental factors than their male counterparts. Experience does not show any definite pattern as regards impact on arrest discretion behaviour whereas the positional variable shows a distinct pattern. Population in supervisory ranks is more likely to impact the arrest discretion behaviour under all three determinants than their junior colleagues.

Analyses of socio-economic survey show that caste, education, house type, landholding, income etc. as social stratifications do not have positive correlation with mobilisation of law to one's advantage. However, offenders with higher degree of legal awareness and access to legal aids are more likely to mobilise law to their advantage.

A number of queries raised in Chapter 1 (section 1.7) have been answered and the hypotheses (para 2.6 of Chapter 2) have been validated by the data analyses. This study is aimed to be interpretive by explaining the results obtained through the analysis of background study of Indian policing, laws and policies in India, and by considering the interplay of multiple variables at play in arrest discretion behaviour of the police. On the basis of these interpretations, certain implications have been generated, which may be of interest to the police leaders and practitioners, policymakers and police researchers in India. This has been dealt in the next chapter.

Notes

1 2014, 8 SCC 283
2 (2014) 8 SCC 283
3 2001 Census Data Office of Registrar General and Census Commissioner, India, MHA, Government of India
4 The Mandal Commission was set up in 1979 by the Government of India with a mandate to identify the socially and economically backward population of India.
5 National Sample Survey is a Government of India set-up to carry out surveys on socio-economic, demographic and allied sectors for national planning and policy requirements.

7 Conclusion

Findings and Recommendations

> Arrest brings humiliation, curtails freedom and cast scar forever. Lawmakers know it, so also the police. There is a battle between the law makers and the police and it seems the police has not learnt its lesson; the lesson implicit and embodied in the CrPC. It has not come out of its colonial image despite six decades of independence, it is largely considered as a tool of harassment, oppression and surely not considered a friend of public. The need for caution in exercising the drastic power of arrest has been emphasised by the Courts time and again but has not yielded the desired result.[1]

The Supreme Court of India, while disposing off a criminal appeal in the year 2014, recorded this commentary on the abuse of arrest power by the police after the 2009 amendment of the CrPC, which casts an obligation on the police to not routinely arrest offenders involved in offences punishable with up to seven years of imprisonment but to serve a notice of appearance. The court painfully observed that the letter and spirit of the law is being flouted by the police with impunity.

7.1 A Brief Summary

This study originates from an intuitive inquiry into the power of arrest which is often abused. Arrest figures in India during the pre- and post-amendment periods remained unchanged in spite of the amendment of a hundred-year-old arrest law in 2009 based on the principles of "reasonableness", "necessity" and "restraints".[2] With the new amendment, arrest figures should have been theoretically reduced by two-thirds, commensurate with the proportion of offences that are punishable for up to or less than seven years of imprisonment as per the substantive laws of India. The Government of India crime statistics[3] show that the arrest per offence figures in the five-year period preceding 2009 was 1.19 and that for the succeeding five-year period was 1.18. The reduction is statistically negligible and does not reflect the legislative intent. Further inquiry showed that statutes, departmental guidelines, court rulings, police manual rules etc. have little influence on the arrest decision

DOI: 10.4324/9781003406679-7

of the police, which leads us to the question of what it is that significantly impacts such behaviour.

Literature review establishes that organisational, situational, subcultural, environmental and individual determinants are at the forefront of influencing arrest decision on behalf of law enforcement (Gaines and Kappeler 2003; Groeneveld 2005; Hidayet 2011).

The organisation through the pillars of policy, process, value and training creates a structure that influences arrest decision (Groeneveld 2005). Subculture is a culture within a broader culture that may deviate in some aspects from the broader culture and influences daily decisions (Herbert 1998). Subcultural ethos is intangible and many of the subcultural ethos negatively influence the decision. Even the way police officers interact with each other informally impacts subculture. In a democratic set-up, the police function in an environment where the media, public opinion, public reaction and political culture create a complex maze within which the police take decisions. Each of these components either independently or in combination influences the decision-making processes of the police. Literature review suggests that the individual characteristics of officers on the one hand and officers' values, beliefs and attitudes on the other are seen as drivers of police decision (Hidayet 2011). Finally, studies have established that situational determinants have considerable influence on arrest decisions (Black 1971; Hidayet 2011). Some of the situational variables are as follows: the seriousness of the crime, offender's prior criminal record, demeanour of the offender and characteristics of an individual officer (Gaines and Kappeler 2003; Walker and Katz 2005).

Out of these five determinants – organisational, situational, subcultural, environmental and individual – only the organisational and to some extent the situational determinants comprise well-defined rules and are tangible. The organisational determinants are constrained by legal variables such as statutory guidelines, court directives, departmental guidelines and manual rules. The situational determinant is partly comprised of legal factors, such as the seriousness of the offence and the offender's criminal record, in addition to certain extralegal factors, such as the demeanour and by social stratification including race, gender and education of the offender. The other three determinants are extralegal, significantly more intangible and subjective in characteristics. Empirical research shows that while legal factors significantly influence arrest outcomes, there are other significant drivers of police behaviour. Worden (1989) notes that the behaviour of the officer is not solely influenced by law, and that "policing is for the most part extra-legal, for while officers work within the constraints of law, they seldom invoke law in performing police work". Black's (1971, 1976) seminal work on the social organisation of law gives an insight into how the law is mobilised (for example, an arrest decision) to protect or ignore the interest of an actor. According to his theory of legal control and the nature of law, arrest decisions are influenced by social stratifications including race, gender and education "People of disadvantage are less likely to be successful in having law mobilised to protect their interest and more likely to have the law successfully applied to their behaviours" (Eitle 2005). Black's theory has generated a number of hypotheses regarding how extralegal characteristics influence the likelihood of the law being implemented. The combination of legal and extralegal factors creates a complex maze in which the arrest decision behaviour is processed and ultimately manifested. This naturally seeks an inquiry into the interplay of factors influencing the arrest decision, the key question here being why police officers choose to take particular decision to the exclusion of other legal alternatives, and whether such decisions are unfettered or bound by law. The first step in finding these answers is the study of literature on police discretion.

One of the most referred to definitions of "discretion" is the one offered by Kenneth Culp Davis (1969). He states that a "public officer has discretion whenever the effective limit on his power leave him free to make a choice among possible courses of action or inaction". This, however, is a very broad definition of the word discretion which makes no distinction between acceptable and unacceptable grounds for discretion. Davis further points out that the discretion that is allowed to the officials is essentially structured or "fettered" by the policies or the guidelines that have been designed to ensure the proper and acceptable exercise of discretion. According to Davis's definition, discretion is not only limited to what has been authorised or what is legal but also includes all that is within the effective limit of the officer's power. This phraseology becomes necessary because a good deal of discretionary decisions can be questioned on the grounds of legality. Another aspect of this definition is that of the choice to do or abstain from doing anything; perhaps inaction decisions are 10 to 20 times as frequent as decisions of action (Palmiotto and Unnithan 2011). Discretion not only is limited to substantive choices but also extends to the procedures, methods, timing, form and a few other subsidiary factors.

The pathbreaking research of American Bar Foundation in the 50s and 60s brought about a paradigm shift in understanding the discretion in criminal justice system. The result shows us that "the idea that the police, for example, made arrest decisions simply on the basis of whether or not a law has been violated – as a generation of police leaders led the public to believe – was simply an inaccurate portrayal of how police worked. The police work is complex, that police use enormous amount of discretion, and that discretion is at the core of police function" (Kelling 1999). Davis (1969) observed that "the police are among the most important policy makers of our entire society. And they make far more discretionary determinations in individual cases than any other class of administrators; I know of no close second". Having accepted that discretion is an inescapable and unavoidable part of policing, lawmakers, courts and the police organisations have been grappling with the issues of regulating and taming discretion so that the decisions are principled rather than being arbitrary and that they respect the basic human and civil rights (Bronitt and Stenning 2011).

Revisiting the initial inquiry into the factors that influence arrest behaviour, it is found that literature review does nudge one towards the idea that there are factors beyond the strict elements of structural and legal control that influences the arrest discretion behaviour. There are intangible embedded extralegal determinants like subculture, environment, individual officer's characteristics, and situation that filter the decision-making processes and influence the outcome.

7.2 Key Findings

To find answers to the questions posed earlier, and to conduct the maiden empirical inquiry testing the determinants of arrest discretion, 360 police officers from across ranks including members of Indian Police Service constitute the sample for this study. The so-called indicators or factors or predictor variables of the determinants of arrest discretion (organisational, subcultural and environmental) were operationalised by devising suitable response statements measurable in the classical Likert scale. The response format was worded such that strong agreement or disagreement with the item indicates higher degree of influence of the indicator. Data on gender, experience and position in the organisation have been culled out from the sample to analyse individual determinants. A socio-economic and legal awareness survey of one-hundred and ninety-five offenders was also conducted to test the situational variables. This data was then analysed by using reliable statistical tools such as frequency tables, cross-table comparison and the multiple regression technique.

A simple snapshot of the methodology shown in Table 4.1 may be referred to appreciate the key findings.

7.3 Organisational Determinants

7.3.1 Policy Dimension

Six response predictors have been operationalised for this dimension. The objective is to test if police respondents acknowledge that the amended Section 41 CrPC on arrest, the court directive in the Arnesh Kumar case, and crime branch circular of the state police are the factors that influence arrest decisions. It was found that an overwhelming percentage of the respondents (more than 80 percent) agree to this proposition. This validates the presupposition that the organisation through issue of guidelines, and the courts through their judicial pronouncements shape the inevitable exercise of discretion and can influence its proper exercise.

7.3.2 Process Dimension

The process dimensions mainly focus on organisational procedures and protocols such as supervisory review and the disciplinary procedures for intentional violations of arrest policy. The process dimension includes organisational imposition of procedures that must be followed while making arrests and puts an accountability mechanism in place for the exercise of unwarranted discretion. The use of such procedures allows the organisation to exercise influence over arrest discretion through supervisory scrutiny and imposition of sanctions against non-compliance. This dimension has been captured by four response predictors broadly falling under two categories: the say of supervisory officers in arrest decisions and the presence of accountability mechanisms for violation of arrest procedures. A statistically significant population endorses that the views or opinions of supervisory officers do influence the arrest decisions made by subordinates. This validates the hypothesis that organisational dimensions like supervisory monitoring and instructions are positively correlated to arrest decision behaviour. Only 51.2 percent of the population agree or strongly agree that internal mechanisms exist in the department to detect violations of arrest procedures. This casts doubt on the proposition if department has internal mechanism in place to detect violations of arrest procedures. The other response statement is meant to test if the organisation places strong emphasis on departmental action for intentional violation of arrest procedures. Here, only 57 percent of the respondents either agree or strongly agree to the statement. The relatively large (43 percent) population either have disagreed or are indecisive on this statement, which casts doubt on the existence of robust accountability mechanisms in the organisation for the abuse of arrest power.

7.3.3 Value Dimension

The organisational dimensions that attempt to influence the arrest processes address the notion of departmental values. Indicators such as operational independence, discretionary choices, training and effect of community policing have been included under this dimension. One of the response statements significant for this study is designed to elicit information on how much operational independence the officer enjoys beyond the four walls of departmental guidelines and rules. More than 73 percent of the respondents either agree or strongly agree to the response statement that investigating officers sometimes make arrest decisions based on their personal judgement as opposed to guidelines. This is revealing of the fact that a larger proportion of population believes that the scope for personal judgement exists within the boundary of the statute. Another statement under this dimension is designed to elicit a response on the oft-criticised police practice to arrest an accused person before the collection of evidence in spite of a litany of court directives and requirements of the statute to do the contrary. About 76 percent of the respondents believe that arrests in some instances precede formalities like collection of evidences. This casts doubt on the efficacy of accountable mechanism of the department against intentional violation of arrest guidelines. Another aspect that is critical for this study is to examine whether the amended provisions of Section 41 CrPC provides enough discretionary choices to negate the legislative intent of reducing the avoidable arrests. The provisions under 41(1)(b)(ii) of CrPC are riders or exception clauses, which state that the police can arrest any person without warrant if such person has committed a cognisable offence punishable with imprisonment up to seven years provided that the police officer is satisfied that such arrest is necessary

(a) to prevent such person from committing further crime, or
(b) for proper investigation, or
(c) to prevent such person from tampering with evidence, or
(d) to prevent such person from making any inducement, and threat to any witness, or
(e) to ensure the presence of such person in the Court whenever required. Otherwise, the person can be served with notice under Section 41A.

An overwhelming 88 percent of respondents endorse that these five conditions under Section 41(1)(b)(ii) provide plenty of scope for the exercise of discretion on whether to arrest an accused person involved in a "noticeable" offence. The rider clauses give enough discretionary choices to the police officer. Interestingly, while on one hand the lawmakers amended the century-old arrest law dubbing it as archaic and being unable to pass the constitutional test of "reasonableness" and that it allows for too much of discretion and subjectivity at the hands of the police, on the other the five rider clauses to the amended provisions of arrest are but wide discretionary latitudes given to the police officer that cannot be vouched for not being subject to potential misuse. About 71 percent of the respondents agreed to the statement that "exercise of discretion" was not a part of their police training. This is a significant finding and gives us an insight into the areas that need to be addressed by policymakers to check discretionary abuse. Community policing ensures a layer of accountability to police functions and is expected to influence decision-making process. An overwhelming 75 percent of the respondents agree that community policing practices will substantially constrain the arrest discretion of officers.

7.4 Subcultural Determinants

Literature review suggests that members of the police organisation are guided by their own set of beliefs, attitudes and behaviour, factors that can be grouped together and referred to as police subculture. "The police subculture is a crucial concept in the explanation of police behaviour and attitudes" (Westley 1970). The subculture, in Westley's view, has characterised the public as hostile, potentially violent and not to be trusted; this outlook requires secrecy, mutual support of peers, and a sense of unity on the part of the police. Researchers and practitioners in this field have devoted a considerable amount of their time in order to understand police subculture. "It is understandable, given that culture is noted as an obstacle to police accountability, as a reason why police reforms fail, as a cause of police abuse of authority, as a mechanism for officers to cope with the hostile and uncertain work environments, and an explanation for discretionary behaviour" (Ingram, Paoline and Terrill 2013). For the purpose of this study, four response predictors have been selected and operationalised in the Indian context: "Dirty Harry dilemma" (criminal justice system is ineffectual, and strong pretrial measures like arrest and detention are the punishment meted to the antisocials), "us versus them" (public potentially hostile and untrustworthy), "thin blue/khaki line" (thin line between order and chaos) and "code of silence" (to maintain solidarity and protect each other). About 61 percent of the respondents either agree or strongly agree to the existence of the subcultural ethos, "Dirty Harry dilemma", in the organisation. This means that more than half of the population endorses the view that police excesses are sometimes justified for larger societal interest. More than 68 percent of the population endorse the trait, "us versus them", perceiving the public to be untrustworthy, hostile and unappreciative. This subcultural ethos is likely to force an officer to resort to avoidable arrest with a view to attracting public approbation for his acts. About 58 percent of the respondents believe that formal arrest should be the norm, and the service of notice should be an exception. This reflects a subcultural trait – thin blue (khaki) line. About 55 percent of the respondents have endorsed the statement that the department and officers should protect each other while there is an allegation of illegal arrest by an officer, as arrest is made for larger public interest. The fact remains that majority of the respondents either agreed or strongly agreed to all the four subcultural traits within the police organisation. Noticeably, the average percentage of "agree" is generally less than the overwhelming "agree" response in the organisational determinants. As discussed earlier, these are intangible and subjective traits vis-à-vis the legalistic factors of organisational determinants and variations in the opinions are in the expected line.

7.5 Environmental Determinants

For the purpose of this study and having regard to the macro external environment in which the police organisation in India is embedded, the political culture, pressure groups and media are taken as factors influencing the decision-making process. Media, public opinion, public reaction and political influences create a complex maze within which the police often take decision and the factors have been operationalised for this study. Each of these components either independently or in combination influences the decision-making processes of the police.

About 85 percent of the respondents either agreed or strongly agreed to the proposition that arrest decisions are often taken after weighing the fall out of such decisions. On whether public perception of police action on specific cases considerably influences arrest decisions, an overwhelming 88.6 percent population of the population endorse the proposition. This being a corollary to the earlier statement, the high endorsement is in the expected line. The influence of media and civil society in arrest decision is validated by 87 percent of the respondents. As regards political influence on arrest decisions, 75 percent of the population either agrees or strongly agrees to the proposition. To sum up, each indicator or predictor variable under environmental determinants exerts considerable influence on arrest discretion behaviour of police, validating the hypothesis that predictors like public perception, media and civil society, and political elements influence the operating environment of the police.

7.6 Relative Significance of the Independent Variables on Arrest Discretion

One of the objectives of this empirical study was to find out which dimension has significant contribution towards influencing the determinants (conceptual space) – that is, organisational, subcultural and environmental – and which among the determinants seems to have the maximum contribution towards influencing arrest discretion behaviour of police.

7.6.1 Organisational Determinants – Policy Dimensions

Four factors or predictors – specific statutory guidelines, court directives, extensiveness of arrest policy and internal review mechanism of arrest procedures – together define the space for policy dimensions. The study intends to explore if these factors (predictor variables) are significant, and which among the four factors has maximum influence on the policy dimensions. The data analysis validates some important aspects of this study. The factors chosen for defining the conceptual space of policy dimensions are highly significant to validate the hypothesis that statutes, departmental guidelines, manual rules and internal review mechanism to ensure compliance to arrest procedures play a critical role in shaping the arrest discretion behaviour (please refer Tables 5.3 and 5.13).

7.6.2 Process Dimensions

The second important dimension to the way that the department attempts to influence officer discretion in arrests can be found in the process or procedural requirements associated with making arrests. Four factors – supervisory monitoring, weightage to supervisory instructions over personal judgement, guidelines to detect violation of arrest procedures and departmental sanction against erring personnel – have been taken as variables to measure the dimension. The analysis validates the selection of factors taken for this study under the process dimensions and the hypothesis that police organisations, through processes like supervisory monitoring and departmental sanction against procedure violations, control the arrest discretion behaviour (please refer Tables 5.5 and 5.13).

7.6.3 Value Dimensions

Indicators such as operational independence, discretionary choices, training and effect of community policing have been included under this dimension. The two response statements for operationalisation of the factors, "independence in decision-making" and "discretionary choices" are as follows: "It is acknowledged that officers have to make arrest decisions sometimes on criteria not covered by written policy or standard procedure" and "arrest in many instances precedes formalities like collection of prima facie evidences". About 73 percent of the respondents either agree or strongly agree to the response statement that investigating officers sometimes have to make arrest decision on their personal judgement as opposed to guidelines, while 76 percent of the respondents believe that arrests in some instances precede formalities like collection of evidences. These are significant study outcomes in that they not only show that officers do acknowledge the presence of wide discretionary boundaries in the arrest law but also go towards validating the hypothesis that there are extralegal factors which considerably influence the arrest decision (please refer Tables 5.7 and 5.13).

7.6.4 Relative Significance of Policy, Process and Value Dimensions Over Organisational Determinants

Literature establishes that the way the organisation creates a structure for arrest discretion flows from three principal sources: official policy, process and values. These dimensions capture the channel through which officers can influence or constrain the arrest discretion behaviour of officers. One of the empirical tasks is to find out which among these three has maximum impact on arrest discretion in the presence of the other two. We see that the mean response for the policy dimension is the highest at 3.950 with the lowest standard deviation among the three dimensions (please refer Table 5.13). The findings give empirical support to the hypothesis that the way the organisation creates a structure for arrest discretion flows from three principal sources: official policy, process and values. These dimensions capture the channel through which the departmental supervisory officers can influence or constrain the arrest discretion behaviour of the officers.

7.7 Subcultural Determinants

Four dimensions of informal organisational or subcultural determinants have been carefully chosen for the study – "Dirty Harry dilemma", "us versus them", "thin blue (khaki) line" and "code of silence". The empirical tests validate the research presupposition that the factors taken to represent the subcultural determinants are highly relevant, relatively independent of each other's sphere of influence and yet collectively define the conceptual space. The factor, "Us versus them" with a mean of 3.61 among the four independent variables is perceived to be a significant influencer of arrest discretion (please refer Table 5.14). It should also be noted that the standard deviations of the responses for subcultural indicators are significantly higher than those of organisational indicators, which goes on to show that there is room for these factors to be interpreted in many different ways, and therefore, in a way, validates the existence of discretionary latitude in arrest decisions.

7.8 Environmental Determinants

Based on literature review and with regard to the Indian context, four dimensions have been chosen to represent the environmental determinants that influence arrest decisions. They are "fall out of the action", "public perception", "media and civil society" and "politics". One of the objectives of this empirical study is to find out which among the factors has most impact on the operating environment of the police. The factors "media and civil society" and "public perception" have the highest means (4.03 and 4.01, respectively) within the environmental determinants, although the differences in means are almost marginal between these and the other two factors (please refer Table 5.15). Media and civil society with highest means comes out to be the most influential of the environmental factors.

7.9 Relative Significance of Organisational, Subcultural and Environmental Determinants Over Arrest Discretion

One of the key assumptions of this study, is that factors such as organisational policy, process and value dimensions, subcultural ethos, operating environment of the police, situational and individual determinants, either individually or in combination, influence the arrest discretion behaviour of the police. Out of the five determinants, the first three determinants – organisational, subcultural and environmental determinants – have been operationalised for statistical analysis with several anchor variables. One of the tasks is to find out the relative importance of the three key determinants – organisational, subcultural and environmental – in influencing the arrest discretion behaviour and to find out which among the three determinants has the maximum influence on the arrest discretion behaviour. Not surprisingly, the environmental factors (mean 3.928) came out as the strongest influencer on arrest discretion, though the organisational determinants (mean 3.727) and the subcultural determinants (mean 3.408) are not far behind (please refer Table 5.16). Out of these three, environmental and subcultural determinants are based on extralegal factors.

The findings on the face of it appear to be counter-intuitive. What could be the intuitive support for environmental and subcultural determinants impacting arrest discretion behaviour almost similarly or even more than organisational determinants which are well defined with rules, regulations, statutes, departmental sanctions etc. in influencing the arrest discretion behaviour? The answer is not far to seek. The organisational determinants are constrained with statutes, rules, departmental regulations, guidelines and court directives, which all can be categorised as legal determinants. They are more objective and hence less likely to be susceptible to individual vagaries, whereas determinants like subculture and environment are intangible in nature, susceptible to individual interpretation and most importantly extralegal in characteristics. Not surprisingly, subcultural and environmental determinants are empirically proved to impact the arrest discretion behaviour in equal measures, if not more than the organisational determinants. In other words, officers react to the organisational determinants more objectively and to the subcultural and the environmental determinants more subjectively. The conceptual diagram of the study (please refer Figure 2.1) also gets an empirical validation from this outcome.

7.10 Individual Determinants

Individual determinants refer to the influences of police officers' own characteristics over their behaviour. Studies on individual factors examine the characteristics such as gender, experience, educational level, race and social class and their influences on officers' response to a situation including discretionary behaviour. The assumption here is that female, more experienced and senior supervisory officers will react differently to the arrest discretion determinants than their male, rookie and non-supervisory counterparts, respectively.

7.10.1 Gender as a Variable

The pattern of response on the organisational variables on gender differentiation does not reveal anything significant. However, subcultural determinants affect the female officer more in decision-making than their male counterparts. One interesting finding that is worth highlighting from the data analysis is the "code of silence", where females outscore males by more than fifty percent, which literally means that the female officers are less likely to speak out against a colleague's misconduct than their male counterparts.

7.10.2 Experience as a Variable

For the purpose of this study, respondents with work experience of up to twenty years and more than twenty years have been taken as variables to find out if the determinants have differential impact with years of experience in the job. Nothing significant came out of data analysis to suggest that both categories react differently to the determinants except in the case of one subcultural variable, "the code of silence". Relatively larger percentage of respondents with up to 20 years of work experience (66 percent) believe in this subcultural ethos in comparison to their more experienced counterparts

(47 percent), showing that with more years of experience in the organisation this subcultural imprint gradually wanes.

7.10.3 Position as a Variable

For the purpose of this analysis, the sample has been split into two groups, one from the rank of Sub-Inspector of Police to the Deputy Superintendent of Police, and the other comprising respondents from the rank of Additional Superintendent of Police to senior IPS officers who are in the ranks of Superintendent to Additional Director General of Police. The former category has been taken as non-supervisory and the latter as supervisory category. Study shows that the supervisory officers are more concerned about the discretionary abuse than their junior colleagues. As regards the subcultural determinants, study establishes that supervisory officers are less likely to be affected by the subcultural determinants than their junior colleagues in the police organisation.

7.11 Relative Significance Within Gender, Experience and Position

From the multiple regression analysis (please refer Table 6.12), it has come out that subordinate officers are more likely to believe that the subculture has a significant impact on arrest discretion and that they are more likely to be influenced by the subculture than their senior counterparts. It may further be interpreted that the officers with less than twenty years of experience are more likely to react to the environment, comprising the societal, media and political factors, than their more experienced counterparts. Female officers are relatively more affected by the impact of subculture than their male counterparts to the extent of nine percent (beta value – 0.088). This finding goes with what is observed in analysing the frequency table (refer Table 6.5) – the subcultural determinants affect the female officer more in decision-making than their male counterparts.

7.12 Situational Determinants

In this study, having regard to the Indian context, the socio-economic status of the offenders has been surveyed to find out if there is a correlation between the poor and marginalised being as such and their more likelihood of being arrested in comparison to their affluent counterparts under similar circumstances as a parallel to "racial profiling" of the West, and whether the former category of respondents is less likely to exert their legal rights with lesser extent of legal awareness. Study establishes that there is no correlation between the poor and marginalised being more likely to be arrested as compared to their affluent counterparts. It further establishes that offenders with a higher degree of legal awareness and access to legal consultation are more likely to mobilise the law to their advantage.

7.13 Discussions on the Hypotheses

Six hypotheses relevant to this study have been carefully formulated on the basis of the literature review and their validation tested empirically.

1: *Organisational determinants positively constrain the arrest discretion behaviour of the police through channels like policy, process and values.*

"Researches on organisational characteristics of police agencies indicate that decisions of police officers are shaped by departmental norms, rules, procedures, and values" (Groeneveld 2005; Smith 1984; Mastrofski 1981). According to Brown (1988), organisational constraints refer to the system of administrative rules, policies and managerial controls designed in conformity with administrative directives. Groeneveld (2005) in his seminal work on arrest discretion of field patrol officers has further classified the variables under organisational determinants of discretion for his research work. He argues that "the way an organisation creates structure for arrest discretion flows from four principal sources: official policy, process, training, and values. These dimensions capture the channels through which organisational management can attempt to influence or constraint the arrest behaviour of officers". Organisational determinants positively constrain the arrest decision of officers by ensuring compliances to the statute and court directives, and by introducing policy, manual rules, regulatory circulars, disciplinary mechanism, training etc. The first hypothesis is formulated based on these literature reviews.

The data analysis of the organisational determinants (Chapter 5) with its three dimensions and factors defining each dimension validates several hypotheses and presuppositions besides establishing the model developed in this study being a good fit to the data (please refer Table 5.13). Firstly, negligible to low relationship exists between the factors and between the dimensions (correlation coefficient, r). This is consistent with the statistical notion that factors or dimensions should be additive, not cloning each other, such that the accumulation of the factors individually captures different aspects of the dimension and collectively they represent the conceptual space defined by the dimension. The policy dimension with the highest mean of 3.950 (on a scale of 5.0) shows that respondents believe it to be a significant predictor of arrest discretion, followed by the value dimension (3.673) and process dimension (3.563). Thus, the study gives empirical support to the hypothesis that the way the organisation creates a structure for arrest discretion flows from three principal sources: official policy, process and values. These dimensions capture the channel through which the departmental supervisory officers can influence or constrain the arrest discretion behaviour of the officers.

2: *Police subculture positively correlates with arrest discretion behaviour.*

Study of literature establishes that the members of the police organisation are guided by their own set of beliefs, attitudes and behaviour, what can be termed as police subculture. "The police subculture is crucial as a concept in order to explain the police behaviour and attitudes" (Westley 1970). The subculture, in Westley's view, has characterised the public as hostile, potentially violent and not to be trusted; this outlook requires secrecy, mutual support amongst the police officers and unity on the part of the police. Four distinct subcultural myths, "Dirty Harry dilemma", "us versus them", "thin blue/khaki line" and "code of silence" have been operationalised in the Indian context to empirically test the impact of subculture on decision-making behaviour. So, the study proposes the next hypothesis that subcultural determinants are significant influencers of arrest discretion behaviour.

The mean response in case of subcultural factors is 3.408 and that of organisational factors is 3.727 (please refer Table 5.16). The correlation coefficient ("r") between any two factors comprising the conceptual space of subculture is low, signifying that each of these dimensions is independent of the influence of the other. Both statistically thus validate the hypothesis that the factors taken to represent the subcultural determinants are highly relevant, relatively independent of each other's sphere of influence and yet collectively define the conceptual space.

3: *The environmental determinants positively affect the arrest discretion behaviour.*

In the context of this study, environmental factors such as media, public opinion, public reaction and political culture that create a complex maze within which the police take decisions have been operationalised as predictor variables. Each of these components either independently or in combination influences decision-making processes of police. The factors, "Media and civil society" (4.03) and "public perception" (4.01) have the highest means within the environmental determinants, although the difference in means is almost marginal between them and the other two factors (please refer Table 5.15). The values of correlation coefficients range between low and marked, which has been explained in section 5.6.3. But with the highest mean value of 3.928 among the three determinants (please refer Table 5.16) it claims to be the forerunner in arrest discretion behaviour.

4: *Subculture and environmental determinants affect the arrest discretion behaviour more than the organisational determinants.*

"An important finding of the organisational theories is that while organisational characteristics have positive correlates with how an officer behaves, the 'constrained organisational' and 'loosely coupled models' imply that non-organisational factors, like environment, subculture, and situations can exert a significant influence on the decision-making processes of rank and file" (Eitle 2005). In investigating the three proposed models, Mastrofski, Worden and Snipes (1995) argued that the size of an organisation is an essential element required in validating the models. They conclude that the decision-making of an officer is widely influenced by the policing environment in the area and the peer culture in larger bureaucratic departments, while the organisational policies have become essential in regulating behaviour in the smaller departments. The police organisations in India are relatively large with vast geographical jurisdiction, each covering more than few thousand square kilometres and with manpower no fewer than tens of thousands. Large or very large being the police organisations in India, the decision-making is more likely to be influenced by the policing environment and subculture than the organisational policies. The fourth hypothesis thus needs an empirical validation. The mean responses in case of subcultural and environmental factors are 3.406 and 3.928, respectively, and that of organisational factors is 3.727 (please refer Table 5.16). The correlation coefficient between any two determinants denotes low relationship. Environment seems to be the most significant influencer among the three major determinants. Subculture with a mean value of 3.408 is not far behind that of the organisation (3.727). Thus, it can be safely deducted from the empirical findings that environment and subculture influence the arrest discretion no less than the organisational determinants.

5: *Individual determinants like officer's gender, work experience and position in the organisation impact differentially to the arrest discretion behaviour.*

Literature studies on individual determinants examine the characteristics like gender, experience, educational level, race and social class and their influences on officers' response to a situation including discretionary behaviour. The assumption for this study is that female, more experienced and senior supervisory officers will react differently to the arrest discretion determinants than their male, rookie and non-supervisory counterparts, respectively.

It is seen from Table 6.12 that the significant p-values at 95 Percent level represent the relationship between subculture – position, and environment – experience, respectively. In other words, it can be said that for every one-unit change of supervisory position to subordinate level, the dependent variable, subculture changes by thirty percent (beta value being 0.291). This can be interpreted by stating that subordinate officers are more likely to believe that the subculture has a significant impact on arrest discretion and that they are more likely to be influenced by the subculture than their senior counterparts. The analysis of frequency tables (Table 6.11) with position and subculture as variables presents a similar finding. Another significant relationship is noticed when experience is regressed with environment. The p-value here is 0.023 (<0.5), which is highly significant. Having considered the beta value (0.136) for this relationship, it may be interpreted that the officers with less than twenty years of experience are more likely to react to the environment, comprising the societal, media and political factors, than their more experienced counterparts. Another relationship, though less significant, emerges while gender has been regressed with subculture. Females are relatively more affected by the impact of subculture than their male counterparts to the extent of nine percent (beta value – 0.088). This finding goes with what is observed in analysing the frequency table (refer Table 6.5) – the subcultural determinants affect the female officer more in decision-making than their male counterparts.

6: *People with socio-economic disadvantage are less likely to be successful in having law mobilised to protect their interest.*

According to Black's (1971, 1976) general theory of legal control and the nature of law, arrest decisions are influenced by social stratification including race, gender and education. "People of disadvantage are less likely to be successful in having law mobilised to protect their interest and more likely to have the law successfully applied to their behaviours" (Eitle 2005). People with more education and greater culture in their lives are more likely to exercise their rights and mobilise the law to protect their interests. Black's theory has generated a number of hypotheses regarding how the extralegal characteristics can influence the likelihood of law being implemented. In the Indian context, it may be hypothesised that the poor and marginal are less likely to exercise their rights and have the law mobilised, to protect their interest. Thus, the final hypothesis for this study examines whether the police in India have an inherent bias against "poor and marginalised" as equivalent of "racial profiling" in the West. A socio-economic survey of 195 offenders has been conducted for an empirical test. The variables under socio-economic status are taken as caste, occupation, level of education, house pattern, land ownership and monthly income. Study establishes that there is no correlation between poor and marginal being more likely to be arrested than their affluent counterparts. However, the study establishes that legal awareness is critical in having the law mobilised to protect one's interest.

7.14 Discussions on the Questions That Need to Be Answered

The study stems from the general inquiry whether the amended provision of CrPC on arrest without warrant during investigation (Section 41 CrPC) resulted in desirable reduction in the arrest figures in India. The preceding discussions and data analysis do not substantiate the legislative intent. The subsequent inquiries flow from this research problem. In Chapter 1 (please refer section 1.7), the following five questions have been raised that need to be answered while exploring the various factors influencing arrest discretion behaviour of the police in India:

Q 1. *Are the discretional latitudes wide enough in the amended arrest law of Sec 41 CrPC to deny realisation of legislative intent?*

Q 2. *Are the determinants of arrest discretion behaviour in the Western literature significant for police in India?*

Q 3. *Do the extralegal determinants like subculture, environment and individual characteristics impact the arrest discretion behaviour of police in India?*
Q 4. *Which among the three determinants, such as organisational, subcultural and environmental determinants, is the dominant one in influencing arrest discretion behaviour?*
Q 5. *Do the police in India have the arrest bias against "socially and economically marginal" people as an equivalent of "racial profiling" in Western literature?*

Q 1. *Are the discretional latitudes wide enough in the amended arrest law of Sec 41 CrPC to deny realisation of legislative intent?*

As already discussed in the preceding sections that the century-old arrest law was amended in the year 2009 on the basis of recommendations made in the 177th Report of the Law Commission of India. The objective is to reduce the number of avoidable arrests based on the legal doctrines of "reasonableness", "necessity" and "restraints". The Law Commission examined the directives given by the Supreme Court on arrests, various reports published by the National Human Rights Commission and the recommendations made by the National Police Commission in its 3rd Report in 1980 on reducing the number of avoidable arrests. The amended Section 41 of the CrPC introduced a new provision of "service of notice" instead of a formal arrest of an accused person, if the commission of the offence is punishable with imprisonment up to seven years. Analysis of substantive laws in India shows that the offences which prescribe punishment up to or less than seven years are two-thirds of the total penal offences. Had the legislative intent been followed in true letter and spirit of the amended law, the arrest figures in India would have been reduced by two-thirds. But analysis of arrest figures for the pre- and post-amendment periods shows that there has been very insignificant reduction in the arrest figures (1.18 arrests per offence in the post-amendment period as against 1.19 in the pre-amendment period; please refer Table 1.3). This raises a query if the amendment law still provides enough discretionary latitude to negate the legislative intent. First, a look at the rider provisions in the amended Section 41 CrPC is necessary to appreciate the discretionary choices available to the investigating officer. The provisions under 41(1)(b)(ii) of CrPC is the rider clause, which states that the police can arrest any person without warrant if such person has committed a cognisable offence punishable with imprisonment up to seven years provided that the police officer is satisfied that such arrest is necessary –

(a) to prevent such person from committing further crime, or
(b) for proper investigation, or

(c) to prevent such person from tampering with evidence, or
(d) to prevent such person from making any inducement, and threat to any witness, or
(e) to ensure the presence of such person in the Court whenever required. Otherwise, the person can be served with notice under Section 41A.

Data analysis shows that an overwhelming eighty-eight percent respondents endorse that the five conditions under Section 41(1)(b)(ii) provide plenty of choices for exercise of discretion whether to arrest an accused person involved in "noticeable" offence. True, the discretion is an inescapable part of criminal justice system and discretionary choices are available to the investigating officer to arrest repeat offenders, habitual criminals and criminals who could influence or intimidate the witnesses even if the offence committed is punishable with an imprisonment up to seven years. Interestingly, while on one hand the lawmakers amended the century-old arrest law dubbing it as archaic being unable to pass the constitutional test of "reasonableness" and that allows too much of discretion and subjectivity at the hands of police, on the other, the five rider clauses to the amended provisions of arrest are but wide discretionary latitudes given to the police officer which cannot be vouched for not being subject to potential misuse. Besides, the investigation officer may take shelter of the rider clauses as lawful safe haven against the colourable exercise of arrest power.

Q 2. *Are the determinants of arrest discretion behaviour in the Western literature significant for police in India?*

One of the objectives of the study is to empirically test, if the determinants of arrest discretion are significant for police in India. Literature on police discretion is relatively unknown in India. Literature review from the West establishes that factors like organisational, subcultural, environmental, individual and situational determinants are at the forefront of influencing the discretional decision made by law enforcement (Gaines and Kappeler 2003; Groeneveld 2005; Hidayet 2011). The study is a maiden attempt to empirically test if these determinants are significant for police in India. The determinants (organisational, subcultural and environmental) have been operationalised in the Indian context with suitable response statements for police respondents. Besides, a socio-economic and legal awareness survey has been conducted in respect of offender respondents for gaining insight into situational determinants. The data analyses have been made with suitable quantitative methodology to gain insight into the inquiry. Details of data analyses are captured in Chapters 5 and 6.

Table 7.1 Frequency distribution and mean values

Determinants	*Dimensions*	*%Agree/Strongly agree*	*Mean values*
Organisational	Policy	82.8	3.727
	Process	65.0	(±0.37)
	Values	78.0	
Subcultural		60.5	3.408 (±0.74)
Environmental		83.9	3.928 (±0.64)

NB: The values in the parenthesis represent the standard deviation

To answer the question if the determinants are significant for police in India, it must be shown that majority of the population endorses the response statements by "agreeing" or "strongly agreeing" with them. Based on the frequency of agreement to a general statement, an inference can be drawn on how much the population agrees to the existence of response predictor that influences the arrest discretion. This requires a simple interpretation of the frequency table. Besides, the mean values (out of 5 on the Likert scale) give a strong indication of the acceptability of the factors. Higher the mean, more is the influence of the factor. Table 7.1 contains the average frequency distribution of agreement (both "agree" and "strongly agree") and mean values of the factors under the determinants: organisation, subculture and environment.

Majority of the population endorse the response statements designed to capture the determinants or dimensions with the frequency distribution varying from 60.5 to 83.9 percent for "agree/strongly agree" responses. The mean values range between 3.408 and 3.928 on a scale of 5.0. This testifies empirically that majority of the population agrees to the existence of the response predictors that influence the arrest discretion. The study thus validates that the determinants of arrest discretion found from the literature of the West are highly relevant to police in India as well.

Q 3. *Do the extralegal determinants like subculture, environment and individual characteristics impact the arrest discretion behaviour of police in India?*

Having empirically tested the validity of the organisational, subcultural, environmental and individual determinants influencing arrest discretion behaviour, the question arises how far the extralegal determinants are responsible in shaping such behaviour. As discussed, extralegal factors are those factors in decision-making which are not regulated or sanctioned by law, yet have influence on shaping the final outcome of the decision. Legal factors include those that are set forth clearly in the written provisions of law for making an arrest, as well as the strategic considerations such as victim preference in making an arrest, the seriousness of the offence committed and the strength of evidence. The organisation with statutes, rules, regulations and court directives tries to influence the arrest discretion by invoking legal factors. The factors like influences of subculture, role of environment in which police operate, like media, political culture and public opinion, and individual characteristics play significant role in decision-making and may be categorised as extralegal factors. The individual determinants, such as gender, position and experience in the organisation impact in varying degrees to the arrest discretion behaviour comprising the organisation, subculture and environment. The empirical validation of hypotheses 4 and 5 answers this question (please refer section 7.13).

Q 4. *Which among the three determinants, such as organisational, subcultural and environmental determinants, is the dominant one in influencing arrest discretion behaviour?*

We find from the responses out of the three determinants that organisational factors have received the most "agree" or "strongly agree" responses. However, we have also seen that once the policy dimension from organisational factors is removed, it is the environmental and subcultural factors that have received more positive responses. Besides, environmental determinants outscore those of the organisation when mean values are taken into consideration. Subculture is not far behind either (please refer Table 7.1).

How could the organisational determinants with statutes, rules, court directives, guidelines, regulations, disciplinary mechanism in place for violation of departmental norms etc. almost similar and in some cases less influence on arrest discretion behaviour as compared to subcultural and environmental determinants? The answer lies in explaining the legal–extralegal conundrum. The factors comprising the organisational determinants are strictly legal ones, processed objectively, and leaving little room for subjective interpretation of a decision. Whereas, the conceptual space for subcultural and environmental determinants is captured by complex and intangible extralegal factors, not regulated or sanctioned by law. Subjectivity of an officer in addressing a situation is key here leaving little scope for objective assessment to arrive at a decision. It is the complex and intangible nature of the subcultural and environmental determinants that have the mischief potential to influence the discretion more than the organisational determinants, structured and fettered by statutes, policies and guidelines and designed to ensure acceptable bases for discretion.

Q 5. *Do the police in India have the arrest bias against "socially and economically marginal" people as an equivalent of "racial profiling" in Western literature?*

While the empirical research leaves very little doubt that the legal factors have a significant influence on arrest outcomes, Worden notes in his assessment of the discretionary context of policing that the behaviour of the police officer is not solely influenced by the law: "policing is for the most part extra-legal, for while officers (often) work within the constraints of the law, they seldom invoke the law in performing police work". Black's (1971, 1976) seminal work on the social organisation of law gives an insight into how the law is mobilised (for example, an arrest decision) to protect or ignore the interest of an actor. According to his general theory of legal control and the nature of law, arrest decisions are influenced by social stratification including race, gender and education. "People of disadvantage are less likely to be successful in having law mobilised to protect their interest and more likely to have the law successfully applied to their behaviours" (Eitle 2005). Racial profiling is a suitable example of the police discretion concerning race.

In this study, conducted in the Indian context, the socio-economic status of offenders has been surveyed to find out if there is a correlation between poor and marginal and their being more likely to be arrested. The awareness about the legal rights or lack of it depends upon the socio-economic condition of the individual. The assumption here is that members of poor and marginal sections of the society are more likely to be at the receiving end of discretionary abuse than their affluent counterparts, as an equivalent of "racial profiling" in the West. A socio-economic survey of 195 offenders has been conducted for an empirical test. The variables under socio-economic status are taken as caste, occupation, level of education, house pattern, land ownership and monthly income. Study establishes that there is no correlation between the poor and marginal being more likely to be arrested in comparison to their affluent counterparts (please refer section 6.6.6 of Chapter 6). The members of scheduled caste, scheduled tribe (refer Table 6.13), people with cultivation as means of livelihood (refer Table 6.14) and with low income (refer Table 6.18) have been able to mobilise law to their advantage with larger percentage of offenders being served notice instead of formal arrest. In other words, it may be said that there is no empirical evidence to validate that police in India have a "poor and marginal" bias in arrest as an equivalent of "racial profiling".

7.15 Implications

As the maiden empirical study on arrest discretion behaviour of the police in India, this study is meant to be exploratory in nature as it provides an overall insight into how the police officers and their supervisory officers perceive the widely discussed determinants of arrest discretion in the Western countries. Additionally, this study aims to be interpretive, which means it is intended to provide substantial explanations for the results which have been obtained in this study. On the basis of these interpretations, certain implications have been generated that can be of interest to the police leaders and practitioners, policymakers and the police researchers in India.

The factors comprising the organisational determinants are strictly legal ones, interpreted by statutes, guidelines, regulations, rules and court directives. Whereas, the conceptual space for subcultural and environmental determinants is captured by complex and intangible extralegal factors, not regulated or sanctioned by law. The identification of dominant independent factors with significant influence over the dependent factors will serve two purposes. First, if it is a legal factor, its influence over arrest discretion behaviour needs to be encouraged as a legitimate controlling factor. And, secondly, if it is an extralegal factor, the mischief associated with it needs to be identified and regulated to prevent potential abuse of discretionary power. Table 7.2 shows the factors or dimensions that have maximum influence over the dependent factors.

The factors in Column 1 are most sensitive variables from among the set of variables operationalised for the study under each of the dimensions or determinants mentioned in Column 2. The first one is the legal factor and the rest three are extralegal ones. The study concludes that environmental determinants are the most sensitive with maximum influence over the arrest discretion behaviour of police. The identification of sensitive variables is critical to understand the arrest discretion behaviour of the police and to recommend measures how to regulate and moderate the extralegal factors which are often intangible and complex and yet being the inescapable part of decision-making.

The study implies that suitable mechanism should be put in place by the police leadership to identify the negative effects of the subculture, decide the changes needed and support the desired changes.

Majority of the police responders endorse that scope for personal judgement exists in arrest decision beyond the boundary of statutes and rules. Still

Table 7.2 Factors with maximum influence over dependent factors

Sl no.	*Factors with maximum influence*	*Dependent factors*	*Nature*
	1	*2*	*3*
1.	Policy dimensions	Organisational determinants	Legal
3.	Us versus them	Subcultural determinants	Extralegal
3.	Media and civil society	Environmental determinants	Extralegal
4.	Environmental determinants	Arrest discretion behaviour	Extralegal

a larger percentage of study population believes that arrests in some instances precede formalities like collection of evidences. This casts doubt on the efficacy of accountable mechanism of the police organisation against intentional violation of arrest guidelines. The study thus empirically establishes the inadequacy of the existing accountability mechanism for police misconduct and suggests what more to be done in this field to enhance legitimacy and credibility of policing.

This study establishes that a large proportion of offenders are neither aware of their legal rights nor are they able to avail of legal assistance. This casts a responsibility on the State to create legal awareness and provide legal aids to indigent offenders.

7.16 Limitations

As with any other study, certain limitations are inherent in this study as well. Firstly, the arrest powers of the police under Section 41 CrPC are the subject matters of this study. Police in India are vested with arrest powers in order to prevent the commission of cognisable offences under Section 151 of the CrPC. The section provides that a police officer knowing of a design to commit any cognisable offence may arrest, without warrant or orders from a Magistrate, the person if it "appears" to such office that the commission of the offence cannot otherwise be prevented. The figures are not available for comparison but the fact remains that a large number of arrests are made by the police under this section of CrPC. The provisions of the section require personal knowledge or belief on the part of the police officer and therefore allow wide discretionary powers. The study has excluded such arrests as a different methodology than the one taken for this empirical test would have been required.

Secondly, the framework for this study is based on theoretical inquiries of Western literature as the literature on police arrest discretion is unknown in India. One of the challenging tasks of the study has been to operationalise the variables under each determinant in the context of Indian police. While there could be more variables under each determinant, the ones found to be relatively critical in the Indian context have been chosen for the purpose of the study. For example, arrest for extraneous consideration could have been an appropriate variable. The National Police Commission (1981a) in its Third Report observes that power of arrest involves the exercise of considerable discretion and gives scope for corruption and malpractices. The difficulty to operationalise this variable and to get the sample population became a constraint to bring this critical factor into the ambit of this study.

Thirdly, under situational determinants, three variables have been operationalised for this study: socio-economic status of the accused, legal awareness and access to legal assistance. Literature review establishes situational factors that have consistently been shown to have a strong effect on the arrest decision. The demeanour of the accused, previous criminal record, strength of the evidence, gravity of the offence, race and ethnicity of the suspect, characteristics of the victim etc. are some of the variables of situational determinants. A large number of variables have been omitted for this study since no suitable tool could be devised for the investigation. Only a few variables related to offenders have been operationalised although victims and police respondents could have been taken as samples.

Finally, as there was no empirical inquiry related to arrest discretion behaviour of the police in India, the framework of this study is based on theoretical inquiries from Western literature. Therefore, this study may serve as an exploratory investigation that may provide useful insights for further studies on arrest discretion behaviour of the police in India.

7.17 Recommendations

As discussed in the preceding chapters, Davis (1969) argues that the police make far more discretionary determinations in individual cases as compared to any other class of administrators. Surprisingly, most police training academies do not teach "discretion" as a discipline. Majority of the police officers are not even aware of the discretionary decisions they routinely make in everyday policing. Training prepares a newcomer to the organisation to contribute to the organisational goal. Therefore, training is expected to play a vital role in making police officers aware of the discretionary choices they make, the value of good judgement and potential abuse of discretionary powers. Study establishes that about 71 percent of the respondents agree to this statement that as a discipline "discretion" is not a part of the police training curriculum in India. While responding to the statement that police training specifically addresses issues like officer's arrest decision, only about 50 percent of the respondents agree, validating the observation that most of the police training curriculum does not place emphasis on this critical aspect of policing. It is strongly recommended that discretion should be part of training curriculum of the police training academies. An andragogical training structure with discussions, case studies, application based, problem-solving approach is more suited for this task.

This study established empirically that subcultural determinants play a dominant role in arrest discretion behaviour of the police in India, equivalent to the legal factors manifested by the organisational determinants. "An adherence to police subculture may foster negative and cynical attitude towards citizens even the legal system" (Cochran and Bromley 2003). The "us and them" and "Dirty Harry dilemma" are the manifestations of such subcultural ethos. Wood (1997) argues that adherence to subculture will reinforce peer loyalty amongst the police officials so that their misconduct goes undetected because of the prevalence of "code of silence" in the organisation. Anthony (2018) suggests that changing culture of a police organisation and of the officers requires training initiatives that will be accepted, supported and implemented by the officers. It is recommended that police leadership consider training on ethics and practice of community policing to improve the department's operational image and to overcome the negative aspects of police culture. The police leaders should first determine the desired culture they wish to instil, compare it with the existing culture to decide the changes needed, create disaffection with the existing culture and support for the desired changes. Included within the broad ambit of value dimension is the predictor variable, community policing. Community policing as a strategy revolves around the philosophy of people-centric policing, partnership with citizens for crime prevention and decentralisation of the organisational hierarchy with a view to providing more decision-making powers to the field officers. Simultaneously, it ensures a layer of accountability to the police functions that are expected to influence decision-making process. Police in India have introduced several tactical dimensions of community policing within the broad policing functions. One of the response statements is intended to explore whether the accountability mechanism that community policing brings into the broad police functions will be helpful in regulating abuse of arrest powers. An overwhelming 75 percent of the respondents either agree or strongly agree to this proposition. Therefore, it is suggested to adopt various components of community policing in the police organisation so that it would forge a partnership with the community and its members and thereby stem the negative effects of subcultural ethos.

A significant outcome of this study is about the interplay of legal and extralegal determinants in arrest discretion behaviour. The organisation with statutes, rules, regulations and court directives tries to influence the arrest discretion by invoking legal factors. The factors like influences of subculture, role of environment in which police operate, like media, political culture and public opinion, and individual characteristics play significant role in decision-making and may be categorised as extralegal factors. Data analysis shows that an overwhelming eighty-eight percent respondents endorse that the five conditions given under Section 41(1)(b)(ii) provide plenty of choices for exercise of discretion whether to arrest an accused person involved in "noticeable" offence. The five rider clauses to the amended provisions of arrest are but wide discretionary latitudes given to the police officer and one cannot be sure against their potential misuse. Besides, the investigation officer may take shelter of the rider clauses as lawful safe haven against the colourable exercise of arrest power. Despite statutory provisions and court pronouncements, 73 percent of the respondents either agree or strongly agree to the response statement that investigating officers sometimes have to make arrest decisions on their personal judgement as opposed to the guidelines. This is revealing in that the larger proportion of population believes that the scope for personal judgement exists within the boundaries of the statute. Extralegal determinants tend to influence the personal judgement. Seventy-six percent of the respondents believe that arrests in some instances precede formalities like collection of evidences. This casts doubts on the efficacy of accountable mechanism of the department against intentional violation of arrest guidelines. Study establishes that it is the complex and intangible nature of the subcultural and environmental determinants that has the mischief potential to influence the discretion more than the organisational determinants, structured and fettered by policies and guidelines and designed to ensure acceptable bases for discretion. This calls for strong accountability mechanism in the organisation.

The Supreme Court in Arnesh Kumar[4] directed "the police officers not to automatically arrest when an offence is registered but to satisfy themselves about the necessity for arrest under the parameters laid down in Sec 41, CrPC." It also directed that all police officers be provided with a "Check List" containing specified subclauses under Section 41(1)(b)(ii), which should accompany every arrest where the accused person has been produced before a Magistrate. The "Check List" should, inter alia, furnish all the reasons and materials which have necessitated the arrest. Odisha State Police introduced a Check List in the year 2014 in compliance to the directive of the Supreme Court (*Appendix L*). The arrest figures of the Odisha police show a declining trend post introduction of the Check List. The arrest per offence in the four-year period prior to introduction of the Check List was 1.40, which was declined to 1.18 in the three-year period post introduction of the Check List.[5]

Data analysis shows that an overwhelming 88 percent respondents endorse that the five conditions given under Section 41(1)(b)(ii) provide plenty of choices for exercise of discretion whether to arrest an accused person involved in "noticeable" offence. True, the discretion is an inescapable part of criminal justice system and discretionary choices are available to the investigating officer to arrest repeat offenders, habitual criminals and criminals who could influence or intimidate the witnesses even if the offence committed is punishable with imprisonment for less than seven years. Interestingly, while on one hand the lawmakers amended the century-old arrest law dubbing it as archaic being unable to pass the constitutional test of "reasonableness" and that allows too much of discretion and subjectivity at the hands of police, on the other, the five rider clauses to the amended provisions of arrest are but wide discretionary latitudes given to the police officer which cannot be vouched for not being subject to potential misuse. Besides, the investigation officer may take shelter of the rider clauses as lawful safe haven against the colourable exercise of arrest power. The check list introduced, following the directives of the Supreme Court in Arnesh Kumar case, may not be sufficient to prevent the discretionary abuse. It is recommended that the police organisation devise mechanism to make the grounds of arrest more objective.

Most of the reported police misconducts are inquired by the departmental hierarchy in India, though statutory bodies like Human Rights Commissions and courts are empowered to do so. But a minuscule proportion of such misconducts are taken up by the statutory bodies because of other pressing mandates. A study of international best practices for police accountability mechanism shows that more and more countries have introduced external oversight agencies to probe into police misconduct. This has been necessitated by the fact that the subcultural ethos, the "code of silence" of the police organisation, acts as a deterrent to getting to the bottom of the allegations against a fellow officer. The Supreme Court of India in Prakash Singh case[6] directed "the States to constitute Police Complaint Authority at the district and State level to look into complaints against police officers. The district level Authority is to be headed by a retired District Judge while the State Level Authority to be headed by a retired Judge of the High Court/ Supreme Court". Importantly, the heads of the authorities will be selected from the panel of names given by the Chief Justice of the High Court. The members of the Authority shall be selected by the State government from a list of names prepared by the State Human Rights Commission/Lok Ayukta/ State Public Service Commission. The composition of the Authority is in line with international best practices and is expected to ensure better accountability mechanism in the police organisation.

Study establishes that out of the four dimensions operationalised for capturing the conceptual space for the environmental determinant, "politics" comes out as a sensitive variable. Not surprisingly, the literature on political influence on the police functions has been so critical of the issues and concerns (National Police Commission 1979; Singhvi 1994; Ghosh and Rustamji 1994). The directives of the Supreme Court[7] on fixed tenure of field police officers, selection of the State police chief and the constitution of the State Security Commission are strongly recommended to keep the police free from undue political influences. The Supreme Court directs the State Governments "to constitute a State Security Commission in every State to ensure that the State Government does not exercise unwarranted influence or pressure on the State police and for laying down the broad policy guidelines so that the state police always acts according to the laws of the land and the Constitution of the country."

In its Eighth Report, the National Police Commission (1981b) emphasises that accountability can be ensured by active supervision and depends upon the awareness of people of their rights and their willingness to exercise the same. This study establishes that majority of the offender respondents are neither aware of their legal rights nor able to mobilise legal aid in the course of arrest. The Constitution of India and Criminal Procedure Code guarantee several rights for the persons accused of an offence(s) or arrested by the police. It is incumbent upon the State as well as non-governmental organisations to undertake legal awareness camps and provide legal aids to the indigent offenders.

Discretion and accountability are linked intrinsically. Pepinsky (1984) argues that "accountability means having to answer for one's actions or inaction. Accountability is synonymous with responsibility. Having to answer for one's action makes sense only if one could have chosen to do otherwise". According to Davis (1969), discretion means choice of action. Pepinsky (1984) concludes that accountability implies the existence of discretion as the public authority exercised one of the choices in exclusion of the others and should be made answerable to the choice acted upon. Besides, as the authority of the police is derived from the people through a social contract and the power that is held in public's trust and confidence (Moll 2006), the police must remain accountable to the public for its action. The National Police Commission recommends that police should remain accountable to the people, to law and to the organisation – in that order. It also emphasises that accountability can be ensured by active supervision and depends upon the awareness of people of their rights and their willingness to exercise the same. This is universally applicable to the police organisations across the nations though varying degrees of accountability mechanisms exist in all police organisations.

If the global outrage one witnessed following the tragic death of George Floyd during his arrest is an indication, the malaise seems to be much deeper. People in the democracies across the world want more say in the way they would like to be policed and, in a way, reject the existing accountability mechanisms of the organisation. Twenty-first century is likely to usher in a new era of police accountability – accountable to the people – two centuries after the advent of the modern police.

Notes

1 Arnesh Kumar v. State of Bihar (2014) 8 SCC 283
2 177th Report of the Law Commission of India, 2001
3 Crime in India, NCRB, MHA, Government of India, 2016
4 2014, 8 SCC 273
5 Figure compiled from White Papers of the Government of Odisha on Home Department
6 Prakash Singh versus Union of India 2006 (8) SCC 1
7 Ibid.

Appendix A

Number of Offences With Punishment Up to or Less Than Seven Years and More Than Seven Years in Indian Penal Code and Minor Criminal Acts

Sl	*IPC/Minor criminal acts*	*Total offences*	*Punishment*	
			>7 years	*<7 years*
1	Indian Penal Code	296	98 (33%)	198 (67%)
2	Minor Criminal Acts (49)	131	45 (34%)	86 (66%)
Total		427	143 (33.4%)	284 (66.6%)

Appendix B
NHRC Guidelines Regarding Arrest

Need for Guidelines

Arrest involves restriction of liberty of a person arrested and therefore, infringes the basic human rights of liberty. Nevertheless, the Constitution of India as well as International human rights law recognise the power of the State to arrest any person as a part of its primary role of maintaining law and order. The Constitution requires a just, fair and reasonable procedure established by law under which alone such deprivation of liberty is permissible.

Although Article 22(1) of the Constitution provides that every person placed under arrest shall be informed as soon as may be the ground of arrest and shall not be denied the right to consult and be defended by a lawyer of his choice and S.50 of the Code of Criminal Procedure, 1973 (CrPC) requires a police officer arresting any person to "forthwith communicate to him full particulars of the offence for which he is arrested or other grounds for such arrest". In actual practice, these requirements are observed more in the breach.

Likewise, the requirement of production of the arrested person before the court promptly which is mandated both under the Constitution [Article 22(2)] and the CrPC (Section 57] is also not adhered to strictly.

A large number of complaints pertaining to Human Rights violations are in the area of abuse of police powers, particularly those of arrest and detention. It has, therefore, become necessary, with a view to narrowing the gap between law and practice, to prescribe guidelines regarding arrest even while at the same time not unduly curtailing the power of the police to effectively maintain and enforce law and order and proper investigation.

Pre-Arrest

- The power to arrest without a warrant should be exercised only after a reasonable satisfaction is reached, after some investigation, as to the genuineness and bonafides of a complaint and a reasonable belief as to both the person's complicity and the need to effect arrest. [Joginder Kumar's case- (1994) 4 SCC 260).

- Arrest cannot be justified merely on the existence of power, as a matter of law, to arrest without a warrant in a cognisable case.
- After Joginder Kumar's pronouncement of the Supreme Court the question, whether the power of arrest has been exercised reasonably or not is clearly a justiciable one.
- Arrest in cognisable cases may be considered justified in one or other of the following circumstances:

  (i) The case involves a grave offence like murder, dacoity, robbery, rape etc. and it is necessary to arrest the suspect to prevent him from escaping or evading the process of law.
  (ii) The suspect is given to violent behaviour and is likely to commit further offences.
  (iii) The suspect requires to be prevented from destroying evidence or interfering with witnesses or warning other suspects who have not yet been arrested.
  (iv) The suspect is a habitual offender who, unless arrested, is likely to commit similar or further offences. [3rd Report of National Police Commission]

- Except in heinous offences, as mentioned earlier, an arrest must be avoided if a police officer issues notice to the person to attend the police station and not leave the station without permission (see Joginder Kumar's case (1994) SCC 260).
- The power to arrest must be avoided where the offences are bailable unless there is a strong apprehension of the suspect absconding.
- Police officers carrying out an arrest or interrogation should bear clear identification and name tags with designations. The particulars of police personnel carrying out the arrest or interrogation should be recorded contemporaneously, in a register kept at the police station.

Arrest

- As a rule, use of force should be avoided while effecting arrest. However, in case of forcible resistance to arrest, minimum force to overcome such resistance may be used. However, care must be taken to ensure that injuries to the person being arrested, visible or otherwise, are avoided.
- The dignity of the person being arrested should be protected. Public display or parading of the person arrested should not be permitted at any cost.
- Searches of the person arrested must be done with due respect to the dignity of the person, without force or aggression and with care for the person's right to privacy. Searches of women should only be made by other women with strict regard to decency (S.51(2) CrPC).
- The use of handcuffs or leg chains should be avoided and if at all, it should be resorted to strictly in accordance with the law repeatedly explained and

mandated in the judgement of the Supreme Court in Prem Shanker Shukla v. Delhi Administration [(1980) 3 SCC 526] and Citizen for Democracy v. State of Assam [(1995) 3 SCC 743].

- As far as is practicable, women police officers should be associated where the person or persons being arrested are women. The arrest of women between sunset and sunrise should be avoided.
- Where children or juveniles are sought to be arrested, no force or beatings should be administered under any circumstances. Police officers, may for this purpose, associate respectable citizens so that the children or juveniles are not terrorised and minimal coercion is used.
- Where the arrest is without a warrant, the person arrested has to be immediately informed of the grounds of arrest in a language which he or she understands. Again, for this purpose, the police, if necessary, may take the help of respectable citizens. These grounds must have already been recorded in writing in police records. The person arrested should be shown the written reasons as well and also given a copy on demand (S.50(1) CrPC).
- The arrested person can, on a request made by him or her, demand that a friend, relative or other person known to him be informed of the fact of his arrest and the place of his detention. The police should record in a register the name of the person so informed. [Joginder Kumar's case (supra)].
- If a person is arrested for a bailable offence, the police officer should inform him of his entitlement to be released on bail so that he may arrange for sureties (S.50(2) CrPC).
- Apart from informing the person arrested of the above rights, the police should also inform him of his right to consult and be defended by a lawyer of his choice. He should also be informed that he is entitled to free legal aid at state expense [D.K. Basu's case (1997) 1 SCC].
- When the person arrested is brought to the police station, he should, if he makes a request in this regard, be given prompt medical assistance. He must be informed of this right. Where the police officer finds that the arrested person is in a condition where he is unable to make such request but is in need of medical help, he should promptly arrange for the same. This must also be recorded contemporaneously in a register. The female requesting for medical help should be examined only by a female registered medical practitioner (S.53 CrPC).
- Information regarding the arrest and the place of detention should be communicated by the police officer effecting the arrest without any delay to the Police Control Room and District/State Headquarters. There must be a monitoring mechanism working round the clock.
- As soon as the person is arrested, police officer effecting the arrest shall make a mention of the existence or non-existence of any injury(s) on the person of the arrestee in the register of arrest. If any injuries are found on the person of the arrestee, full description and other particulars as to the

manner in which the injuries were caused should be mentioned in the register, which entry shall also be signed by the police officer and the arrestee. At the time of release of the arrestee, a certificate to the above effect under the signature of the police officer shall be issued to the arrestee.

- If the arrestee has been remanded to police custody under the orders of the court, the arrestee should be subjected to medical examination by a trained Medical Officer every 48 hours during his detention in custody by a doctor on the panel of approved doctors appointed by Director, Health Services of the concerned State or Union Territory. At the time of his release from the police custody, the arrestee shall be got medically examined and a certificate shall be issued to him stating therein the factual position of the existence or non-existence of any injuries on his person.

Post-Arrest

- The person under arrest must be produced before the appropriate court within 24 hours of the arrest (Ss 56 and 57 CrPC).
- The person arrested should be permitted to meet his lawyer at any time during the interrogation.
- The interrogation should be conducted in a clearly identifiable place, which has been notified for this purpose by the Government. The place must be accessible and the relatives or friend of the person arrested must be informed of the place of interrogation taking place.
- The methods of interrogation must be consistent with the recognised rights to life, dignity and liberty and right against torture and degrading treatment.

Enforcement of Guidelines

1. The guidelines must be translated into as many languages as possible and distributed to every police station. It must also be incorporated in a handbook which should be given to every policeman.
2. Guidelines must receive maximum publicity in the print or other electronic media. It should also be prominently displayed on notice board, in more than one language, in every police station.
3. The police must set up a complaint redressal mechanism, which will promptly investigate complaints of violation of guidelines and take corrective action.
4 The notice board which displays guidelines must also indicate the location of the complaints redressal mechanism and how that body can be approached.
5. NGOs and public institutions including courts, hospitals and universities must be involved in the dissemination of these guidelines to ensure the widest possible reach.

6. The functioning of the complaint redressal mechanism must be transparent and its reports accessible.
7. Prompt action must be taken against errant police officers for violation of the guidelines. This should not be limited to departmental enquiries but also set in motion the criminal justice mechanism.
8. Sensitisation and training of police officers are essential for effective implementation of the guidelines.

Appendix C

Interview Schedule for Odisha Police Officers

Name:
Designation:
Gender:
Place of posting:
Years of completed service:
Contact No and Mail id:

Each respondent has to indicate the extent of agreement and disagreement by ticking the appropriate response (Strongly Agree, Agree, Cannot Say, Disagree, Strongly Disagree)

1. *The amended provisions of Sec 41 Cr PC (arrest in cognisable offences) are very specific and provide detailed guidelines on arrest in cognisable cases*

Strongly Agree	Agree	Cannot Say	Disagree	Strongly Disagree

2. *Guidelines of the Supreme Court in "Arnesh Kumar" case made the compliance to the amended provisions of arrest more specific and accountable*

Strongly Agree	Agree	Cannot Say	Disagree	Strongly Disagree

3. *Department Arrest Policy circulated in Crime Branch Circular 350/2014 gives clear guidelines for decision to arrest in cognisable offences*

Strongly Agree	Agree	Cannot Say	Disagree	Strongly Disagree

4. *The Crime Branch guidelines of 2014 provided more clarity on the arrest decision than before*

Strongly Agree	Agree	Cannot Say	Disagree	Strongly Disagree

5. *Way back in 1996, The Police Manual Rule 221 mentions that except in heinous offences arrest should be avoided, even service of notice would be proper in certain cases. But provision of PMR was not complied due to lack of awareness and knowledge.*

Strongly Agree	Agree	Cannot Say	Disagree	Strongly Disagree

6. *The department has strong internal review mechanism of compliance to arrest procedures*

Strongly Agree	Agree	Cannot Say	Disagree	Strongly Disagree

7. *Supervisory officers like IIC or SDPO/ACP or SP/DCP often take decision on arrest procedures in specific cases*

Strongly Agree	Agree	Cannot Say	Disagree	Strongly Disagree

8. *Supervisory officers' opinions or instructions on arrest decision take precedence over personal judgement*

Strongly Agree	Agree	Cannot Say	Disagree	Strongly Disagree

9. *The department has mechanism in place to detect violations of arrest procedures*

Strongly Agree	Agree	Cannot Say	Disagree	Strongly Disagree

10. *The department places strong emphasis on disciplinary action for any officer that intentionally violates arrest procedures*

Strongly Agree	Agree	Cannot Say	Disagree	Strongly Disagree

11. *It is acknowledged that officers have to make arrest decisions sometimes on criteria not covered by written policy or standard procedure*

Strongly Agree	Agree	Cannot Say	Disagree	Strongly Disagree

12. *Arrest in many instances precedes formalities like collection of prima facie evidences*

Strongly Agree	Agree	Cannot Say	Disagree	Strongly Disagree

13. *Although the amended Sec 41 CrPC provides for issuance of notice to a person who commits an offence for which maximum punishment extends up to seven years, the investigating officer can arrest the person if he has the reason to believe that arrest is necessary to 1) prevent such person from committing further crime or 2) for proper investigation or 3) prevent the person from tampering with evidence or 4) threat to witnesses or 5) to ensure his presence in the court. All these five choices provide enough scope to the Investigating Officer whether to arrest or serve notice.*

Strongly Agree	Agree	Cannot Say	Disagree	Strongly Disagree

14. *Arrest discretion was part of formal Police training*

Strongly Agree	Agree	Cannot Say	Disagree	Strongly Disagree

15. *Department training specifically addresses the use of officer's discretion in arrest decision*

Strongly Agree	Agree	Cannot Say	Disagree	Strongly Disagree

16. *Community policing practices will substantially constrain the arrest discretion of officers*

Strongly Agree	Agree	Cannot Say	Disagree	Strongly Disagree

17. *Arrest and judicial custody during investigation is the only punishment meted out to antisocials as they are most likely to get acquitted*

Strongly Agree	Agree	Cannot Say	Disagree	Strongly Disagree

18. *The choice of serving notice to an accused person involved in an offence for which the punishment is less than seven years is likely to be attributed motive by the public*

Strongly Agree	Agree	Cannot Say	Disagree	Strongly Disagree

19. *Formal police arrest, not service of notice for appearance, is essential to maintain order in the society*

Strongly Agree	Agree	Cannot Say	Disagree	Strongly Disagree

20. *Department and officers should protect each other while there is allegation of malafide arrest by an officer as arrest is made for larger public interest*

Strongly Agree	Agree	Cannot Say	Disagree	Strongly Disagree

21. *Arrest decisions are often taken having regard to the fall out or outcome of such decisions in the law and order scenario*

Strongly Agree	Agree	Cannot Say	Disagree	Strongly Disagree

22. *Public perception of police action on specific cases considerably influences arrest decision*

Strongly Agree	Agree	Cannot Say	Disagree	Strongly Disagree

23. *Media and response of the civil society to a specific offence weigh on the officer's arrest decision*

Strongly Agree	Agree	Cannot Say	Disagree	Strongly Disagree

24. *Arrest decisions are sometimes taken on political consideration or influence*

Strongly Agree	Agree	Cannot Say	Disagree	Strongly Disagree

Appendix D

Interview Schedule

(For IPS officers of Other States)

Name:

Cadre/Organisation Designation:

Gender: Male/Female

Place of posting:

Years of completed service:

Contact No and Mail id:

Each respondent has to indicate the extent of agreement and disagreement by ticking the appropriate response (Strongly Agree, Agree, Cannot Say, Disagree, Strongly Disagree)

1. *The amended provisions of Sec 41 Cr PC (arrest in cognisable offences) are very specific and provide detailed guidelines on arrest in cognisable cases*

Strongly Agree	Agree	Cannot Say	Disagree	Strongly Disagree

2. *Guidelines of the Supreme Court in "Arnesh Kumar" case made the compliance to the amended provisions of arrest more specific and accountable*

Strongly Agree	Agree	Cannot Say	Disagree	Strongly Disagree

3. *Department Arrest Policy circulated following Arnesh Kumar gives clear guidelines for decision to arrest in cognisable offences*

Strongly Agree	Agree	Cannot Say	Disagree	Strongly Disagree

4. *The police organisation has adequate departmental guidelines to ensure compliance to arrest procedures*

Strongly Agree	Agree	Cannot Say	Disagree	Strongly Disagree

5. *Supervisory officers like IIC or SDPO/ACP or SP/DCP often take decision on arrest procedures in specific cases*

Strongly Agree	Agree	Cannot Say	Disagree	Strongly Disagree

6. *Supervisory officers' opinions or instructions on arrest decision take precedence over personal judgement*

Strongly Agree	Agree	Cannot Say	Disagree	Strongly Disagree

7. *The police department has clear set of guidelines in place to detect violations of arrest procedures*

Strongly Agree	Agree	Cannot Say	Disagree	Strongly Disagree

8. *The department places strong emphasis on disciplinary action for any officer that intentionally violates arrest procedures*

Strongly Agree	Agree	Cannot Say	Disagree	Strongly Disagree

9. *Investigating Officers have to make arrest decisions sometimes on their personal judgement but not necessarily as per guidelines*

Strongly Agree	Agree	Cannot Say	Disagree	Strongly Disagree

10. *Arrests in some instances are carried out before formalities like collection of prima facie evidences*

Strongly Agree	Agree	Cannot Say	Disagree	Strongly Disagree

11. *Although the amended Sec 41 CrPC provides for issuance of notice to a person who commits an offence for which maximum punishment extends up to seven years, the investigating officer can arrest the person if he has the reason to believe that arrest is necessary to 1) prevent such person from committing further crime or 2) for proper investigation or 3) prevent the person from tampering with evidence or 4) threat to witnesses or 5) to ensure his presence in the court. All these five choices provide enough scope to the Investigating Officer whether to arrest or serve notice.*

Strongly Agree	Agree	Cannot Say	Disagree	Strongly Disagree

12. *Subject like "Exercise of Discretion" is not part of formal Police training*

Strongly Agree	Agree	Cannot Say	Disagree	Strongly Disagree

13. *Police training specifically addresses issues like officer's arrest decision*

Strongly Agree	Agree	Cannot Say	Disagree	Strongly Disagree

14. *Community policing practices will help reduce abuse of arrest power*

Strongly Agree	Agree	Cannot Say	Disagree	Strongly Disagree

15. *Arrest and pre-trial custody during investigation is the only punishment to the antisocials as they are most likely to get acquitted*

Strongly Agree	Agree	Cannot Say	Disagree	Strongly Disagree

16. *The choice of serving "notice of appearance" to an accused person involved in offences for which the punishment is up to seven years is likely to be attributed motive by the public*

Strongly Agree	Agree	Cannot Say	Disagree	Strongly Disagree

17. *Formal police arrest, and not service of notice for appearance, helps to maintain law and order in the society*

Strongly Agree	Agree	Cannot Say	Disagree	Strongly Disagree

18. *Department and officers should protect each other while there is allegation of illegal arrest against an officer because arrest is made for larger public interest*

Strongly Agree	Agree	Cannot Say	Disagree	Strongly Disagree

19. *Arrest decisions are often taken having regard to the fall out or outcome of such decisions in the law and order scenario*

Strongly Agree	Agree	Cannot Say	Disagree	Strongly Disagree

20. *Public perception of police action on specific cases considerably influences arrest decision*

Strongly Agree	Agree	Cannot Say	Disagree	Strongly Disagree

21. *Media and response of the civil society to a specific offence weigh on the officer's arrest decision*

Strongly Agree	Agree	Cannot Say	Disagree	Strongly Disagree

22. *Arrest decisions are sometimes taken on political consideration or influence*

Strongly Agree	Agree	Cannot Say	Disagree	Strongly Disagree

Appendix E
Interview Schedule for Offenders

A Socio-Economic Status

1. What is your Age: 1.18–30 2.31–45 3.46–60 4.60+
2. What is your mother tongue: 1. Odia 2. Hindi 3.Bengli 4.Telgu 5.Any other (specify)
3. What is your marital status: 1. Unmarried 2. Married 3. Widower 4. Divorced
4. What is your Religion: 1. Hinduism 2. Islam 3. Christianity 4. Any other (specify)
5. Category: 1. SC, 2. ST 3. OBC 4. General
6. What is your occupation: 1. Cultivation 2. Wage labour 3. Household Industry 4. Fishing 7. Trade/Business 6. Govt Service 7. Any other (Specify)
8. What is the level of education attained by you (specify): 1. Up to Class V 2. Up to Class VIII 3. High School Certificate 4. + 2 5. Graduation 6. Postgraduation 7. Professional Degree
9. What is your habitat pattern: 1. Rural 2. Urban 3. Semi-urban
10. Say about your House pattern: 1. Thatched 2. Asbestos 3. RCC Building 4. Any other
11. Say about your Land Ownership: 1. Landless 2. Less than one acre 3. Between 1 and 2 acres 4. Between 2 and 4 acres 5. Above 4 acres
12. What is your Monthly Income in Rupees: 1. Up to 1000 2.1000–2000 3.2000–5000 4.5000–10000 5.10000–15000 6.15000–20000 7.20000–25000 8. Above 25000

B Awareness of the Rights

1. Police have the power to arrest but only after collection of evidences: 1. Yes 2. No 3. Can't say
2. Police normally should not arrest but issue an appearance notice if the punishment for the offence involved is not more than seven years: 1. Yes 2. No 3. Can't say

3. Getting bail at the police station is a matter of right of the accused person involved in a bailable offence: 1. Yes 2. No 3. Can't say
4. Court grants bail in non-bailable offences: 1. Yes 2. No 3. Can't say
5. Police can't detain a person in custody for more than 24 hours if arrested in connection with any offence: 1. Yes 2. No 3. Can't say
6. Upon arrest the police should inform the arrested person about the ground of arrest and inform the relatives about the arrest: 1. Yes 2. No 3. Can't say

C Legal Assistance

1. When I knew about police looking for arrest in connection with a case, I consulted: 1. Lawyer 2. Person who knows the police procedure 3. Person who knows the police 4. None
2. When I went to the police station before arrest, I was accompanied by: 1. My lawyer, 2. Friend 3. Relative 4. A local leading person 5. None
3. When police interrogated me, my lawyer was present: 1. Yes 2. No

Appendix F

Sampling Method of Officers From Odisha Police

Step-1: Select fifteen districts out of thirty districts by adopting Simple Random Sampling Without Replacement (SRSWOR), considering five districts from each RDC Division, that is, Central/Northern/Southern Divisions.
Step-2: Select two other Police districts out of 4 extra Police districts by adopting SRSWOR.
Step-3: Select seventeen districts (15 + 2) including extra Police districts for the study.
Step-4: Select three Police Stations from each selected seventeen districts as follows:

i) One Police Station of Headquarters
ii) Two by adopting SRSWOR
iii) Select fifty-one total Sample Police Stations (3 PS x 17 districts = 51)

Step-5: i) Select two Sub-Inspectors (SI) – preferably one male and one female (by own choice) from each selected PS. Total SIs is 102 (2x51)
(If there is no woman Sub-Inspector, a male counterpart will be chosen)
ii) Select one Inspector (Officer-In-Charge) from each selected PS. Total Inspector is fifty-one (1x51)
iii) Select twenty-five Deputy Superintendents of Police (DSP) as supervisors having jurisdiction over the selected police stations by own choice.

Appendix G

Sample List of Field Police Administrative Units in the State (Selected by Adopting SRSWOR)

District Name	*Subdivision Name*	*Police STN Name*
1. Balasore	Balasore Sadar	Balasore Town
	Nilagiri	Oupada
	Jaleswar	Jaleswar
2. Bolangir	Bolangir Sadar	Bolangir Town
	Bolangir Sadar	Puintala
	Patanagada	Lathor
3. Cuttack	Cuttack Sadar	Gobindapur
	Athagarh	Badamba
	Salipur	Mahanga
4. Dhenkanal	Dhenkanal Sadar	Dhenkanal Town
	Dhenkanal Sadar	Hindol
	Kamakhyanagar	Bhuban
5. Ganjam	Chhatrapur	Chhatrapur
	Purushottampur	Kabisuryanagar
	Aska, Hinjili	Sorada
6. Jajpur	Jajpur	Jajpur Town
	Jajpur Road	Dharmasala
	Jajpur	Mangalpur
7. Kalahandi	Kalahandi Sadar	Bhawanipatna Town
	Dharmagada	Junagarh
	Dharmagada	Ambapani
8. Kendrapara	Kendrapara	Kendrapara
	Pattamundai	Pattamundai
	Pattamundai	Aul
9. Keonjhar	Keonjhar Sadar	Town
	Badbil	Rugudi
	Anandpur	Ghasipura
10. Koraput	Koraput Sadar	Koraput Town
	Sunabeda	Semiliguda
	Nandapur	Nandapur
11. Malkangiri	Malkangiri	Malkangiri
	Malkangiri	Padia
	Chitrakonda	Chitrakonda
12. Nabarangpur	Nabarangpur	Nabarangpur
	Papadahandi	Papadahandi
	Umerkote	Raighar

(*Continued*)

(Continued)

District Name	*Subdivision Name*	*Police STN Name*
13. Nayagarh	Nayagarh	Nayagarh
	Khandapara	Fategarh
	Saranakula	Saranakula
14. Rourkela	Rourkela	Plantsite
	Rourkela	Sector-19
	Bonai	Bonai
15. Sambalpur	Sambalpur Sadar	Town
	Kuchinda	Govindapur
	Rairakhol	Charmal
16. Sundergarh	Sundergarh Sadar	Town
	Rajgangpur	Bargaon
	Biramitrapur	Hatibari
17. UPD Cuttack	Zone-I	Choudwar
	Zone-III	Markatnagar
	Zone-IV	Baranga

Appendix H

Explanatory Note on How to Fill Up the Written Interview Schedule

There are 22 statements in the written interview schedule. Response to each statement has five options, viz., Strongly Agree, Agree, Cannot Say, Disagree and Strongly Disagree. You have to respond to each statement by ticking against one of the five responses. What you feel from your experience as the correct response should guide your answers instead of what should be the legally correct answer. Your name and personal details will be kept confidential.

Before responding to the schedule, it will be profitable to recapitulate and discuss on few factors that influence the arrest discretion of the police officer. For the purpose of this study, arrests made in cognisable offences have been considered, which means arrests after the drawl of FIR.

Discretion is generally defined as the freedom that a decision-maker enjoys to choose between alternatives. Discretion denotes "good judgement" and implies choice exercised by a decision-maker based on proper reasoning and supported by intelligible standards. Following examples may clarify the concept of exercise of discretion in police functions: the question of when to arrest an offender largely depends on personal judgement of the IO, whether to arrest an old and ailing mother-in-law in his eighties who is accused in an offence of dowry death, whether to book a two-wheeler rider without helmet and whether to bring an accused on remand for custodial interrogation. In all these instances, the police officer uses his discretion having regard to the facts and circumstances of each case. The law permits the exercise of discretion but such exercise should be just, fair and conform to public policy as the decisions are bound by law, rules, norms and guidelines.

Following recommendations of the 177th Report of Law Commission of India (2001), the provisions of arrest without warrant were amended in the Criminal Procedure Code of India (CrPC) in the year 2009. The Law Commission argued that the language of the provisions of arrest without warrant enjoined in Section 41 of the CrPC (pre-amendment) falls short of the constitutional guarantees of fundamental rights of an individual and leaves the sole and absolute discretion with the police officer making arrest. Besides, taking into account the recommendations of the National Police Commission

Report on arrest and avoidable arrest, and having due regard to the rulings of the Supreme Court in Joginder Kumar and D.K. Basu, the Law Commission of India suggested sweeping amendments to the provisions of arrest without warrant. The provisions of Section 41 CrPC were amended in the year 2009. The amended law provides that police may arrest without warrant a suspect involved in offences that prescribe maximum punishment of up to seven years only after certain conditions are justified in writing by the investigating officer, otherwise a notice can be served on the suspect with undertaking to produce himself for investigation as and when required. The lawmakers thus introduced a new category of offence by this amendment, that is, "noticeable". The legislative intent was to reduce the number of avoidable arrests, overcrowding of the prisons, reduce police arbitrariness and regulate the discretion in arrest law.

The new amendment had little or no impact on the arrests made by the police till 2014 when the Supreme Court in Arnesh Kumar v. State of Bihar ruled that the amended provisions of Section 41CrPC should be strictly followed by the investigating officers who must be held accountable for arrests in offences punishable up to seven years of imprisonment and prescribed filling up of a Check List in such cases for the scrutiny of the Courts.

But the decisions whether to serve notice or to arrest an offender are influenced by a number of factors encountered in the field including circumstances of each case. True, statutory provisions, the Supreme Court and High Court rulings, Police Manual provisions, departmental circulars etc. should guide the arrest discretion, but research has proved that several other factors influence this discretion. Public outcry (for example, death in road accident or dowry harassment cases which prescribes less than seven years of imprisonment but the victim insists on the arrest of the offenders), media pressure, pressure from political and influential persons or even sometimes the senior supervisory officers' views count on the arrest decision of the IO.

The police often have to work in a potentially hostile environment for long hours within the constraints of resources and with an objective to maintain order in the society. Researches have established that the members of the police organisation are guided by their own set of beliefs, attitudes and behaviour, what is known as police subculture. For example, police view the criminal justice system as ineffective and therefore believe that strong police action or excesses in certain instances are justified to maintain order in the society and needed for overall societal good and that officers should protect each other against allegation of police excesses. The strong undercurrent of police subculture leaves its mark on the arrest decision behaviour too.

Discretion and accountability are linked intrinsically. Accountability means having to answer for one's actions or inaction. Accountability is synonymous with responsibility. When an officer has several choices to act upon legally, he must justify his preferred course of action as to why he chose one option in exclusion of others. Otherwise, no differentiation can be made between proper exercise of discretion and abuse thereof.

The interview schedule is based on the factors that influence the arrest discretion behaviour of police officers. Please be truthful in your views and need not be legally correct. Your honest and truthful views are expected to throw useful insight into the objective of the study and to suggest measures to regulate the arrest discretion behaviour.

Appendix I
District-Wise Respondents of Odisha Police

Sl no.	*District*	*No. of respondents*
1	Balasore	15
2	Bolangir	11
3	Cuttack	15
4	Dhenkanal	14
5	Ganjam	15
6	Jajpur	11
7	Kalahandi	13
8	Kandhamal	12
9	Kendrapara	12
10	Keonjhar	16
11	Koraput	13
12	Nayagarh	12
13	Nawarangpur	14
14	Rourkela	13
15	Sambalpur	12
16	Sundargarh	12
17	UPD, Cuttack	12
		Total: 222

Appendix J

Number of Respondent IPS Officers With Cadre

Sl no.	*Name of cadre*	*No. of respondents*
1	Andhra Pradesh	2
2	Arunachal Pradesh	2
3	Assam	7
4	Bihar	6
5	Chhattisgarh	8
6	Delhi/UT	14
7	Gujarat	4
8	Haryana	3
9	Himachal Pradesh	1
10	Jharkhand	8
11	Karnataka	3
12	Madhya Pradesh	19
13	Maharashtra	11
14	Manipur	5
15	Mizoram	1
16	MHA	1
17	Odisha	1
18	Punjab	6
19	Rajasthan	3
20	Sikkim	1
21	Tamil Nadu	2
22	Telangana	3
23	Tripura	1
24	Uttar Pradesh	20
25	Uttarakhand	2
26	West Bengal	1
27	No name and address	3
		Total: 138

Appendix K

Sample Details for the Situational Determinants

Sl no.	*Area*	*Arrest-1*	*Notice-2*
1	Dkenkanal	12	4
2	Ganjam	8	5
3	Kandhamal	14	10
4	UPD Cuttack	12	6
5	Sundargarh	11	4
6	Nayagarh	9	6
7	Balangir	9	6
8	Kalahandi	10	6
9	Sambalpur	11	5
10	Balasore	8	6
11	Kendrapara	12	5
12	Keonjhar	11	5
	Total: 195	**127**	**68**

Appendix L
Check List

The "Check List" is prepared and circulated by Odisha Police to all police stations (Crime Branch Circular 350/2014) in July 2014 that requires the following information to be furnished by the investigating officer.

1. Police District
2. Police Station with case reference
3. Name and designation of the Arresting Officer
4. Offence
5. Name and parentage of the Person arrested with address
6. Maximum punishment prescribed
7. Notice u/s 41-A CrPC served, if any
8. Appearance of the persons noticed, if any
9. Which of the following reasons satisfied the Arresting Officer to effect arrest of the accused person?
    (a) To prevent such person from committing any further offence, or
    (b) For proper investigation of the offence, or
    (c) To prevent such person from causing the evidence of the offence to disappear or tampering with such evidence in any manner, or
    (d) To prevent such person from making any inducement, threat or promise to any person acquainted with the facts of the case so as to dissuade him from disclosing such facts to the Court or to the police officer, or
    (e) As unless such person is arrested, his presence in the Court whenever required cannot be ensured.
10. The reasons for arrest, the brief facts of the case and the materials justifying the arrest
11. Signature of the Arresting Officer:

References

Alpert, G. P., et al. (2006). *Police officers' decision making and discretion: Forming suspicion and making a stop document no. 213 004*. Washington, DC: US Department of Justice.

Alpert, G. P., Dunham, R. G., and Piquero, A. (1997). On the study of neighborhood and police. In G. P. Albert and A. Piquero (Eds.), *Community policing: Contemporary readings* (pp. 309–326). Prospect Heights, IL: Waveland.

Alvesson, M., and Sveningsson, S. (2015). *Changing organizational culture: Cultural change work in progress*. New York, NY: New York University Press.

Anthony, L. D. (2018). *Police culture and decision making*. Walden University Scholar Works. http://scholarworks.waldenu.edu/dissertation (accessed on January 1, 2019).

Arnold, D. (1986). *Police power and colonial rule, Madras 1859–1947*. New Delhi: Oxford University Press.

Ayyar, R. V. V. (2009). *Public policy making in India*. New Delhi: Dorling Kindersley (India) Pvt. Ltd.

Bayley, D. H. (1969). *The police and political development in India*. Princeton, NJ: Princeton University Press.

Bayley, D. H., and Bittner, E. (1989). Learning the skills of policing. 47 *Law and Contemporary Problems*, 35–59.

Bellew, S. S. (2001). *Media influence on executive police decision-making – thesis for master of science*. University of North Texas (accessed on April 26, 2019).

Black, D. J. (1971). Social organization of arrest. *Sanford Law Review*, 23, 1087–1111.

Black, D. J. (1976). *The behaviour of law*. New York: Academic Press.

Bronitt, S. H., and Stenning, P. (2011). Understanding discretion in modern policing. *Criminal Law Journal*, 35(6), 319–332. http://sites.thomsonreuters.com.au/journals/files/2011/12/CrimLJ_v35_pt06_Dec2011_offp rint_bronnit_stenning1.pdf (accessed on June 16, 2016).

Brown, M. K. (1988). *Working the street: Police discretion and the dilemmas of reform*. Beverly Hills and New York: Sage.

CHRI. (2002). Police organisation in India. https://www.humanrightsinitiative.org/publications/police/police_organisations.pdf (accessed on April 17, 2017).

Cochran, J. K., and Bromley, M. L. (2003). The myth (?) of the police sub-culture. *Policing: An International Journal of Police Strategies & Management*, 26(1), 88117.

Cockcroft, T. (2012). *Police culture: Themes and concepts*. New York, NY: Routledge.

Cox, S. M. (1996). *Police practices, perspectives and problems*. Boston: Allyn & Bacon.
Crank, J. P. (2004). Understanding police culture (2nd ed.). Ohio: Anderson Publishing Co.
Curry, J. C. (1932). *The Indian police*. London: Faber & Faber Limited.
Davis, K. C. (1969). *Discretionary justice a preliminary enquiry*. Baton Rouge, LA: Louisiana State University Press.
Davis, K. C. (1975). *Police discretion*. Minnesota: West Publishing Co.
Dworkin, R. M. (1967). The model of rules, Faculty scholarship series, Paper 3609. *The University of Chicago Law Review*, 35(1).
Eitle, D. (2005, October). *The influence of mandatory arrest policies, police organizational characteristics, and situational variables on the probability of arrest in domestic violence cases crime and delinquency* (Vol. 51, No. 4, pp. 573–597). Washington, D.C: US Department of Justice.
Fisk, J. G. (1974). The police officer's exercise of discretion in the decision to arrest: Relationship to organisational goals and societal values. *Government and Public Affairs*, 5(188), 1–102.
Fyfe, J. J. (1981). Observations on police deadly force. *Crime and Delinquency*, 27(3), 376–389.
Gaines, L. K., and Kappeler, V. E. (2003). *Policing in America* (4th ed.). Cincinnati, OH: Anderson Publishing.
Galligan, D. J. (1992). *Discretionary powers: A legal study of official discretion*. New York: Oxford University Press.
Garrett Henry, E. (1926). *Statistics in psychology and education*. New York: Longmans, Green & Co.
Ghosh, S. K., and Rustamji, K. F. (1994). *Encyclopaedia of police in India (Ed) Vol II Part A*. New Delhi: Ashish Publishing House.
Goldstein, H. (1975). *Police corruption: A perspective on its nature and control*. Washington, DC: Police Foundation.
Goldstein, H. (1977). *Policing a free society*. Cambridge, MA: Ballinger.
Goldstein, J. (1960, March). *Police discretion not to invoke the criminal process* (Vol. 69, pp. 543–594). Connecticut: The Yale Law Journal Company, Inc.
Groeneveld, R. F. (2005). *Arrest discretion of police officers: The impact of varying organizational structures*. New York, NY: LFB Scholarly.
Halliday, L. G. (2009). Law enforcement & justice administration. *Western Journal of Criminal Justice-Western Illinois University*, 1, 2–11.
Herbert, S. (1998). Police subculture reconsidered. *Criminology*, 36(2), 343–370.
Hidayet, T. (2011). *Personal perception and organizational factors influencing police discretion: The case of Turkish patrol officers' responsiveness*. Doctoral Dissertation (Open Access). University of Central Florida.
Ingram, J. R., Paoline, E. A., and Terrill, W. (2013). A multilevel framework for understanding police culture: The role of the workgroup. *Criminology*, 51(2), 365–397.
Jauregui, B. (2013). Cultures of legitimacy and postcolonial policing: Guest editor introduction. *Law & Social Inquiry*, 38(3), 547–552.
Joshi, G. P. (2013). *Policing in India*. New Delhi: Atlanta Publishing.
Kelling, G. L. (1999). *Broken windows and police discretion*. Washington, DC: Research Report National Institute of Justice.
Kelling, G. L., and Coles, C. M. (1996). *Fixing broken windows: Restoring order and reducing crime in our communities*. New York: The Free Press.

Kleinig, J. (1996). *Handled with discretion: Ethical issues in police decision making.* Lanham, MD: Rowman& Littlefield Publishers.
Klinger, D. A. (1996). More on demeanor and arrest in Dade County. *Criminology*, 34, 61–79.
Klinger, D. A. (1997). Negotiating order in patrol work: An ecological theory of police response to deviance. *Criminology*, 35(2), 277–306.
Klockars, C. B. (1980, November). Annals of the American academy of political and social science. *The Police and Violence,* 452, 33–47. www.kyoolee.net/Dirty_Harry_Problem the_-_Klockars.pdf (accessed on May 21, 2017).
Klockars, C. B. (1985). The dirty Harry problem. In F. A. Elliston and M. Feldberg (Eds.), *Moral issues in police work*. Totowa, NJ: Rowan and Allanhold.
Lasley, J. (2012). *Los Angeles police department meltdown: The fall of the professional reform model of policing*. New York: Routledge.
Law Commission of Report. (2001). *One hundred and seventy-seven report on law relating to arrest.* New Delhi: Law Commission of Report.
La Fave, W. (1969). The need for discretion law & the lawless: A reader in criminology. *Random House*, 299–303.
Manning, P. K. (1977). *Police work: The social organization of policing*. Cambridge, MA: MIT Press.
Mastrofski, S. D. (1981). Policing the beat: The impact of organizational scale on patrol officer behavior in urban residential neighborhoods. *Journal of Criminal Justice*, 9, 343–358.
Mastrofski, S. D., Worden, R. E., and Snipes, J. B. (1995). Law enforcement in a time of community policing. *Criminology*, 33, 539–563. file:///C:/Users/O.P/Downloads/459159.pdf (accessed on January 23, 2016).
McConville, M., and Shepherd, D. (1992). *Watching police, watching communities.* London: Routledge.
Mohanty, S. (2019). Police subculture and its influence on arrest discretion behaviour; An empirical study in the context of Indian police. *SVPNPA Journal*, LXVIII(2), 41–61.
Mohanty, S., and Mohanty, R. K. (2014). *Community policing as a public policy: Challenges and recommendations.* Newcastle upon Tyne, UK: Cambridge Scholars Publishing.
Moll, M. M. (2006). Improving American police ethics training: Focusing on social contract theory and constitutional principles. *Forum on Public Policy.* www.forumonpublicpolicy.com/archievessum07/moll.pdf (accessed on January 16, 2016).
Mollen Commission. (1994). *Report of the commission to investigate allegations of police corruption and anti-corruption procedures of police department.* City of New York: Mollen Commission.
National Police Commission. (1979). *II Report. Interference and misuse of police by illegal or improper orders of pressure from political, executive and other Extraneous sources remedial measures Chapter XV.* New Delhi: National Police Commission
National Police Commission. (1981a). *III Report. Chapter XXII, Corruption in police.*New Delhi: Mational Police Commission.
National Police Commission. (1981b). *VIII Report, Chapter LXI, Accountability and police performance.* New Delhi: National Police Commission.
Palmiotto, M. J., and Unnithan, P. N. (2011). *Policing & society: A global approach.* New York: Delmar Cengage Learning.

Pepinsky, E. Harold. (1984). Better living through police discretion. *Law and Contemporary Problems*, 47(4), 249–267.
Pound, R. (1940). Discretion, dispensation, and mitigation: The problem of the individual special case. *New York University Law Review*, 35.
Punch, M. (1985). *Conduct unbecoming: The Social construction of Police deviance and control.* London and Tavistock: Oxford University Press.
Ratho, P. C. (2000). *The Odisha police manual.* Cuttack: Legal Associates.
Reiner, R. (1992). *The politics of police Hamel Hempstead: Harvester wheatsheaf.* New York: Harvester Wheatsheaf.
Richard, F. A. (2016). Pattern of use of police discretion. *International Journal of Education and Social Science*, 3(4), 1–3.
Satish, M. (2016). *Discretion, discrimination and the rule of law: Reforming rape sentencing in India.* New York: Cambridge University Press.
Scaramella, G. L., Cox, S. M., and McCamey, W. P. (2011). *Introduction to policing.* California: Sage.
Selke, W., and Bartoszek, G. (1984). Police and media relations: The seeds of conflict. *Criminal Justice Review*, 9(2), 25–30.
Sherman, L. W. (1984). Experiment in police discretion: Scientific boon or dangerous knowledge? *Law and Contemporary Problems*, 47(4), 67–87.
Singhvi, G. C. (1994). Police as the agent of law and not the party in power. In *Encyclopaedia of police in India Vol II, part a.* New Delhi: Ashish Publishing House.
Skolnick, J. H., and Fyfe, J. J. (1993). *Above the law: Police and the excessive use of force.* New York: Free Press.
Smith, D. A. (1984). Organizational context of legal control. *Criminology*, 22, 19–38.
Smith, D. A. (1987). Police response to interpersonal violence: Defining the parameters of legal control. *Social Forces*, 65, 767–782.
Smith, D. A., and Visher, C. (1981). Street level justice: Situational determinants of police arrest decisions. *Social Problems*, 29, 167–177.
Sparrow, M., Moore, M. H., and Kennedy, D. M. (1990). *Beyond 911: A new era for policing.* New York: Basic Books.
Stalans, L., and Finn, M. A. (1995). How novice and experienced officers interpret wife assaults: Normative and efficiency frames. *Law and Society Review*, 29, 287 - 321.
Terrill, W., and Mastrofski, S. D. (2002). Situational and officer-based determinants of police coercion. *Justice Quarterly*, 19(2), 215 - 248.
Terrill, W., Paoline, E. A., and Manning, P. K. (2003). Police culture and coercion. *Criminology*, 41(4), 1003–1035.
Tyagi, S. P. (2014). *Criminal trial.* New Delhi: Vinod Publishing House.
University of Calcutta. (1913). *History of police organisation in India and Indian village police.* Calcutta: Calcutta University Press.
Walker, S., and Katz, C. M. (2005). *The police in America: An introduction* (5th ed.). New York, NY: Mc-Graw – Hill Companies.
Walker, S., Spohn, C., and DeLone, M. (1996). *The color of justice: Race, ethnicity and crime in America.* Belmont, CA: Wadsworth.
Westley, W. (1970). *Violence and the police.* Cambridge, MA: MIT Press.
White, V., and Robinson, S. (2014). Leading change in policing: Police culture and the psychological contract. *The Police Journal*, 87(4), 258–269.
Williams, G. H. (1989). Police discretion: A comparative perspective. *Indiana Law Journal*, 64(4).

Wilson, J. Q. (1968). *Varieties of police behavior: The management of law and order in eight communities*. Cambridge, MA: Harvard University Press.

Wood, J. R. T. (1997). *Final report of the royal commission into the New South Wales police service: Vol 1: Corruption (Code of silence: And "us and them")*. Government of the State of New South Wales.

Worden, R. E. (1989). Situational and attitudinal explanations of police behavior: A theoretical reappraisal and empirical assessment. *Law and Society Review*, 23, 667–711.

Worden, R. E. (1990). A badge and a baccalaureate: Policies, hypotheses, and further evidence. *Justice Quarterly*, 7, 565–592.

Wortley, R. K. (2003). Measuring police attitude towards discretion. *Criminal Justice & Behaviors*, 30(5), 538–558.

Young, B. B. (2011). *Police discretion in contemporary America, MA thesis faculty of the school of continuing studies*. Washington, DC: Georgetown University. https://repository.library.georgetown.edu/bitstream/handle/10822/553420/youngBerniceBr ooks.pdf?s (accessed on January 16, 2016).

Index

For Product Safety Concerns and Information please contact our EU representative GPSR@taylorandfrancis.com
Taylor & Francis Verlag GmbH, Kaufingerstraße 24, 80331 München, Germany

www.ingramcontent.com/pod-product-compliance
Ingram Content Group UK Ltd.
Pitfield, Milton Keynes, MK11 3LW, UK
UKHW022043061126
477531UK00009B/510
* 9 7 8 1 0 3 2 5 2 4 3 4 4 *